SCOTLAND IN THE
REIGN OF
ALEXANDER III
1249–1286

SCOTLAND IN THE REIGN OF ALEXANDER III 1249-1286

Edited by
NORMAN H. REID

JOHN DONALD PUBLISHERS LTD
EDINBURGH

DEDICATION

The untimely death in December 1988 of Dr Marinell Ash deprived her many friends and colleagues of a source of challenge and inspiration. The remaining contributors to this book feel great sadness that she did not live to see it published. The essay which appears here, along with the other fine and varied work which she leaves behind, is a pointer to the loss which Scottish historical study has sustained. We dedicate this volume to her memory.

ISBN 0 85976 218 1

British Library Cataloguing in Publication Data
Scotland in the reign of Alexander III.
1. Scotland, 1057–1314
I. Reid, Norman H.
941.102

Typeset by Pioneer Associates, Perthshire
Printed and Bound in Great Britain by
Billing & Sons Ltd., Worcester

PREFACE

This book came about through a fortuitous combination of circumstances. The meeting in January 1986 of the Conference of Scottish Medieval Historical Research, of which I was then the Secretary, adopted as its theme, 'Alexander III'. The theme had been chosen in order to ensure that the reign of this most important monarch was commemorated in the year which fell seven hundred years after his death. During 1985, while that meeting was at the planning stage, a person quite unconnected with the Conference suggested that the septicentenary should be celebrated in print. This volume is the result. Three of the essays, 'Noble Families and Political Factions', 'Alexander III: A Silver Age?', and 'Norwegian Sunset, Scottish Dawn', were presented as papers to the 1986 meeting, and have been revised to varying degrees for publication. The remaining five essays were commissioned specially for the volume. All of the contributors are or were members of the Conference. It should be noted that all significant editorial work on the essay, 'The Church in the Reign of Alexander III' by Marinell Ash, was complete and approved by her before her death, and that it thus represents entirely her own, unaltered contribution to the volume.

Those of us who have contributed to the book each owe a debt of gratitude to the many people who have assisted us in a variety of ways. Some of these are acknowledged in the notes to the individual essays. We are, however, collectively indebted to the following: Anita Ebanks and the Cayman Islands National Museum, the use of whose computer equipment has greatly eased the latter stages of the editorial process; John Tuckwell of John Donald Publishers Ltd., both for his part in initiating the project, and for his constant enthusiasm, forbearance and help; and my wife, Elspeth, who has read the entire work several times, and whose editorial assistance has been invaluable.

1990   Norman H. Reid

CONTRIBUTORS

Marinell Ash
(Late) Consultant Historian

Geoffrey Barrow
Sir William Fraser Professor of Scottish History and Palaeography, University of Edinburgh

Edward J. Cowan
Professor of History and Chair of Scottish Studies Programme, University of Guelph, Ontario

Richard Fawcett
Principal Inspector of Ancient Monuments, Historic Buildings and Monuments Directorate

Hector L. MacQueen
Lecturer in Scots Law, University of Edinburgh

Nicholas J. Mayhew
Senior Assistant Keeper, Ashmolean Museum, Oxford

Norman H. Reid
Archivist, Heriot-Watt University, Edinburgh

Alan Young
Senior Lecturer in History, College of Ripon and York St John, York

CONTENTS

ILLUSTRATIONS

ABBREVIATIONS

Unless specified otherwise, the abbreviations used in the notes conform to those in the *List of Abbreviated Titles of the Printed Sources of Scottish History to 1560*, published as a supplement to the *Scottish Historical Review*, October 1963. The following list contains divergences from and additions to that publication.

Barrow, *Anglo-Norman Era*
  G. W. S. Barrow, *The Anglo-Norman Era in Scottish History* (Oxford, 1980)

Barrow, *Bruce*
  G. W. S. Barrow, *Robert Bruce and the Community of the Realm of Scotland* (3rd. edn., Edinburgh, 1988)

Barrow, *Kingdom*
  G. W. S. Barrow, *The Kingdom of the Scots* (London, 1973)

Barrow, *Kingship and Unity*
  G. W. S. Barrow, *Kingship and Unity: Scotland 1000–1306* (London, 1981)

Barrow and Royan, 'James Stewart'
  Barrow, G. W. S. and Royan, Ann, 'James Fifth Stewart of Scotland, 1260?–1309', in Stringer, *Nobility Essays*, 166–194

Book of Fees
  The Book of Fees commonly called Testa de Nevill (London, 1920–31)

Brown, *Fifteenth Century*
  Scottish Society in the Fifteenth Century, ed. J. M. Brown (London, 1977)

Cal. Inquisitions Post Mortem
  Calendar of Inquisitions Post Mortem . . . preserved in the PRO (London, 1904–; in progress)

CFR
Calendar of Fine Rolls, 1272–1337 (London, 1911–13)·

Charter Rolls
Calendar of the Charter Rolls preserved in the PRO (London, 1903–27)

Chron. Guisborough
The Chronicle of Walter of Guisborough, previously Edited as the Chronicle of Walter of Hemingford or Hemingburgh, ed. H. Rothwell (Royal Historical Society, London, 1957)

Close Rolls
Close Rolls of the Reign of Henry III, preserved in the PRO (London, 1902–38); *Calendar of the Close Rolls of Edward I, 1271–1307* (London, 1900–1908)

Cowan and Easson, *Religious Houses*
I. B. Cowan and D. E. Easson, *Medieval Religious Houses: Scotland* (London, 1976)

CPR
Calendar of the Patent Rolls preserved in the PRO (London, 1891–; in progress)

Duncan, *Kingdom*
A. A. M. Duncan, *Scotland: The Making of the Kingdom* (Edinburgh, 1975)

Fergusson, *Alexander III*
James Fergusson, *Alexander III* (London, 1937)

Formulary E
Formulary E: Scottish Letters and Brieves, 1286–1424, ed. A. A. M. Duncan (University of Glasgow, 1976)

Grant, *Independence*
Alexander Grant, *Independence and Nationhood: Scotland 1306–1469* (London, 1984)

HS
The Saga of Hacon and a Fragment of the Saga of Magnus with appendices, trans. G. W. Dasent (Rolls Series, *Icelandic Sagas*, iv; London, 1894)

Historical Atlas
  An Historical Atlas of Scotland, ed. P. G. McNeill and R. Nicholson
  (St Andrews, 1975)

Liberate Rolls
  Calendar of Liberate Rolls (London, 1916–1964)

Nicholson, *Scotland*
  Ranald Nicholson, *Scotland: The Later Middle Ages* (Edinburgh,
  1974)

NLS
  National Library of Scotland, Edinburgh

Paris, *Chron. Maj.*
  Matthew Paris, *Chronica Majora*, ed. H. R. Luard (Rolls Series,
  1872–3)

PRO
  Public Record Office, London

RCAHMS
  Royal Commission on the Ancient and Historical Monuments of
  Scotland

Rot. Parl.
  Rotuli Parliamentorum (London, 1783)

RRS: Alexander III
  G. G. Simpson, *Handlist of the Acts of Alexander III, the Guardians
  and John, 1249–1296* (*RRS*, 1960)

SRO
  Scottish Record Office, Edinburgh

Simpson, *Quincy*
  G. G. Simpson, *An Anglo-Scottish Baron of the Thirteenth Century:
  The Acts of Roger de Quincy, Earl of Winchester and Constable of
  Scotland* (unpublished Ph.D. thesis, University of Edinburgh, 1965)

Simpson, 'The *Familia* of Roger de Quincy'
  G. G. Simpson, 'The *Familia* of Roger de Quincy, Earl of Winchester
  and Constable of Scotland', in Stringer, *Nobility Essays*, 102–29

Skene, *Celtic Scotland*
W. F. Skene, *Celtic Scotland: A History of Ancient Alban* (2nd. edn., Edinburgh, 1886–90)

Stell, 'The Balliol Family'
G. Stell, 'The Balliol Family and the Great cause of 1291–2', in Stringer, *Nobility Essays*, 150–65

Stones, *Relations*
E. L. G. Stones, *Anglo-Scottish Relations, 1174–1328* (2nd. edn., London, 1970)

Stones and Simpson, *Edward I*
E. L. G. Stones and G. G. Simpson, *Edward I and the Throne of Scotland 1290–1296* (Oxford, 1979)

Stringer, *Nobility Essays*
Essays on the Nobility of Medieval Scotland, ed. K. J. Stringer (Edinburgh, 1985)

Watt, *Fasti*
D. E. R. Watt, *Fasti Ecclesiae Scoticanae Medii Aevi ad annum 1638* (2nd draft, Edinburgh, 1968)

Watt, 'Minority'
D. E. R. Watt, 'The Minority of Alexander III of Scotland', *Transactions of the Royal Historical Society* (ser. 5), xxxi (1971), 1–23

Young, 'Walter Comyn'
Alan Young, 'The Political Role of Walter Comyn, Earl of Menteith, during the Minority of Alexander III of Scotland', in Stringer, *Nobility Essays*, 131–149

INTRODUCTION

Alexander III is a name known to many Scots. Some associate with it the idea of a 'golden age'; others may remember only the traditional tale that he died as a result of a fall from his horse at the cliffs of Kinghorn. Few, however, will realise the significance of Alexander's kingship, in terms of the length and stability of his reign, and the growth and consolidation of a national identity which not only weathered the storms of the ensuing decades, but was indeed strengthened by them. For most, the romantic appeal of the more spectacular events which followed 1286 has overshadowed Alexander III, a fact which has hindered study of the reign. Sir James Fergusson's *Alexander III: King of Scotland* (1937) remains the only full-scale published treatment of the reign. Comparison of it with the present work, and with other recent studies of medieval Scotland, strikingly displays the changes in historical methodology which have taken place during the past fifty years. Sir James himself, whilst acknowledging the shortcomings of his work, due mainly to the paucity of source material, and expressing the hope that further study would follow, was nonetheless in no doubt that the stature of this king demanded his pioneering attempt.[1]

The present volume does not attempt to provide a biography of the king; nor could it be termed a 'history' of the reign. It aims rather to examine some of the themes which reveal the character of this period, which is itself so crucial for a true understanding of the formative years which followed. The first five essays are concerned with areas of study vital to an appreciation of the essential nature of the reign. They deal, respectively, with personal and political relationships within the noble governing community; the interrelationship of crown and church; the economy; law and legal administration; and foreign relations, particularly with regard to the definition of the frontier in the west. The next two essays develop other, complementary themes: the national army, which was to play so vital a role in the years to follow; and ecclesiastical architecture, which is today perhaps the most striking legacy of the period and which gives testimony to the settled and confident nature of the reign. The final contribution examines the historiography of the reign, explaining the growth of the idea of a 'golden age', a term with which tradition has long since endowed the reigns of Alexander III and his father.

As mentioned above, there have been great strides made in historical methodology in recent years. This collection demonstrates some of the current trends in Scottish historical study, and we hope that it will stimulate an increased awareness of the riches of Alexander III's reign.

NOTE

1. Fergusson, *Alexander III*, p. ix.

1

NOBLE FAMILIES AND POLITICAL FACTIONS IN THE REIGN OF ALEXANDER III

Alan Young

John of Fordun's chronicle, perhaps the main strand in the standard narrative account of Scottish medieval history, describes the nobles who kidnapped young King Alexander III at Kinross in 1257 as 'disaffected men, who did all as they pleased and naught as was lawful, and reigned over the people, right or wrong'.[1] This statement encapsulates many commonly accepted images of the Scottish medieval nobility — politically irresponsible aggressors, overmighty subjects,[2] 'warring factions' and natural enemies of the crown.[3] Vigorous research has recently exposed the frailties of such assumptions,[4] and has attempted to view the nobility from inside the baronial milieu. Such an approach, by adding both breadth and depth to our understanding of aristocratic lives and ambitions, has opened up new avenues for enquiry and consequently new perspectives on Scottish medieval history. It has also highlighted some of the problems and prejudices which have militated against a balanced view of the nobility in medieval Scotland. The political importance of Alexander III's reign, on the eve of such a dramatic and formative period in Scottish history, requires this type of treatment.

There are several factors which have tainted the traditional view of the nobility in this reign. Firstly, the minority period, as is invariably the case with political crises, has tended to dominate discussion.[5] It also, of course, caused atypical behaviour on the part of the protagonists, and thus subsequent interpretation has tended to veer to the extremes. Another factor is the natural tendency of Scottish medieval historiography to concentrate on the development of an independent kingdom in this period[6] which has led inevitably to a monarchocentric standpoint, emphasising the problems caused to the crown by the nobility. This view has been bolstered by Fordun's chronicle, so heavily used by later historians, the main theme of which is the importance of the monarchy in the growth of the Scottish nation.[7] As a result, in the context of

Alexander III's minority, there has been a tendency to emphasise the violent factiousness of the nobility and their role as overmighty subjects because this was a threat to monarchy and the development of the kingdom. When discussion of the nobility is extended to the whole of Alexander III's reign, proponents of such views are left with a dilemma. How do they explain why such a disruptive nobility (with most of the same families and even the same individuals involved) suddenly developed into a responsible aristocratic governing community acting in co-operation with the crown during the maturity of Alexander III?[8] A view from the baronial milieu is perhaps necessary to explain this apparent paradox.

Hindsight also poses a problem. The period of constitutional difficulty which followed, with internecine strife and even civil war, has caused historians to seek in Alexander III's reign the roots of the baronial conflicts and alliances which were so much a feature of the later period. It is assumed that the Bruce–Balliol conflict, and the Balliol–Comyn alliance, for example, were of long standing: such a view is not borne out by the evidence.[9] The prolonged war with England which was to follow Alexander III's reign has also caused its problems: the English interests of many of the Scottish nobility have been seen as a source of conflict in this context. And finally, the available source material cannot be absolved of blame. The monarchocentric view of Fordun has already been noted, and other sources are even less helpful. In general terms, political crises seem to increase both the amount and the bias of narrative sources. Thus comments on King Alexander's minority range from the distinctly xenophobic Matthew Paris, to the narratives of Fordun, Bower[10] and the Melrose chronicler,[11] all of which highlight the factiousness of the nobles. Another strong influence is the substantial amount of material from English sources, much of it in the period 1255–57 representing the at times almost hysterically paternal view of Henry III that Scotland was on the verge of civil war.[12] In marked contrast to the minority period, narrative sources of all kinds are thin for the period of Alexander III's maturity. Fordun continues to chronicle the development of monarchy and nation, but the *Melrose Chronicle* peters out in the 1270s, and in fact gives little information beyond 1266. Walter Bower concentrates his narrative largely on ecclesiastical matters though he does give snippets of information about nobility in political offices and on royal missions[13] as well as valuable information on baronial disputes.[14] The early part of the *Lanercost Chronicle* has little to say about secular matters in Scotland.

All of these factors have tended to lead historians to an unjust view of the nobility as unprincipled aggressors[15] and overmighty subjects[16] split into 'native' and 'English' factions,[17] and even constituting an English 'fifth column'. 'The truth is, and it must be confessed with shame and sorrow, that the Scottish nobility as a body were not true to Scotland'.[18] These views do not bear scrutiny when the evidence from a baronial perspective is taken in the context of the whole of Alexander III's reign. A blend of charter evidence, narrative sources and evidence from Scottish, English and French sources (where noble families held land in more than one country) provides the optimum range of material in presenting the nobility in a social and economic context as families, landowners and estate managers as well as in a political context as officials in local and national government. Only by such a study can the full range of baronial ambitions and aspirations be gained. Unfortunately, it is unusual to achieve a balance of chronicle and charter evidence when studying an individual baron or noble family,[19] and much more research must be undertaken before a fully comprehensive picture of the aristocracy in Alexander III's reign can be achieved. Nonetheless, if the major pitfalls are signposted, an extra dimension can be explored by viewing the nobility from inside the baronial milieu.

Inevitably, discussion must start with the minority of Alexander III, a period which has already received more than enough debate to make an overall perspective on the nobility in the reign difficult to achieve. Every standpoint seems to have been adopted except a baronial one. It would, therefore, be wise to ask what the nobility themselves sought in this period. Baronial activities should be understood in the context of family history, and advancement through two main avenues. Firstly, marriage: native dynasties holding earldoms could further increase their landed wealth by this means; through marriage into one of the thirteen earldoms of Scotland, noble families could themselves gain access to the title 'earl', with its social and political status closest to the king himself.[20] Through marriage the Comyns became the first 'Norman' earls in Scotland, as earls of Buchan c. 1212, the Umphraville family acquired the earldom of Angus in 1243, and the Bruces acquired the earldom of Carrick in 1272. Noble families could be destroyed just as easily, however, by lack of male heirs, as was the case with the Quincy and Durward families.

Though marriage was important in noble lives and ambitions, increasingly significant in the thirteenth century were offices such as justiciar and sheriff. It was very much in the interests of the nobility to enhance or retain their positions in society by friendship and co-operation with the crown, the giver of such offices. The Scottish bureaucracy and administrative machinery in this period was less advanced than its English counterpart, causing a greater reliance on the nobility in Scotland to make royal power effective, especially in the outlying regions. Further, there were relatively few magnates in Scotland with great territorial influence, and there were thus great prizes available in crown patronage. A delicate balancing arrangement was called for in order to ensure the appointment of men of sufficient weight to be respected by the nobility in general, whilst avoiding the possibility of some families gaining a near monopoly of crown patronage. It is nonetheless clear that crown and nobility both had a lot to gain from successful co-operation.

What was the baronial situation in 1249? The Comyns, a tightly-knit family group of three branches[21] with vast territorial strength, had direct control over the earldoms of Menteith and Buchan, indirect control over the earldom of Mar (the family also controlled the earldoms of Angus and Atholl until 1242), and possession of the important lordships of Badenoch and Lochaber, Kirkintilloch and East Kilbride. In 1249, however, they did not have possession of the office of justiciar of Scotia,[22] 'a crucially important channel through which to exercise royal authority and dispense royal favour and patronage'.[23] The importance of this office is key to an understanding of Alexander III's minority, during which there seem to have been attempts to exalt the justiciarship of Scotia (Scotland north of the Forth) into a justiciarship of Scotland.[24] The office of justiciar, the wide-ranging duties of which were to

> . . . know how, and be able, to provide the law and justice to poor as well as rich, and to preserve and control the rights of the king in all matters which pertain to his crown . . .[25]

was held from 1244 by Alan Durward, a man with little or no political influence prior to 1244 but with ambitions to increase his family's territorial influence in northern Scotland (the major base of the Comyns also) by acquisition of an earldom. The Durwards, lords of Lundie in Angus, Coull in Mar and Urquhart on Loch Ness, had pressed for the earldoms of Atholl and Mar earlier in the thirteenth century. For a time in the 1230s Alan Durward had held the title earl of Atholl, but it remained in the Comyn family until 1242.[26] Thomas Durward had pressed a claim to the earldom of Mar when it fell vacant c. 1210 —

c. 1220, but had had to be content with the considerable lordship of Coull between the rivers Don and Dee.[27] The earldom of Mar itself did not cease to be the prime Durward objective. When it came under Comyn influence c. 1242–44 through the marriage of William, earl of Mar to a daughter of William Comyn, earl of Buchan, Durward resentment was understandable.[28] Durward ambitions to break into the forefront of the Scottish nobility were at the very heart of the unrest during the minority. Through the office of justiciar of Scotia, Durward had one very promising avenue to explore in order to achieve his family's ambitions. Access to royal favour was strengthened further by the marriage of Alan Durward to Alexander II's illegitimate daughter, Marjory. This two-fold access to royal favour was vigorously used in the minority to break into the baronial establishment and threaten Comyn territorial influence in the north.

The situation, however, should not be seen too narrowly as a dispute between Comyns and Durwards. It should be noted that when, in 1249, Durward sought to formalise his position as head of government during the minority by knighting the young Alexander before he was enthroned as Alexander III, it was not only the Comyns who objected. It was the majority of the Scottish nobility who protested 'with one voice',[29] obviously suspicious of the encroachment on the authority of the traditional baronial establishment. The appointment of Alan Durward as the justiciar of Scotia did not appear, from the events of 1249, to fulfil one of the essential criteria for such an important royal post, the capacity to be obeyed by the baronage as a whole.[30] It seems that the Scottish nobility by the mid-thirteenth century were already well entrenched and less than welcoming of forceful aspirants to that elite.

From 1249 to 1251 it is clear that the Durwards had insufficient support to control the country. It was a joint magnate/clergy invitation to Henry III which led to a change of government in 1251, with the Comyns gaining control. Durward was accused of too vigorous a pursuit of one particular avenue for promotion open to him and his family — relationship with the royal family. The *Melrose Chronicle* contains an accusation that he had attempted to legitimise the daughters born to his wife, illegitimate half-sister of the new king, in order to secure further his family's position within the royal circle, and even make succession to the throne a possibility.[31] Henry III's intervention at this point, sealed by the marriage of his daughter Margaret to Alexander III, may be seen from a crown standpoint as a blow to the development of an independent Scottish kingdom, for which the nobility deserved censure. In the political crisis which the minority caused, however, there was a common regard by the magnates of Scotland for the English king as a bringer of stability. Without that stability no-one could enjoy the prizes of power. Stability in the minority meant having a government with the support of the majority of the nobility and clergy,[32] and, in this particular case, also the confidence of the English king. While it is perhaps surprising that Walter Comyn, earl of Menteith and acknowledged leader of the Comyn party, did not himself take over the justiciarship of Scotia, by 1253 at the latest Alexander Comyn, earl of Buchan, an increasingly influential member of the family, was in this office.[33] Alexander had been preceded by joint justiciars, Philip Meldrum and Michael Mowat, both of whom were probably in the Comyn following,[34] but perhaps not of sufficient aristocratic weight for this key post in a minority period.

Given the general support of nobility and church in 1249 and between 1251 and 1255, the black picture painted by Fordun of the Comyn government[35] cannot be supported. There is no evidence that the Comyns were working against the interests of the kingdom. They were, however, politically astute enough to ensure further support from the church by pushing successive claims of two of their supporters to the see of St Andrews, thus ensuring influence over the premier see in Scotland and at the same time quashing the influence of Alan Durward in its cathedral chapter. General support in Scotland, however, was not quite enough, without the continued confidence of the king of England. Alan Durward had skilfully ingratiated himself with Henry III by serving with him in Gascony,[36] and the English king thus supported Durward's counter-coup: the Comyn government was removed in 1255 to be replaced by a council of fifteen Durward supporters.[37] The composition of this council is quite revealing, as it shows much narrower support than that of the Comyn government which it replaced. The new council comprised persons who were predominantly from the south and south-west of Scotland, though, as has been seen, Durward himself had strong territorial influence in the north. That he felt this northern influence was not strong enough is demonstrated by the renewal of his claim to the earldom of Mar.[38] He seems to have been attempting to use the high office of justiciar of Scotia, which he had immediately reclaimed in 1255, to alter the balance of baronial power in the north. Yet lack of broad-based support became crucial between 1255 and 1257. Durward was unable either to gain the earldom of Mar, or to prevent the consecration of Gamelin, the Comyn government's chancellor, to the see of St Andrews.[39] Comyn reaction was once more to seek Henry III's support for their broader-based and church-supported 'party', but this time without success. This failure, combined with Durward's strong-arm tactics,[40] led to the much-discussed Comyn-inspired kidnapping of Alexander III at Kinross.

It seems, however, that the Comyns too lacked general support for their actions in 1257. There is an interesting lack of confidence in the treaty into which they entered with the Welsh in 1258, which names few nobles from outside the Comyn family, and shows the Comyns to be self-conscious that they did not have majority support, and hesitant to act without the backing of their king:

> If it should happen that we are compelled to enter into a peace or truce with the King of England or anyone else opposed to Llewelyn, by command of our lord king of Scotland, we shall strive to see that this is done to Llewelyn's honour and advantage, nor shall we do anything contrary to this league unless it be by our lord the king's strictest compulsion, but rather we shall do our best to bring the lord our king into this alliance.[41]

The events of 1257 and 1258 were extraordinary and should be judged as such. The minority period as a whole displays a natural inclination to work through the normal channels of government despite the crisis. Though family interests rather than any political ideals guided the actions of the nobility in Scotland in these difficult years,[42] the reverence for royal authority is unmistakeable, even during 1257 and 1258. The relationship between crown and nobility, under severe strain during the minority, still survived. The nobility of Scotland also showed a clear awareness that the support of Henry III was necessary for stability in Scotland. The nobility were not a particularly coherent group, but were generally very conservative, acting in unison only when attempts were being made to intrude into the already well-established baronial clique.

The compromise council of 1258,[43] in which supporters from both Comyn and Durward groups were apparently willing to work together, is normally taken as a sign that the unsettled minority period was drawing to a close,[44] to be replaced by a period when the aristocracy were firmly under royal control, allowing the Scottish kingdom to develop with royal authority increasing in the west and the north, and with greater political independence being won from England. Certainly, Alexander III seems to have emerged in full command of Scottish government by 1260,[45] two years before his twenty-first birthday. It is perhaps unwise, however, to make too great a distinction between the years of Alexander III's minority and those of his maturity. Attempts have been made to explain the apparently dramatic change in the nobility's role and attitude after the minority was over. One view is that the Comyns were in decline: it has been suggested that there is no evidence of Comyn domination in the period 1260 to 1286, and that historians must resist the temptation to 'read in the events of 1286–1306, when the Comyns were the most important single family in Scotland, and when their every marriage added to the complex of their powers, a similar domination of the reign of Alexander III'.[46] Such an argument sees Alexander III denying his patronage to disruptive barons, and restricting the monopoly of power enjoyed by the Comyns by encouraging a junior branch of the family, the Comyns of Kilbride, to be more visible at his court than the more senior Buchan and Badenoch lines, and also by promoting other 'new men' in the royal circle, such as Simon Fraser, Reginald Cheyne, Thomas Randolph and Hugh Berkeley.[47]

While the removal of baronial malcontents and their replacement by 'new men' seems a logical way to explain a more responsible attitude on the part of the nobility between 1258 and 1286, an analysis of offices held and royal missions accomplished in this period presents a different picture. Alan Durward, a major participant in the politics of the minority, did not, it is true, hold major office after 1258. He was nonetheless recognised as one of the leading members of the nobility in the late 1250s and early 1260s by, amongst other things, his membership of the provisional regency council set up in 1261.[48] He seems to have retired, however: he witnessed relatively few royal charters and does not seem to have been involved in royal business from c. 1268 until his death in 1275. When the fortunes of the Comyn 'faction' after 1258 are reviewed, however, a surprising picture emerges. Far from being eclipsed, the Comyns dominated political and public offices, royal missions and witness lists to royal charters. It is striking that those very members of the Comyn party so roundly condemned in 1257 and 1258 retained the offices which they then held. The premier political office, the justiciarship of Scotia,[49] was held by Alexander Comyn, earl of Buchan, from 1258 until his death in 1289. The chief of the Badenoch branch of the family was justiciar of Galloway in 1258 (and after?) and again before 1275. Other members of the Comyn following[50] who held justiciarships were Thomas of Normanville, justiciar of Lothian c. 1259–60, Hugh Berkeley, justiciar of Lothian c. 1279–c. 1292, and Aymer Maxwell, justiciar of Galloway in 1264. William Wishart retained the post of chancellor between 1258 and

1273, and Aymer Maxwell retained the post of chamberlain,[51] which then remained in Comyn hands until 1290.

Comyn dominance of offices of state becomes even more apparent when possession of sheriffdoms is analysed.[52] Comyn men dominated the sheriffdoms of Roxburgh, Dingwall, Forfar,[53] Kincardine (or Mearns), Elgin,[54] Berwick and Cromarty for most of Alexander III's reign, and at times Comyns or their supporters also held the sheriffdoms of Fife,[55] Dumfries, Peebles, Perth, Lanark, Dumbarton, Wigtown and Ayr. Some key Comyn men held a multiplicity of offices: Alexander Comyn, as well as being justiciar of Scotia, was sheriff of Wigtown, c. 1263–66 and sheriff of Dingwall c. 1264–66, from c. 1275 constable of Scotland, and dominated the witness lists of Alexander III's charters; Aymer Maxwell was chamberlain c. 1259–c. 1260, justiciar of Galloway c. 1264, sheriff of Roxburgh c. 1249?, sheriff of Peebles c. 1262 and sheriff of Dumfries 1264–66; Thomas Randolph was chamberlain c. 1269–77, sheriff of Roxburgh in 1266 and sheriff of Berwick c. 1264–66, and was a frequent witness to the king's charters; William Soules, son of Nicholas Soules (related to the Comyns through marriage), was justiciar of Lothian 1279–92/3, sheriff of Roxburgh by 1289 and before 1289–91 sheriff of Inverness, while John Soules was sheriff of Berwick by 1289; David Graham, who had been deputy justiciar of Lothian in 1248, was sheriff of Berwick c. 1264 while his son Patrick was very prominent in royal witness lists of the 1270s and 1280s and was to be sheriff of Stirling by 1289. Both Patrick Graham and John Soules took part in Alexander III's search for a second bride in 1284. Other examples are too numerous to detail.

It is interesting to find similar Comyn domination of ecclesiastical offices between 1260 and 1286. Again familiar names recur: Henry Cheyne was bishop of Aberdeen 1282–1328; William Comyn of Kilconquhar was bishop of Brechin 1275–7; William Wishart (from a family prominent in the 1255 list of Comyn supporters) was bishop of Glasgow 1270–71 and bishop of St Andrews 1271–9, while Robert Wishart was bishop of Glasgow 1271–1316; and Gamelin was bishop of St Andrews 1255–71.[56]

Neither offices held nor evidence from royal witness lists support the notion that Alexander III was deliberately elevating the junior Comyn line, the Comyns of Kilbride, above the main branches of Badenoch and Buchan. Alexander Comyn, earl of Buchan, was the most regular of all witnesses to Alexander III's charters, while the Badenoch branch, represented by John Comyn, both father and son, was also present in the royal circle, though not very frequently. The prominence of William Comyn of Kilbride in royal witness lists is a sign of yet another member of the family coming to prominence rather than of the eclipse of the two main branches. Absence of Kilbride representation in the political actions of the Comyn party from 1251 to 1258 should not be taken as a sign that there was no active support from this branch for the two more senior branches of the family. William Comyn's father, David (d.1247) was clearly a member of Earl Walter Comyn's party in 1244. Charter evidence certainly suggests that William Comyn was an active member of the Comyn party and maintained close connections with the Badenoch line.[57]

Analysis of offices held and presence in the royal circle, then, indicates a clear dominance by the Comyns and noble families known to be in their following. Other families who emerged in the period c. 1260–86 are of less certain, unknown, or no affiliation. Members of the Moray family gathered political strength as the period progressed: Alexander Moray was sheriff of Inverness after 1264 and sheriff of Ayr by 1288, Malcolm Moray was sheriff of Perth 1257x1289 and Walter and William Moray were witnesses to several royal charters. Their affiliation is not clear. Walter Moray was in the Durward party of the 1250s and appears to have been justiciar of Lothian 1255–57,[58] but Freskyn Moray was in the Comyn following of 1258 and other members of the family (Walter and Malcolm) appeared as witnesses to charters of Alexander Comyn, earl of Buchan in the 1260s.[59] The family of Stewart certainly had no Comyn association. With their hereditary position as Steward of Scotland and their vast estates derived from the first royal grants to the family in the twelfth century,[60] the Stewarts were already a powerful family by the middle of the thirteenth century, with access to the royal council. In Alexander III's reign after c. 1260 they stepped more firmly to the forefront of the political stage. Walter Stewart, a younger member of the family, became earl of Menteith in controversial circumstances c. 1261, was sheriff of Ayr by 1264, sheriff of Dumbarton between 1271 and 1288 and was also very prominent in royal witness lists in the 1280s. Alexander Stewart and his son James appeared regularly in the royal circle from the 1250s to the 1280s. From a less prominent background and with no known affiliation, the Fraser family, especially in the person of Simon Fraser, emerged in the 1260s and 1270s to real importance.[61] Other prominent nobles in the royal circle included John Lamberton, sheriff of Stirling c. 1265 and a regular witness to royal charters, especially in the mid-1260s. It is also noticeable that the Bissets emerge again in the person of William Bisset, a regular witness to royal acts in the 1270s.

Of the elite thirteen earls of Scotland, a number have already been referred to as holding political offices, Alexander, earl of Buchan and William, earl of Mar especially, but Walter Stewart, earl of Menteith also being significant. William's successor as earl of Mar, Donald, also appeared regularly in royal witness lists of the 1280s. Patrick, earl of Dunbar, to be joined in later years by his son, was a more frequent witness to Alexander III's royal acts in the 1260s and 1270s than any other individual magnate apart from Alexander, earl of Buchan, yet he remained without any political office or apparent responsibility. Evidence from royal witness lists hardly indicates that he dropped 'out of sight' or was wholly ignored,[62] but his role is a mystery. It is interesting, however, that he apparently became tied to the Comyn family by marriage to one of the daughters of the earl of Buchan.[63] Both Malise, earl of Strathearn and Gilbert Umphraville, earl of Angus appeared as witnesses, although not very frequently; the appearances in the royal circle of the earls of Fife in this period, Colban, Malcolm and Duncan, were few, as were those of the earls of Atholl. The earls of Carrick, Adam and, after 1272, Robert Bruce, appeared infrequently, although Robert Bruce was beginning to make some impact after 1274. It is perhaps appropriate to end this analysis with the names Balliol and Bruce. Members of the Balliol family made very occasional appearances in the Scottish king's circle; the name Bruce made little impact on Scottish politics until the 1270s. Neither held political office or had obvious political influence in Scotland; neither looked like disturbing the Comyn grip on the Scottish political scene.

Marriage further sealed Comyn dominance in the second half of the thirteenth century. Alexander Comyn's sisters had made 'good' marriages: Elizabeth married William, earl of Mar, his half-sister Jean had married William, earl of Ross, Idonea had married Gilbert Hay, and Agnes had married Philip Meldrum. Five of Alexander Comyn's daughters married major Scottish barons: Patrick, earl of Dunbar, Malise, earl of Strathearn, Gilbert Umphraville, earl of Angus, William Brechin and Nicholas Soules, while Alexander's son and heir, John, married Isabella, daughter of Colban, earl of Fife.[64] Alexander Comyn's place at the head of the aristocratic establishment of Scotland was secure, both socially and politically.

Due attention should be paid to baronial patronage in this period, as well as royal patronage. Noble families could rise through association with the Comyn family through either marriage or political support, as well as through the patronage of the king: take, for example, Hugh Abernethy, sheriff of Roxburgh in 1264 and a very frequent witness to royal acts in the 1260s and 1270s, and in the inner core of Comyn support in the difficult years for the family, 1257 and 1258. Earl Alexander's prominent presence, usually first, in the witness lists to private deeds is to be noted especially in those deeds which concern one of his supporters: he headed the witness list to an important marriage contract between Hugh Abernethy and William, lord of Douglas in 1259,[65] and was also first witness to a royal grant to Hugh at Scone in 1265.[66] Hugh appears to have been regularly in Earl Alexander's company.[67]

The clear Comyn dominance hardly suggests a delicate balancing operation between rival baronial factions. Had the poachers, therefore, of the minority period become the gamekeepers of Alexander III's maturity? Certainly it was the same Alexander Comyn associated with the violent hounding of the Bissets in 1242, the kidnapping of King Alexander III in 1257 and the treaty with the Welsh of 1258, who was to become the justiciar of Scotia and the king's chief royal officer throughout his reign.

The loss of the earldom of Menteith from Comyn control after 1258 does not seem to have affected Comyn dominance, but the episode,[68] if viewed from the baronial standpoint, can shed some light on the realities of the relationship between crown and nobility in Alexander III's reign. When, after the death of Walter Comyn, earl of Menteith in 1258, his widow married John Russell, a large body of magnates, according to Fordun, 'took this in high dudgeon'.[69] They thought she had disdained the noble lords of Scotland who wanted to wed her in order to marry a low-born English knight. This is another of the comparatively rare episodes which illustrate the conservative aristocratic elite acting in unison to protect its status from new or low-status intruders. Nevertheless, the leading magnates of the realm did, at the request of the king, sanction the marriage, which meant that the head of the Badenoch branch of the Comyn family, John Comyn, earl Walter's nephew, would succeed only to the lordship of Badenoch. When John Comyn then seized the countess and her second husband and forced them to resign the earldom to him, the general baronial response is worth noting. At an assembly of king and magnates, eleven of whom were known members of the Comyn 'party', a compromise was agreed upon: Walter Stewart, on his wife's behalf (she was perhaps a cousin of Countess Isabella), should be invested with the earldom. If narrow factional interest was all-important to the nobility, then surely a Comyn-dominated court would have made a decision in favour of John Comyn.[70] The decision reached may have been *contra justitiam,*[71] and was not an end to the affair,[72] but a politically sensible decision had been made, aimed at promoting stability 'while the king was still a minor'.[73] The Comyns themselves may have recognised that they had a 'black sheep' in the family, a man described by Fordun as 'prone to robbery and rashness'.[74] He was to cause annoyance to fellow magnates in 1269 when he upset the earl of Atholl by building a castle at Blair in Atholl.[75] His loss of the earldom of Menteith by 1260-61 was a personal setback to him in Scotland, not a setback for the Comyn family. These events explain, perhaps, why John Comyn was not as regularly in the royal circle as might have been expected, given his tenure of the office of justiciar of Galloway, and his standing in the Comyn family. They also explain why he spent much time seeking advancement in England during the 1260s.[76]

The alliance between the monarchy and this mighty family is of fundamental importance to an understanding of the administration of Scotland during the reign of Alexander III. Comyn landowning power throughout Scotland, largely a result of consistent royal patronage, undoubtedly made Alexander Comyn's authority more effective as justiciar of Scotia, and indeed throughout the country. A further sign that the justiciarship of Scotia was being elevated into a justiciarship of Scotland is seen in the king's licence, dated at Kilwinning in 1260, commanding the earl of Buchan 'and his (i.e. the king's) bailies of Carrick' to hold an inquest 'to inquire whether Hector son of Hector of Carrick was vested and seized *per dies et annos* in five pennyworths of the land at "Ackinsauhile" (Auchensoule in Barr, Ayrshire) and how he was ejected therein'.[77] Earl Alexander is not known to have had interests in Carrick until after 1264.[78] His role as justiciar, certainly very useful to the king administratively, judicially and financially,[79] was significantly extended into a military role in 1263 when he played a leading part in the defence of the country against a Norwegian threat, and in the extension of royal authority in the Western Isles.[80] Alexander Comyn also took part in a reorganisation of royal control in the south-west and north of the kingdom. In the 1260s an extension of the general pattern of sheriffdoms was made,[81] Wigtown and Dingwall being erected into sheriffdoms in 1253-6 and placed under Alexander Comyn's control, apparently as hereditary offices. The territorial influence of the Buchan branch of the family in the south-west was greatly increased on the death of Roger Quincy in 1264, through the vast inheritance won by Alexander Comyn's wife, one of the co-heiresses to the estate.[82] It is interesting to note that the custody of Earl Roger's lands went not to royal clerks but in part to a great magnate like Earl Alexander, who was also one of the interested parties. He also acquired the office of constable, again as a result of the Quincy inheritance, an office which provided him with yet more land,[83] and established him still more closely to the king. Even prior to the Quincy inheritance, the Badenoch branch of the family already had an interest in that region. John Comyn, head of that branch after 1258, had important influence in Peebleshire and Dumfriesshire,[84] and was justiciar of Galloway in 1258 and again in 1275. He also played a military role as one of the leaders of a royal expedition against Man in 1275.[85] Comyn presence in the south-west was further emphasised by William Comyn's role as sheriff of Ayr c. 1265 and the importance attached to his contribution to the development of royal authority in the west is perhaps gauged by his regular appearances in the royal circle, especially in the 1270s.

In the north, as noted above, Earl Alexander was sheriff of Dingwall c. 1264–6, but his role in this part of the country was even more clearly seen in 1282 when he was sent on urgent royal business to the northern isles. In a letter to excuse his absence from conflicting responsibilities in England, Alexander III made it very clear to the English king that the earl's activities in the north were indispensable to both Scottish king and kingdom.[86] The involvement of Comyn associates in the extension of the kingdom in both south-west and north was also important. Thus William, earl of Mar was sheriff of Dumbarton c. 1264–6, Aymer Maxwell was sheriff of Dumfries c. 1264–5, and the sheriffdom of Cromarty was founded c. 1266 as another hereditary office for the Mowat family.

To study the Comyn family after 1258, then, is to study a family who were the very pillars of monarchy. Despite the accusations made about the behaviour of the nobility in the period of Alexander III's minority, this should not be regarded as atypical. The Stewarts, for instance, were another family to benefit from royal patronage, and particularly from the desire of Alexander III to define further his authority in the west. Already powerful through the honorary title *Senescallus Scotiae*, which gave them automatic access to the king, the family had much territorial influence through the generosity of David I to the first

Stewart, and were especially powerful in Renfrewshire and the northern half of Kyle, Bute and Cowal. The Stewarts gained extra status when Walter, a younger brother, gained the earldom of Menteith in 1260–1. This same Walter was sheriff of Ayr sometime before 1264 and sheriff of Dumbarton between 1271 and 1288. The Stewarts played a prominent part not only in the defence of the kingdom against Hakon IV, but also in the extension of royal authority in the south-west highlands. By 1262 Walter Stewart, extending his influence through royal authority, had acquired interests in Knapdale and Arran at the expense of the Macsweens and may also have ousted the Bissets from Arran.[87] The possession of the two key sheriffdoms of Ayr and Dumbarton also emphasises the firm royal backing for the Stewarts in this area. Alexander Stewart played a significant role too when he was commander of the Scottish army at the battle of Largs. Both he and his son James feature regularly in the royal circle in Alexander III's reign.

Mutual self-interest and interdependence was a feature also of the relationship between the crown and the Morays in the north. The delegation of power to the Morays by the crown in order to achieve a greater measure of royal authority in that area was a feature of the thirteenth century generally.[88] By the mid-thirteenth century the family already held the earldom of Sutherland, the lordships of Duffus (near Elgin) and Petty (near Inverness) and lands in Strathspey. It is hardly surprising, given Alexander III's anxiety to increase royal authority in the north, that the Morays became further involved in royal service in this reign. Alexander Moray was sheriff of Inverness by 1264x6, Malcolm Moray was sheriff of Perth 1257x89 and no less than four members of the family appear as witnesses to royal acts. The family's increasing influence throughout Alexander III's reign is highlighted by Andrew Moray's position as sheriff of Ayr by 1288, and after Alexander Comyn's death, justiciar of Scotia c. ?1289x93–?1296.

Comyns, Stewarts and Morays were ideal candidates for advancement through royal service in Alexander III's reign. All had sufficient territorial influence for their authority, wielded on behalf of the king, to be accepted in the north, the south-west, or, in the case of the Comyns, both. The crown was dependent on its magnates for wielding royal power and authority in the provinces, and the sharing of government between crown and aristocracy was in the circumstances mutually beneficial. Interdependence was the logical outcome of a situation where the Scottish king had enough material resources to reward magnates, but not enough to overawe them, and where the nobility did not (unlike the nobility of England) have to suffer the consequences of an aggressive and expensive foreign policy with its heavy aides, scutages and tallages. It is not difficult to see why confrontation between crown and magnates was a more common feature in thirteenth-century England than it was in Scotland.

The nobility of Scotland, of course, had a real interest in preserving the integrity of the Scottish kingdom and extending the authority of a king who could give them and their followers rich rewards. Evidence of aristocratic involvement in the growth of a stronger nation, more independent of England, is also apparent. The nobles, as part of the governing community, were used as messengers of state on various occasions,[89] and those magnates involved in the power struggles of the minority gave experienced counsel in 1260–1, for example, when Alexander III allowed his wife to go to England to stay with her mother during her confinement prior to the birth of the heiress to the Scottish throne.[90] On that occasion the dangers of a minority were clearly recognised, as shown by agreements which tried to counter any possibility of the Scottish government disintegrating: in particular, the clause stipulating that if the king of Scotland should die, a body of thirteen men (in effect a regency council of four bishops, five earls and four barons) or three or four of them would take his heir to Scotland and have responsibility for government, was surely a sign of a responsible aristocratic governing community. The perpetuation of kingship and kingdom loomed large again when the succession was threatened by the deaths of Alexander's son David in 1281, his daughter Margaret in 1283 and his eldest son, the prince Alexander, in 1284. In February 1284, in a parliament at Scone, the most important magnates in Scotland (thirteen earls and twenty-five barons) gave solid affirmation of the principle of primogeniture when they bound themselves to maintain the succession of Margaret, 'Maid of Norway'.[91] Such formal and mature constitutional procedures in the period 1260–86, together with the refusal of Alexander III to acknowledge English overlordship in 1251 and 1278,[92] and many other lesser actions,[93] seem to point to a growing sense of nationality in Scotland.

It is difficult, however, to assess the importance of this notion to the nobility. The warfare which was to follow, and the consequent polarisation of allegiances, has clouded the issue, particularly with regard to that significant group of nobles who held land in both Scotland and England.[94] It has been pointed out[95] that out of thirteen Scottish earldoms nine were held by cross-border magnates during the thirteenth century, and that in this period also senior offices such as the justiciarships of Scotia and Lothian, and chamberlain, were usually occupied by nobility with land in England. Most major baronial families were included within this group,[96] the aspirations and ambitions of which must therefore be taken into account.

Historians, relying on hindsight, have tended to emphasise the political problems liable to arise (after 1290) from nobles in Alexander III's reign holding land on both sides of the border, or have concentrated on linking the nobility with the developing idea of nationality. From a baronial viewpoint, it was probably of much greater concern to seek full advantage from lands owned in both realms, whether gained through marriages or through royal patronage. Access to the larger resources of the Angevin monarchy and the greater wealth of the kingdom of England were attractive considerations for the nobility. Landholding in Scotland also had attractions for magnates: it could be economically very profitable, as studies of Roger Quincy and the Balliols have shown,[97] and it did not suffer from the harsh royal taxation levied in England. Alexander III's reign saw a long period of peace and very good relations between the two kingdoms. The realities of peace rather than the potentialities of war governed baronial attitudes, preventing any chance of serious conflicts of loyalties, and giving cross-border families maximum opportunity to exploit their landed resources. All Anglo-Scottish magnates benefited from, and thus had a common desire for, peace. Their role was a stabilising one. In the minority period when, as has been seen, there was a common regard for the English king as a bringer of stability, members of the Anglo-Scottish baronage played a prominent part: magnates such as Roger Quincy, Robert Ros, John Balliol, and Malise, earl of Strathearn were frequently used on embassies between the two countries in the minority period; John Balliol and Robert Ros, lord of Wark, Helmsley and Sanquhar were guardians of the young king and queen of Scotland between 1251 and 1255;[98] and Malise, earl of Strathearn was given responsibility for safeguarding the queen of Scotland's interests in 1258.[99] Naturally, when the relationship between the kings of Scotland and England was particularly warm and close, magnates holding land on both sides of the border reinforced this 'tie of indissoluble affection'[100] by involving themselves, their families and officials in their cross-border enterprises. This seems to have been the case even when estates were separated by great distances: the chief landholding of the Comyn earls of Buchan was in northern Scotland, but the family's interests and commitments were still vigorously pursued on the other side of the border, both by attorneys,[101] and by the family's personal presence on their English estates.

Anglo-Scottish magnates were not a coherent group in Scottish society. They exhibited varying degrees of attachment to the kingdoms in which their lands lay, though they all accepted the commitments which went with landownership on both sides of the border. Even within one family, different branches developed different policies and aspirations, dependent on individual circumstances. Again, the Comyn family is a good example. All three branches of the family, Buchan, Badenoch and Kilbride, had substantial estates in England. The widespread Scottish interests of the Buchan line have already been noted, and the Quincy inheritance also brought substantial landed interests in Dorset, Leicestershire, Warwickshire, Huntingdonshire, Berkshire, Cambridgeshire, Bedford, Essex, Worcester, Cumberland and Oxfordshire.[102] Though Alexander Comyn was actively and heavily engaged in Scottish government, he showed himself to be most anxious to secure the full rights of his wife in England, the break-up of the English Quincy estates being a protracted affair.[103] During the period 1264–79 frequent safe-conducts were issued for Earl Alexander, his wife and envoys to come to England.[104] He was constantly asking and receiving permission to appoint attorneys in his place.[105] While he was slow to come to the king's court in person to do homage for Elizabeth's property,[106] a sign perhaps of the distance involved or his responsibilities in Scottish government, it would not be fair to call him an absentee landlord. He was present at Shepshed, one of his administrative centres in the Midlands, to receive the homage of William of Brideport in 1281,[107] and his sons were involved in their father's English estates before his death in 1289.[108] It should also be noted that the attorneys used by Earl Alexander were drawn from both his Scottish and English estates, and appear alongside each other in the records.[109]

Alexander Comyn's ready acknowledgement of the commitments, both military and financial, which were owed to the king of England for his English lands was a sign of the importance of his English inheritance. In 1276 he was among 178 tenants-in-chief summoned to meet Edward I at Worcester in order to fight the Welsh, and although he did not serve personally, he paid the scutage of 50 marks (one third of two knights' fees).[110] Similarly in 1282, his recognition of his duty to serve the king of England was clearly shown in his letter to Edward I which expressed his regret at being unable to serve personally against the Welsh.[111] (On this occasion his son Roger served in his stead.) This episode is also interesting in that it shows how dual allegiance was dealt with in practice, for this was the occasion on which he had been sent by the Scottish king to the northern isles on urgent business.[112]

A different set of circumstances governed the activities in England of John Comyn, chief of the Badenoch branch of the family. This branch also had much landed influence throughout Scotland, and in England held land in Tynedale, south-west Northumberland.[113] When the family suffered the setback of the loss of the earldom of Menteith, it is perhaps more than coincidental that John Comyn, although still appearing in the Scottish king's circle in the early 1260s, was more conspicuous by his appearance in the English king's court during the 1260s and early 1270s. He was clearly taking advantage of the opportunities open to him for advancement in England when he appeared to be out of favour in Scotland. He was in the English king's household in 1262, 1264 and 1265,[114] and served Henry III personally in 1264 at the battle of Lewes, being captured there along with other Scottish magnates such as John Balliol and Robert Bruce.[115] The reward for personal service in England was great,[116] and John Comyn was handsomely rewarded. In 1262 he received a royal confirmation of his important Tynedale lands;[117] for serving Henry III in 1264 and 1265 he received 100 marks;[118] in 1267, for 'his laudable service', John Comyn and his heirs were granted the lands of Simon Veer, the king's enemy,[119] and again later in the same year the king 'will complete for him "before all others" 300l. yearly of land which he has granted to him'.[120] The English records mention numerous other grants and favours, and John was still receiving royal gifts in 1272.[121]

In complete contrast to the Badenoch involvement in England was the attitude of the Kilbride branch of the family. They held the lordship of Kilbride, land in Peebleshire and around Falkirk,[122] and in England had land in Northumberland, Norfolk, Suffolk, Essex and Hertford.[123] David Comyn, like Alexander Comyn, had scrupulously acknowledged his commitments and obligations to the English king in his anxiety to succeed to his full English inheritance, which had similarly been the subject of a protracted legal dispute in the English courts between 1215 and 1247.[124] David's son William took a different attitude to his English lands. He was frequently involved in court cases between 1257 and 1279 either to answer for his scutage or as defendant for cases involving land dealings.[125] His disregard for his obligations to the king of England was most apparent in the 1260s when not only did he fail to serve Henry III against his baronial opposition (as did John Comyn,

Robert Bruce and John Balliol), but actually sided with Simon Montfort against the English king. As a result, his English lands were forfeited.[126] Clearly, the advancement of William Comyn of Kilbride and his branch of the family was in Scotland, through the patronage of the Scottish king.

A few examples serve to highlight the personal advantage of having interests in both countries. In 1264 Margaret, queen of Scotland, appealed to her father, Henry III, to procure the release of Richard Comyn, brother of John Comyn, who had been made a prisoner in the king's service.[127] Even William Comyn of Kilbride, who had so flagrantly disregarded his commitments to the English king, benefited when in 1268 Henry III restored William's forfeited English lands *ad instanciam regis Scotiae.*[128] In 1282 William Comyn of Kirkintilloch, son of John Comyn (d.1278) pleaded with Edward I to use his influence with the king of Scotland and his son in favour of his claim to the earldom of Menteith. Amicable letters were sent to Alexander III and his son,[129] and as a result in 1285 William gained half of the earldom, but not the title.

Many other families took advantage of the extra source of patronage offered by the king of England. Nobles ousted from Scotland by political ill-fortune during the minority period found Henry III and England a suitable and often profitable refuge. Alan Durward, David Lindsay, Walter Moray and Malise, earl of Strathearn all received favour from the English king, usually in return for some service.[130] Alan Durward in particular frequently appears in the English records during the minority period, especially between 1251 and 1255, when he was ousted by the Comyns from Scottish government. After he faded from the Scottish political scene again just after the mid-1260s, he was still in receipt of English royal gifts from 1268 until shortly before his death in 1275.[131] Clearly Durward found more favour in England than in Scotland in his later years. The names Bruce and Balliol appear only irregularly in Scottish records of the 1250s and 1260s. Playing only brief roles in the changing governments of the minority period, they held no political offices during Alexander III's maturity, but were both deeply involved in English politics in the 1250s and 1260s. Marriage to Devorguilla, daughter of Alan of Galloway, in 1233 had ensured that the Balliols had acquired vast estates in both countries by the mid-thirteenth century, through Devorguilla's paternal and maternal inheritances.[132] The family thus had a secure territorial base for advancement in both countries, but in the 1260s was prominent only on the English political scene. By the 1270s they were amongst the top-ranking English nobility. Potential in Scotland had not yet been realised, though their position there was further strengthened through the marriage c. 1280 of a sister (Eleanor) of John Balliol II (future king of Scotland) to John Comyn, lord of Badenoch (d.1303).[133] The Bruces, too, were more active on the English political scene, at least until the 1270s. The family held positions of responsibility such as the governorship of Carlisle castle,[134] served in Henry III's army in 1264, was keen to promise future service,[135] and was in regular receipt of Henry III's patronage. Marriages had already brought them sufficient territorial power to have a political platform in both England and Scotland,[136] but they were seen very little in the Scottish royal circle in the 1250s and 1260s, and it was not until the marriage of the Competitor's son to the countess of Carrick in 1272 that this significant step into the elite of the Scottish nobility gave the family the opportunity to realise its potential in Scotland, and the name of Robert Bruce became more familiar on the Scottish political scene.

While the closeness of the kingdoms and the undoubted influence of Henry III in Scotland occasionally worked to the detriment of Anglo-Scottish nobles, it cannot be disputed that their interests were usually well served by retaining land and influence on both sides of the border. The two kings and kingdoms also benefited from being able to call upon extra assistance from outside their kingdoms in times of crisis: England received the benefit of support from Anglo-Scottish families, including Bruces, Balliols and Comyns, when Henry III had to face baronial opposition between 1258 and 1264,[137] and a number of Anglo-Scottish magnates served English kings in support of Angevin policy across the Channel. In Scotland too, Anglo-Scottish nobles were frequently used as a calming influence during the minority of Alexander III, and it is worth pointing out the active role of John Vesci, lord of Alnwick and Sprouston, in the definition of royal authority in the west, as one of the leaders of Alexander III's expeditionary force to the Isle of Man in 1275.[138]

The widespread incidence of cross-border land ownership meant that identification with nation does not appear to have been an overriding concern. A number of families, and not just those of great substance in both kingdoms,[139] would have been faced with a great dilemma if they had been forced to choose between the kingdoms. In the settled conditions of Alexander III's reign, aristocratic priorities were their families, their lands and status in either kingdom; their greatest fears were lack of male heirs, minority of heirs and the partition of inheritances.[140]

The essence of the nobility in Scotland in the later years of Alexander III's reign is effectively captured in the list of thirteen earls and twenty-five barons who swore in 1284 to uphold the succession of Margaret of Norway to the Scottish throne.[141] This aristocratic hierarchy was a very diverse group comprising native dynasties, 'settler' families (though some families established in Scotland since the early twelfth century do not, perhaps, deserve this description), families whose territorial strength was almost entirely based in Scotland, and many who held lands on both sides of the border. The place of these families in the aristocratic elite of Scotland had been won in a variety of ways. The majority of the earldoms were still held by native dynasties who retained a status in line with the dignity of the title 'earl'. A number of families who had settled in Scotland in the twelfth century — Stewart, Comyn, Bruce — had acquired this dignity through marriage by the end of the thirteenth century. Certain families featured particularly strongly in the 1284 list: the Comyns, who had dominated the baronage for most of the thirteenth century, were represented by two members of the family, with the pre-eminent nobleman of the reign, Alexander Comyn, earl of Buchan, Constable and justiciar of Scotia, heading the list. Comyn leadership of the baronial community in Scotland is well attested by the number of names in the list connected to the family by marriage, political association, or both — Patrick, earl of Dunbar, Malise, earl of Strathearn, Gilbert, earl of Angus, Balliol, Brechin, Soules, Hay, Graham, Maxwell and Cheyne. The Stewarts, important in the twelfth century, had moved right to the forefront of the political stage by the acquisition of an earldom and through valuable royal service for Alexander III. The Bruces had come to the fore through good marriages which had gained them an earldom and much territorial influence, rather than through royal service. The same was true of the Balliols, who were also represented on the list by two members. Relatively 'new' families who had risen mainly by royal service included the Frasers, St Clairs and Morays.[142] Native families who had similarly risen to prominence either through association with the dominant families[143] or through royal service were represented by Alexander Ewenson Macdougall, lord of Lorn, Alan Macruaidhri, lord of Garmoran, and Angus Mor Macdonald, lord of Islay. The first two had been leaders of Alexander III's expedition in 1275 to suppress the Manx revolt. The Macdougalls and Macdonalds had much power in Argyll and Kintyre, and it seems that in about 1284 Alexander Macdougall was given responsibility over the west highlands and islands by Alexander III.[144] The Macdougalls, it seemed, enjoyed benefits similar to the Morays, Stewarts and Comyns in the service of the Scottish king and kingdom.

The leadership of Alexander III's expedition to Man in 1275 reinforces an impression of the diversity of the Scottish nobility: Alan, lord of Garmoran, Alexander, lord of Lorn, John Comyn, justiciar of Galloway and John Vesci, lord of Alnwick and Sprouston. Despite their diversity, however, the nobility in Alexander III's reign all saw great benefit for themselves in co-operation with the crown and access to royal patronage. They proved to be a responsible governing community. Traditional accounts of self-seeking factions causing difficulties for the monarchy during the minority period, being 'tamed' by royal authority during Alexander III's maturity, and lapsing once more into factional fighting after his death in 1286, are disproved by detailed analysis. While most of the credit for the development of the Scottish kingdom between 1260 and 1286 has been given to Alexander III himself for his skilful eclipse of the 'overmighty' Comyns and the careful balancing of rival baronial factions, evidence of the period has pointed neither to an eclipse, nor to an attempt to balance baronial factions. The king, in truth, relied on his mighty magnates such as the Comyns, Stewarts and Morays, who naturally became even more powerful as a result. The Comyns and their associates in particular dominated political offices and the royal court throughout the period of Alexander III's maturity. The achievements of Alexander III's reign were the result of an effective alliance between the crown and the nobility. The authority of the king, accepted by the nobility even in the minority period, was a strong factor for stability between 1260 and 1286, but the dominance of the Comyns and the acceptance of them as leaders of a well-established aristocratic governing community by the nobility in general, was another important factor in the interests of stability, which should not be ignored.

There was little sign before 1286 of the great conflicts of the 1290s and the War of Independence. It is misleading to concentrate on the potential rivalries rather than the actual baronial scene of Alexander III's reign. Potential rivalries there inevitably were in a world of aggrandisement, status and power. Marriages which brought noble families to great territorial influence and power could also dictate the political direction of baronial ambition: the marriage of John Balliol's sister to John Comyn, lord of Badenoch (d.1303) in the early 1280s, for example, was to govern the political stances of these two families in the crisis after 1286. It was also, of course, the claims to the throne of Balliol and Bruce through their families' marriage links with the royal family which was to ignite their rivalry in a later period. There were, however, no signs of actual rivalry between them in Alexander III's reign, and, as has been seen, concentration on them has distorted our view of the baronial scene in this reign.

The reality was of an aristocratic governing community dominated by the Comyns and their associates with their ascendancy showing little sign of challenge before 1286. Noble families in Scotland during Alexander III's reign had wide-ranging social, economic and political aspirations and a number of peaceful avenues through which to pursue these fully, both in Scotland and in England. The balance of government would have to be seriously upset before the Scottish nobility would follow the precedent set by the English magnates in 1258; stability between the two kingdoms would have to be equally upset for the problem of suzerainty and English claims in this regard to become a central issue, destroying the good relationship which had been to the mutual benefit of both kings and nobility. The worst did happen, and the common enemy of both king and nobility, lack of male heirs, created crisis for both the kingdom and the baronial establishment. It provided the circumstances for both Balliols and Bruces to spring to the centre of the political arena. The events of the 1290s should not be allowed, however, to cast too great a shadow over the realities of the baronial world in Alexander III's reign, with a small, well-established elite of noble families able to take advantage of settled conditions to prosper and act in concert with the king for mutual benefit.

NOTES

1. *Chron. Fordun*, i, 298 (ii, 293). Fordun was writing in the latter part of the fourteenth century, but there appears to be an otherwise unknown but self-consistent source in Fordun providing information about political events in the mid-thirteenth century.
2. For the 'Challenge of the House of Comyn' see Watt, 'Minority'.
3. '. . . the inveterate hostility of great houses to the Crown and to each other': A. M. Mackenzie, *The Kingdom of Scotland* (Edinburgh, 1948), 113.

4. In general, see Barrow, *Anglo-Norman Era* and Stringer, *Nobility Essays.* For specialist studies: K. J. Stringer, *Earl David of Huntingdon 1152–1219: A Study in Anglo-Scottish History* (Edinburgh, 1985; henceforth Stringer, *Earl David*); Simpson, *Quincy*; A. Young, *The Political Role of the Comyns in Scotland and England in the Thirteenth Century* (unpublished PhD thesis, University of Newcastle upon Tyne, 1974; henceforth Young, *Comyns*); C. J. Neville, *The Earls of Strathearn from the Twelfth to the Mid-Fourteenth Century with an Edition of their Written Acts* (unpublished PhD thesis, University of Aberdeen, 1983).

For the later middle ages, see J. Wormald, 'Taming the Magnates?' in Stringer, *Nobility Essays*; J. Wormald, *Court, Kirk and Community: Scotland 1470–1625* (London, 1981); N. Macdougall, 'The Sources: A Reappraisal of the Legend', in Brown, *Fifteenth Century.*

5. Watt, 'Minority'; Duncan, *Kingdom*, 553–76; Young, 'Walter Comyn'.

6. See, for example, Barrow, *Kingship and Unity*; Barrow, *Kingdom*; Duncan, *Kingdom.*

7. *Chron. Fordun*, i, 293, 295–8 (ii, 289, 290–3).

8. A. A. M. Duncan, *The Nation of Scots and the Declaration of Arbroath* (Historical Association Pamphlet, General Series no. 75, 1970; henceforth Duncan, *Declaration of Arbroath*), 8.

9. Stell, 'The Balliol Family', particularly at 151 and 158; Young, *Comyns*, 313.

10. *Chron. Bower.*

11. *Chron. Melrose* (Stevenson).

12. A great number of embassies (*CDS*, i, nos. 1899, 1966, 1986, 1990, 2063) were sent, and safe conducts (*CDS*, i, nos. 1996, 2003–5, 2035) issued, especially between 1255 and 1257.

13. *Chron. Bower*, ii, 105–11 (for office of chamberlain), 113, 124–5 (royal missions).

14. Ibid., 110 (dispute between the earl of Atholl and John Comyn over the latter's castle at Blair); 120 (dispute between John Comyn and Walter Stewart over the earldom of Menteith).

15. *Chron. Fordun*, i, 295–8 (ii, 290–3); *Chron. Bower*, ii, 85; Buchanan, *History*, 240.

16. Watt, 'Minority', 2; a Comyn perspective is given in Young, 'Walter Comyn'.

17. Paris, *Chron. Maj.*, v, 656; Fraser, *Menteith*, 18.

18. Stevenson, *Documents*, p. lii.

19. Compare, for instance, the mainly charter-based evidence regarding Roger Quincy (see Simpson, 'The *Familia* of Roger de Quincy', 104), with the evidence for Walter Comyn, Earl of Menteith, which is much more heavily weighed towards narrative sources (see Young, 'Walter Comyn').

20. In general, Barrow, *Anglo-Norman Era*, 61–90; Stringer, *Earl David*, 186–9, 192; Stringer, *Nobility Essays*; Duncan, *Kingdom*, 542–3.

21. Young, 'Walter Comyn', 132, 136.

22. The Comyns probably had control over this office between 1241 and 1244 through Robert Mowat and Philip Melville. Mowat certainly and Melville probably were in the Comyn following (SRO, RH 1/2/32; *St Andrews Liber*, 250-3).

23. Barrow, *Kingdom*, 136. The following section owes much to Ch. 3, 'The Justiciar', 83-138.

24. *Chron. Fordun*, i, 293, 297 (ii, 289, 292); see Barrow, *Kingdom*, 85.

25. Barrow, *Kingdom*, 126.

26. Alan Durward held the title earl of Atholl between c. 1233 and c. 1235 (Watt, 'Minority', 5 and n.; A. A. M. Duncan, 'The Earldom of Atholl in the Thirteenth Century', *The Scottish Genealogist*, vii (1960), 2). His right here was probably based on wardship of the heir rather than marriage to the heiress.

27. *RRS*, i, 31; *Scots Peerage*, v, 572-4.

28. Durward vigorously revived his claim to the earldom of Mar in 1255-7 (*CPL*, i, 349, 351; cf. Watt, 'Minority', 16).

29. *Chron. Fordun*, i, 293 (ii, 289). It has been pointed out that in similar circumstances in England, Henry III had been knighted in 1216 by William Marshall who was then asked to take the office of *rector regis et regni* (Watt, 'Minority', 6-7).

30. Barrow, *Kingship and Unity*, 150.

31. *Chron. Melrose* (Stevenson), 179. The chronicle presumably means the legitimisation of Durward's wife.

32. For church support in this government see *CDS*, i, no. 2013. The Comyns had established a good reputation with the church through the munificence of William Comyn, earl of Buchan (*Chron. Melrose* (Stevenson), 177 — note the support for the Comyns in this chronicle).

33. Barrow, *Kingdom*, 137.

34. Mowat: *St Andrews Liber*, 251-3; SRO, RH 1/2/32; Meldrum: Philip married Agnes, daughter of William Comyn, earl of Buchan (*SHS Misc.*, iv, 318, 347-8), and was regularly in the Comyn following (SRO, GD 101/2, RH 1/2/31; *St Andrews Liber*, 250-3).

35. *Chron. Fordun*, i, 296-7 (ii, 291-2).

36. *Chron. Melrose* (Stevenson), 180. Henry had difficulty in getting men to undertake this campaign.

37. Stones, *Relations* [30]-[34]; cf. Duncan, *Kingdom*, 567.

38. *CPL*, i, 349, 351.

39. *Chron. Melrose* (Stevenson), 181.

40. *Chron. Fordun*, i, 297 (ii, 292-3).

41. *Foedera*, i, 653; see also G. W. S. Barrow, 'Wales and Scotland in the Middle Ages', *Welsh History Review*, x (1980-1), 311-12.

42. Young, 'Walter Comyn', 144-5.

43. There are two sources for this council, one version including Walter Comyn (*CPR, 1258-66*, 2), the other being headed by Earl Alexander Comyn (*Close Rolls, 1256-9*, 461-2). It seems that one version was drawn up before the news of Walter's death, whereupon another version was prepared.

44. E.g. Watt, 'Minority', 21–23.
45. In 1259 an embassy, including Alexander Comyn and Alan Durward, was prepared to travel to England to recover the document of 1255 in which the Scots had agreed to the continuation of the minority under Henry III's supervision until 1262 (Paris, *Chron. Maj.*, v, 740). Documents were issued in the king's name between May and December 1260 (*RRS: Alexander III*, 11).
46. Duncan, *Kingdom*, 589.
47. Ibid., 587–9.
48. *Foedera*, i, 715; see also *Chron. Fordun*, i, 301 (ii, 296).
49. For the list of all justiciars, see Barrow, *Kingdom*, 137–8.
50. For lists of Comyn supporters in 1244, see *CDS*, i, nos. 2671–2; in 1255, *CDS*, i, no. 2013; in 1257, *Chron. Bower*, ii, 91; and in 1258, *CDS*, i, no. 2155.
51. For lists of chancellors and chamberlains, see *HBC*, 174 and 178.
52. For the majority of sheriffs in this period, see *ER*, i, 1–51.
53. Through the Mowat family, who were prominent in the following of William Comyn, earl of Buchan (SRO, RH 1/2/32; *St Andrews Liber*, 250–3). The family were also sheriffs of Cromarty.
54. Through the Munfort family, who were also prominent in the following of William Comyn, earl of Buchan (SRO, GD 101/2; RH 1/2/31; *Glas. Reg.*, i, 101).
55. Through the Lascelles family, who were in Alexander Comyn, earl of Buchan's following (SRO, GD 52/388; *Aberdeen Registrum*, ii, 276–7; *Arbroath Liber*, 185–7; *Inchcolm Chrs.*, 25, 26, 141; *St Andrews Liber*, 282–3).
56. Watt, *Fasti*, 2, 39, 146, 293.
57. SRO, Maitland Thompson Transcript Notebook, vi, 37; *Glas. Reg.*, i, 195; *Kelso Liber*, i, 152.
58. *CDS*, i, 10, 1987, 2013, 2121; Barrow, *Kingship and Unity*, 52–3.
59. *Arbroath Liber*, 265–6; *Inchcolm Chrs.*, 25, 26, 141; SRO, RH 6/52.
60. Barrow and Royan, 'James Stewart'.
61. See, e.g., Duncan, *Kingdom*, 588 and Watt, *Fasti*, 293.
62. Duncan, *Kingdom*, 573–4.
63. *Chron. Wyntoun* (Laing), ii, 310.
64. Ibid.; Young, *Comyns*, 274 and family tree.
65. *Fraser Facsimiles*, no. 57.
66. SRO, GD 45/26/4. Hugh was beneficiary to another royal grant in 1265 (*Fraser Facsimiles*, no. 60).
67. *Aberdeen Registrum*, i, 29–30 (1273); Ibid., ii, 272–3 (1277 at Forfar); SRO, RH 6/58 (1279 at Stirling).
68. Theiner, *Monumenta*, 93; *Chron. Fordun*, i, 298 (ii, 293).
69. Ibid.
70. A markedly different account of these events is to be found in Duncan, *Kingdom*, 583–4. For the relationship of Walter Stewart's wife, Mary, to Countess Isabella, see Watt, 'Minority', 22 n. 127.
71. Theiner, *Monumenta*, 93.

72. *Scots Peerage*, vi, 131; *CDS*, iv, no. 1763.
73. Theiner, *Monumenta*, 93. This seems to suggest that the king was not fully in control of government c. 1260/1.
74. *Chron. Fordun*, i, 298 (ii, 293).
75. *Chron. Bower*, ii, 110.
76. See below, p. 19.
77. *CDS*, i, no. 2193.
78. *ER*, i, 27–28. Alexander Comyn had married Elizabeth Quincy, co-heiress to Roger Quincy, earl of Winchester and constable of Scotland (d.1264).
79. For the profits of the justiciarship, totalling £405–13s–4d for 1264–6, see *ER*, i, 18.
80. *ER*, i, 18, 20, 30–31; *Chron. Fordun*, i, 301 (ii, 296). Earl Alexander was the first layman to append his seal to the Treaty of Perth in 1266.
81. C. A. Malcolm, 'The Office of Sheriff in Scotland', *SHR*, xx (1922–3).
82. *ER*, i, 31, 33; *Close Rolls, 1268–72*, 8.
83. Simpson, *Quincy*, 69–70.
84. *Melrose Liber*, 280–1; PRO, SCI 18/147.
85. Anderson, *Scottish Annals*, 382 (Annals of Furness).
86. PRO, SCI 16/93; PRO, SCI 20/158.
87. Barrow, *Kingship and Unity*, 113, 116; Barrow, *Kingdom*, 373; Barrow, *Anglo-Norman Era*, 68.
88. Barrow, *Kingship and Unity*, 52–53, 149.
89. Paris, *Chron. Maj.*, v, 740.
90. *Foedera*, i, 715.
91. Ibid., ii, 266.
92. For 1251: Paris, *Chron. Maj.*, v, 268; for 1278: Stones, *Relations*, [40]–[41].
93. Paris, *Chron. Maj.*, v, 266–70; Duncan, *Kingdom*, 587.
94. The following section owes much to Stringer, *Earl David*, ch. 9, 'Anglo-Scottish Proprietorship: A Wider View', 177–211.
95. Ibid., 190.
96. For example, the earls of Huntingdon, Strathearn and Dunbar, and the families of Comyn, Bruce, Quincy, Forz, Balliol, Moray, Vesci, Durward and Umphraville all had interests in both kingdoms.
97. For the Balliols, see Stell, 'The Balliol Family', 156–7; for Roger Quincy, see Simpson, *Quincy*, 214–16. The estimated value of Roger's demesne lands was approximately £400 in Scotland and £500 in England; cf. the income of Duncan, earl of Fife in 1294–5 of £525 from all sources.
98. Paris, *Chron. Maj.*, v, 501.
99. *CDS*, i, no. 2125. Malise, earl of Strathearn married Marjory, daughter and co-heiress of Robert Muschamp (*Scots Peerage*, viii, 246; *CDS*, i, no. 1792.
100. From a letter of Alexander III to Edward I in 1284 (Stones, *Relations*, [42]).
101. *CDS*, ii, nos. 216, 369, 421.
102. Young, *Comyns*, 261–4.

103. *Close Rolls, 1272-9,* 236.
104. *CPR, 1258-66,* 460, 560; *CPR, 1266-72,* 17, 117.
105. In 1268-71, 1274, 1276, 1279, 1281 and 1282: Ibid., 300, 581; *Close Rolls, 1272-9,* 126, 136, 429, 529; *CPR, 1272-81,* 423; *CPR, 1281-92,* 18.
106. *Close Rolls, 1272-9,* 138.
107. *Cal. Inquisitions Post Mortem,* iv, 171, no. 138.
108. For Roger, see *Placito de Quo Warranto* (Rec. Comm. 1818), 559; for John, see *Cal. Inquisitions Post Mortem,* ii, 460, no. 753 and *CDS,* ii, no. 421.
109. In 1276, for example, Robert Leslie, Richard of Pocklington (in the East Riding of Yorkshire), Richard Aleyn and Matthew of Wigston (Leicestershire) were named as Earl Alexander's attorneys: *Close Rolls, 1272-9,* 429.
110. *CFR,* i, 85.
111. PRO, SCI 16/93.
112. See above, p. 14 (n. 86).
113. *Charter Rolls,* ii, (1257-1300), 40-41.
114. *Liberate Rolls,* v, 90, 198.
115. *CDS,* i, no. 2678.
116. Cf. Alan Durward's personal service in Gascony in 1254, above, p. 6.
117. *Charter Rolls,* ii, (1257-1300), 40-41.
118. *Liberate Rolls,* v, 198.
119. *CDS,* i, no. 2431; *CPR, 1266-72,* 110.
120. Ibid., 175.
121. Ibid., 633.
122. *Morton Registrum,* ii, 3-4; *Newbattle Registrum,* 135-6.
123. *Book of Fees,* i, 919; Ibid., ii, 911, 1118; *CDS,* i, nos. 1523, 1558.
124. Ibid., nos. 632, 1172, 1183, 1251, 1313, 1341, 1391. David acknowledged his summons to fight on Henry's behalf against the King of France, but gave 20 marks (reduced to 10) instead of serving personally (*Close Rolls, 1237-42,* 528; *CDS,* i, no. 1578).
125. Ibid., nos. 2096, 2278, 2638; Ibid., ii, no. 148. Even his widow married again without the English king's consent (Ibid., no. 376).
126. *Close Rolls, 1264-8,* 437.
127. *CDS,* i, no. 2678.
128. *Close Rolls, 1264-8,* 437.
129. *Scots Peerage,* vi, 129-31. It is interesting that William is recorded as about to go abroad in 1281 — perhaps on the English king's service? (*CDS,* ii, no. 198).
130. Ibid., i, nos. 2120, 2121, 2156.
131. Ibid., nos. 1888, 1895, 1956, 1984-5, 2022, 2043, 2099; in 1260, ibid., nos. 2218, 2221-2; in 1268, ibid., nos. 2492-3; in 1274, ibid., ii, no. 18.
132. Stell, 'The Balliol Family', 155-8.
133. Ibid., 153, 158.
134. *CDS,* i, nos. 1994, 2472.
135. Ibid., nos. 2357-9, 2429.

136. Robert Bruce the Competitor was described as *nobilis tam in Anglia quam in Scotia baro* (*Chron. Lanercost,* 159); see also Barrow, *Bruce,* 23–26 and Stringer, *Earl David,* 185–6, 188–9.

137. Exceptions were William Comyn of Kilbride and Guy Balliol, both of whom fought on Simon Montfort's side against Henry III. This emphasises the need to study not only individual baronial families, but also individual branches of families.

138. Anderson, *Scottish Annals,* 382 (Annals of Furness).

139. Duncan, *Declaration of Arbroath,* 10.

140. This theme is well treated in Duncan, *Kingdom,* 584–6.

141. *Foedera,* ii, 266–7.

142. The Sinclairs and Morays may have had some affiliation to the Comyns. For Sinclair, see *Morton Registrum,* ii, 5; SRO, RH 1/2/31–2; *St Andrews Liber,* 254. For Moray, see n. 59 above.

143. Hugh Abernethy, not in the 1284 list, is a good example of a native lord favoured by the Comyns (see above, p. 12) who rose to prominence (Barrow, *Kingship and Unity,* 137–8).

144. Barrow, *Kingdom,* 383; also Barrow, *Kingship and Unity,* 119.

2

THE CHURCH IN THE REIGN OF ALEXANDER III

Marinell Ash

On the nineteenth of June 1250 the young king, Alexander III, along with his mother and the leading clergy and nobility of Scotland gathered at the royal abbey of Dunfermline for a ceremony to mark the translation of the relics of Margaret, the saintly ancestor of the house of Canmore. After nearly five years of negotiations at the papal court, largely carried out by Robert Kenleith, abbot of Dunfermline, Margaret had been canonized,[1] and the placing of her remains in a jewel-covered shrine and their removal to a newly built reliquary chapel behind the high altar was an event of supreme national religious and political significance. It was a ceremony filled with references to the past and prognostications for the future.

First of all it was a celebration of an ancient royal cult, assiduously fostered by the royal line since the time of Margaret and Malcolm's sons in the early eleventh century. In a description of the ceremony in the fifteenth-century *Book of Pluscarden*, written by a monk of Dunfermline, it is said that when the queen's tomb was opened the church was filled with the scent of flowers. Then as the monks began to move the relics to their new home they were unable to move past the tomb of King Malcolm. Once a bystander suggested that they take up the body of the king as well they were able to move both remains easily.[2] Despite the lateness of this account there is no reason to doubt that something like the events described in the *Book of Pluscarden* actually occurred at the translation ceremony. Such a carefully staged event would have been replete with meaning for the churchmen and the representatives of the house of Canmore present at the ceremony, adding visible power to the cult of St Margaret by referring back to her own favourite saint, Cuthbert of Durham. The relics that refused to move were a direct reference to the story connected with the ending of the long wanderings of St Cuthbert's relics, when the coffin in which they had been carried about Northumbria took root at Durham and refused to move further. From that incident dated the beginning of Durham Cathedral and the shrine of St Cuthbert, a cult to which the house of Canmore were particularly devoted: when Cuthbert's relics had been examined and translated in 1104 the future Alexander I, king of Scots, was the only layman present at that ceremony.[3]

Nevertheless such self-conscious antiquarianism was but a small part of the ceremony's significance. In other more important ways, it signified a kind of coming of age of the national church, as well as the beginning of a subtle change in the long and close relationship between king and church which would lead to significant changes in the future. Increasingly (and in common with the trend throughout Europe), relations between king and church became less personal and more bureaucratic. This change would have occurred in any case, but it was accelerated by the growing factionalism surrounding the young king, which had first become apparent at the enthronement ceremony at Scone in 1249, a year before the translation of the relics of Alexander's saintly ancestor.

Playing a leading part in both these ceremonies was the ageing bishop of St Andrews, David Bernham (1239–1253), the first native-born Scot to hold this office since Bishop Fothad in the time of Queen Margaret herself. Bishop and king represented the two halves of an ancient national and religious identity that stretched back to Celtic times and had survived remarkably well into the thirteenth century. Unlike England there had been no major church–state confrontations; no statement of Scottish ecclesiastical rights had to be wrung from a reluctant crown. On the other hand, the rights of the king of Scots in church affairs were far-reaching and often decisive, stretching from rights to temporalities during episcopal vacancies,[4] to the appointment of new bishops.[5] Such rights were rigorously enforced by a strong king, such as Alexander II had been; during the minority of his son they would continue to be exercised by those acting in the king's name, and the ensuing conflicts would help to produce a new relationship between crown and church when the king came of age.

Royal rights in the Scottish church had grown not only from the role played in the twelfth-century reorganisation of the Scottish church by Margaret's sons, but also from the failure to obtain metropolitan status for St Andrews, due largely to English influence at the papal court in the 1150s and 1160s. Scotland's position as an acephalous church meant that the relationship between Scotland and the papacy was extremely close. From the late twelfth century both the church hierarchy and the Crown became adept in their recourse to the papal court, often looking there for support to head off English claims to superiority over Scotland. It was probably in response to moves by King William the Lion, alarmed by newly revived claims by York to authority within Scotland, that in 1192 Pope Celestine III issued the bull *Cum universi*, recognising the Scottish church as a special daughter (*filia specialis*) of the papal see and providing that no-one except the pope or a papal legate could pronounce an interdict, that appeals could only go outside of Scotland to the papal court, and that only a Scot or someone specially sent from the papal court could act as legate in Scotland.[6]

The practical consequences of the Scottish church's anomalous position as a national church without a metropolitan could be seen in such things as episcopal elections; candidates elected by their chapter had not only to be acceptable to the crown, they also had either to travel to the papal court for confirmation and consecration, or the papacy could delegate local scrutineers, usually three bishops, to inquire into the election, the fitness of the candidate, and if all were found to be in order, to proceed with the consecration.

The Scottish need and use of the papal court as a defender and upholder of its rights, however, had its price, and this rose throughout the thirteenth century as papal claims to plenitude of power increased. These claims had begun to grow in the late twelfth century and achieved their earliest definitive expression in the fourth Lateran council of 1215. Scottish bishops attended the Council and one, the bishop of St Andrews, remained abroad for three years, probably at the papal court. It was almost certainly due to his efforts that *Cum universi* was reissued in 1218. He also, perhaps, began the negotiations for the issue of the bull *Quidam vestrum* of 1225,[7] which allowed the Scottish church to govern itself as an autonomous national church by the remarkable device of a national provincial council with the nine Scottish bishops responsible for carrying out the council's mandates within their respective dioceses.[8]

The functioning of this new council is unclear — and may have been deliberately left unclear by contemporaries. For the king a regularly functioning council with well defined rights and administration was a threat to his own authority within the church. On the other hand, if the church attempted to define the scope of the council's activities, it might provoke the king into taking an even closer interest in its affairs than he did already. It seems possible, for example, that a number of the council's meetings in the reign of Alexander II were initiated by the king himself.[9]

Such an *ad hoc* situation worked reasonably well under conscientious bishops, such as Bernham, who had a good working relationship with the crown. Under the pressure of the minority of the new king, however, a new and more ordered consensus about the functioning of the *ecclesia Scoticana* began to emerge; indeed the unprecedented exercise (and attempted exercise) of royal authority over it may have been used by the church to bring about a further definition of its own administrative structure and powers.[10] The results of this shift only begin to become clear, however, after the commencement of Alexander's adult reign. A crucial point in the working out of this new relationship was the king's appeal in 1267 to Bishop Gamelin of St Andrews (1255–1271) against the excommunication of Sir John Dunmore who had had a long-standing series of quarrels with St Andrews Priory.[11] Dunmore, in common with Gamelin, had been a Comyn supporter, but by 1267 had become a trusted royal servant;[12] nevertheless Gamelin refused to lift his bann and in fact excommunicated all who had advised the king to make this request. The king was forced to acquiesce: he was involved in resisting the claims of Cardinal Ottoboni at the time and needed the support of the church,[13] which may have exploited the situation to reassert its rights. Professor Duncan has argued that this case led to the first appearance of the 'Conservator of the Statutes', an official charged initially with the exercise of the laws and discipline laid down by provincial councils of the Scottish church.[14]

This was a marked change from the ill-defined nature of the council earlier in the century, and it may well stand as representing the nature of the overall change that took place during this reign: in common with the rest of Europe the Scottish church was moving away from a closely interconnected, and often ill-defined, relationship of men and institutions, towards a church and a crown working together within a more defined structure, and with each aware of the limits of their power and prerogatives. So far as the church was concerned this change was not solely due to the difficult times through which it had passed during the minority; it also owed much to a church hierarchy and bureaucracy which was increasingly legally trained and minded. The age of the university educated churchman had arrived.

University graduates were but one sign of Scotland's integration into the mainstream of European culture; another was the speed with which the mendicant orders had come into Scotland and the important role they played in the life of the church during the reign of Alexander III. Indeed, some of the Scots who went on to university in England and on the continent must have received their early training in the schools established by the mendicants in Scotland. It is well to recall that it was almost certainly during Alexander III's reign that young John Duns 'Scotus' first entered the Franciscan house at Berwick. Although the mendicants were truly international they placed great stress on the staffing of their houses by local men: a mixture of the international and national that was an important aspect of the later thirteenth-century church in Scotland. The Franciscans and Dominicans had been introduced into the kingdom, under royal patronage, by the early 1230s, the latter under the direction of the distinguished Scottish-born Dominican, Clement, who was provided to the see of Dunblane in 1233; the first Dominican bishop in Britain.[15]

Alexander III followed his father in his encouragement of the mendicants. In 1251, for example, he reissued Alexander II's grant to the Dominicans of Perth,[16] and when he began his personal rule he pressed strongly, but ultimately unsuccessfully, for the creation of a separate Scottish Franciscan province.[17]

The campaign for the Franciscan province was but one expression of the desire for national integrity in church matters. There were others, including a number of attempts to assert rights over daughter houses of foreign monasteries on Scottish soil. Bishop Gamelin attempted, largely unsuccessfully, to exploit a power struggle at Durham between 1258 and 1260 to assert his rights as diocesan over Coldingham priory.[18] Another instance was the priory of May, a daughter house of the Cluniac house of Reading.[19] Despite its distance from Scotland, Reading took a close interest in priory affairs, and during Alexander III's minority there had been controversy with the bishop of St Andrews over procurations, and complaints regarding the unjust alienation of the priory's possessions. Matters reached a head on the death of Prior Hugh in 1269 when a monk of Reading was provided to the vacant office. The king accepted him *pro tunc* but also began attempts to buy the priory, although this was not achieved until after Alexander's death.[20] At last, in 1289, a papal indulgence was issued ordaining that only natives were to be admitted to religious houses in Scotland and forbidding the appointment of foreigners to the rule of a monastery.[21]

This sense of national identity and integrity was reinforced by a heightened interest in Scottish church history. The ceremony at Dunfermline was but one example of a mood of ecclesiastical antiquarianism abroad in mid-thirteenth century Scotland. In addition the new gothic shrine of St Kentigern, designed to cater for a substantial pilgrim traffic, was nearing completion in Glasgow during the early years of the young king's reign.[22] It is symptomatic of the new spirit abroad in the church, demanding the definition and protection of rights, that in 1259 the cathedral chapter of Glasgow asked that a copy of the widely-imitated cathedral constitutions of Salisbury be sent to them as a model for their reorganized cathedral chapter: the spirit and the law combined.

Margaret and Kentigern were not the only Scottish saints to be marked out for special attention during this period. In 1253, for example, the remains of St Duthac of Tain were said to have been translated from Ireland (where he had died in 1065) back to the place of his birth which became a thriving pilgrimage centre.[23]

An important aspect of this revival of interest in church history was a desire to push the roots of Scottish christianity back to the earliest possible period. Thus the 1279 version of the legend of St Andrew opens with the story of the siege of Patras by Constantine's son in 345.[24] Something similar seems to have happened in the rival diocese of Glasgow, during the time of its expansionist bishop, John Cheam.[25] At some time about 1261 a 'stately and venerable cross' bearing the inscription *Locus Sancti Nicholai Episcopi* was found at Peebles, and soon after a stone urn containing the ashes and bones of a man 'torn limb from limb as it were . . . it is believed that it was hidden by some of the faithful about the year 296 while Maximinian's persecution was raging in Britain'.[26] It was said that the king, at the prompting of Bishop Cheam, had a handsome church built on the site. Fordun's account of the finding of the cross at Peebles comes from a century later, but probably represents a real event; certainly there was a house of Trinitarian Friars at the Cross Kirk by 1296, possibly founded by the king; this would be consistent with the vogue for Trinitarian foundations during this period.[27]

By the time Alexander III was involved in the foundation of the Cross Kirk, however, he had been master of his kingdom for several years. It had been otherwise at the time of the translation of the relics of St Margaret, when the glitter of the ceremony barely masked the deepening political crisis brought about by the factional conflict between the Durwards and Comyns. Bishop Bernham was identified with the Comyn faction, but the whole of his career up to the death of Alexander II had been one of close and largely harmonious relationship with the crown. Now he saw this working consensus being torn apart by the instability and factionalism of the royal minority. Indeed, Dunfermline's abbot,

Robert Kenleith, who had been most active in the campaign to secure Margaret's canonization, was a Durwardite. It was this allegiance, as well as his familiarity with the papal court, that led to Kenleith's appointment as royal chancellor early in the reign, charged with bringing the canonization process of Margaret to a successful conclusion and attempting to obtain papal agreement to the anointing and crowning of the Scottish king.[28]

But even if the translation ceremony had not been coloured by factionalism the impending fragmentation of the Scottish church was already very apparent by June 1250. Early in the reign there had been invasion of church property, probably that of the Durwardite cathedral chapter of St Andrews, and at some point during the first year of the new reign a church council had met at Edinburgh. Although its date is uncertain its concerns are known from the terms of a letter drawn up afterwards and probably issued at the time of the Dunfermline ceremonies.[29] The Edinburgh council had produced a number of ordinances and some of them, concerning the respective jurisdictions of sacred and secular authorities, eventually found their way into the statutes of the Scottish church.[30]

In the deepening crisis the Dunfermline letter was ignored, and by the end of 1250 the political and ecclesiastical split was open. The Comyns were on the ascendant, helped early in 1251 by the Durward-inspired papal refusal of Henry III's demands for the use of the Scottish crusading tenth for his Sicilian venture and that the Scottish king should not be anointed or crowned without his consent.[31]

In 1251 a further Scottish appeal to Innocent IV led to a letter being sent to the bishops of Lincoln, Worcester and Litchfield asking them to inquire into the complaints against the Scottish king and his counsellors. The list of some of the charges shows the extent of the problem: excommunications had been revoked by royal command, cases about church possessions and church patronage had been summoned before secular courts and recourse to papal judges delegate had been forbidden.[32]

Soon after the marriage of the young king at York during Christmas 1251 the Comyns achieved ascendancy. So far as the church was concerned this political change coincided with a shift from the concerns expressed in the Dunfermline letter to conflict over provision to episcopal offices. The first controversy followed the death of David Bernham in April 1253.[33] The Durwardite cathedral chapter of St Andrews proceeded unilaterally to elect Robert Stuteville, dean of Dunkeld, despite orders from the court to elect the Comynite Gamelin, a canon of Glasgow who had become chancellor of the realm following the deposition and disgrace of Robert Kenleith early in 1252. Abel Gullane, archdeacon of St Andrews 'by the favour of some that ruled the court' (the Comyns),[34] produced an inhibition and a mandate for the canons to proceed to a new election of Gamelin. When they refused and appealed to the papal court, Abel travelled there and managed to obtain the office for himself. It was a notable climax to a long career as a pluralist and church politician.[35]

Abel's success was short-lived. He returned to Scotland in midsummer 1254 and was dead by the end of the year. By now the Comyns' position was deteriorating, but still they managed to obtain Gamelin's election by the chapter of St Andrews (augmented by two secular canons of the collegiate church of St Mary of the Rock) in February 1255.[36] Proctors were sent to Rome and the election confirmed by the new pope, Alexander IV. Letters were sent to Gamelin's old mentor, Bishop Bondington of Glasgow, delegating him to carry out the consecration.

In the summer of 1255 the Durwards succeeded in gaining control of the king and queen. Henry III moved north and from his headquarters at Wark orders were issued removing the Comyns, Bishop Bondington and Gamelin from Alexander's council.[37] Nevertheless Gamelin was consecrated by Bishop Bondington on 26 December 1255, an act of defiance that led to the new bishop's exile. A contributory cause was, however, apparently Gamelin's refusal to hand over the temporalities of the see which he had administered in the name of the king during the vacancy following the death of Bishop Abel. After being refused passage through England Gamelin went to France and the king's counsellors invaded the temporalities of the see.[38] Ambassadors were sent to the papal court to seek Gamelin's deposition, but this was refused by the pontiff, who ordered instead that Gamelin's accusers were to be excommunicated.[39]

This papal decision was the first step in the resurgence of Comyn fortunes, culminating in their seizure of the king and queen at Kinross in late October 1257. Gamelin was able to return to Scotland during the spring or early summer of the following year. With the cessation of the factional fighting around the king by the end of 1258, and his assumption of full control of his government by 1260, this period of instability in both church and state was drawing to a close.

The minority had a number of consequences for the church. One of the most notable was the increased recourse of both clergy and laity to the papal court; the insecurity of the times made the added expense and effort of appealing outwith Scotland worthwhile.[40] Another consequence of the factionalism of the minority can be seen in the composition of the Scottish episcopate. Besides Gamelin a number of other 'factional' appointments were made during these years, and continued to be made thereafter.[41] Comyn influence, and probably also that of Henry III, may be seen in the ineffectual attempt to provide Ralph, a canon of Lincoln, to Moray in 1252 and it seems likely that the Englishman, Robert of the Provender (*de Prebenda*), Bishop of Dunblane (1259–1284), came to Scotland following the accession (or marriage) of the young king: he first appears in royal government at the time of the first Comyn ascendancy. His political allegiances, however, were dictated more out of concern for his own advancement than with competing political factions. He went to the papal court as one of the proctors to secure the confirmation of Gamelin's election in 1256 and remained there, where he became a papal chaplain and was instrumental in gaining the papal verdict in favour of Gamelin in 1257. Amongst his Scottish benefices were canonries at Dunblane and Glasgow. Robert was back in Scotland early in 1259 as bishop-elect of Dunblane and presided over the pre-election arrangements of Glasgow cathedral chapter. After the election to Glasgow of Nicholas Moffat, archdeacon of Teviotdale, the two bishops-elect travelled to the papal court.[42]

Nicholas's election was overturned by the curia. According to the *Chronicle of Melrose*, Nicholas had been given royal confirmation in Scotland but failed to secure confirmation in Rome 'because he refused to produce a certain sum of money, which the pope and the cardinals demanded . . . and because those who had come with him, as if to help him, did on the contrary oppose him, with all their might'.[43] Obtaining papal confirmations of elections was, indeed, an expensive business. Gamelin's proctors had been given the right to contract a loan of £500 for their expenses, and in addition Gamelin had received a papal dispensation to continue to hold all his benefices for up to two years after his postulation to St Andrews because of the debts of his church and 'other expenses' (of which the major part was certainly the proceedings at the papal court).[44]

The *Chronicle of Melrose* claims that Robert of the Provender hoped that if Nicholas's election was quashed he would himself become bishop of Glasgow. In fact, it was the Englishman, John Cheam, who was provided by the pope. He was a notable careerist and pluralist, a papal chaplain, canon of St Paul's and dean of Bath,[45] who had spent much time at the papal court and was familiar with its ways. Cheam was consecrated, probably at the curia, before 28 October 1259, by which time papal letters had already been sent to King Alexander requesting that he be put in possession of the temporalities of the see.[46]

The election of Cheam, coming as it did just at the time that the king was beginning his effective personal reign, was a test of the crown's rights over the church. The king requested that the pope revoke the provision of Cheam but this was refused, and Alexander had to fall back on the rather weaker position of refusing to grant the temporalities of the see until the new bishop had taken an oath of fealty to him. In reply the pope wrote to the bishops of Lincoln and Bath ordering them to put Cheam in possession of the temporalities of Glasgow. The king then sent envoys to the papal court to complain of this proceeding. Much of their pleading must have referred back to the relevant passages of *Cum universi* and the legal integrity of the Scottish church as defined by the papacy itself. Pope Alexander IV was forced to rescind his letter to the English bishops and Cheam came to Scotland in 1260, took his oath to the king, and began his active career as diocesan.

Despite the threat to royal authority posed by the manner of his provision, Cheam seems to have established good relations with Alexander III. Nevertheless the papal provision of John Cheam was something of a *cause celebre* in the thirteenth century Scottish church, and not just because it showed the possible dangers arising from the exercise of papal prerogatives during a period of local weakness. Alexander learned the lesson, and throughout the rest of his reign his grip on episcopal elections was tight. For example, the two major sees, St Andrews and Glasgow, went almost without exception to royal servants. Gamelin had been royal chancellor; he was followed in 1271 by another, William Wishart, who had been provided to Glasgow in the previous year but had not yet been consecrated. In 1279 Wishart in turn was succeeded by another royal chancellor, William Fraser. At Glasgow Nicholas Moffat had been elected again following Cheam's death in 1268, but he died before he could be consecrated. William Wishart had not been consecrated to Glasgow before he gained St Andrews, but upon his transferral to that see he made sure that his nephew (or perhaps his son), Robert Wishart, followed him at Glasgow.[47]

Royal officials were less frequently found in smaller sees, but the royal role in their filling was still decisive. In Argyll, an area still being brought under effective royal control, the evangelistic work of the mendicants was a useful adjunct to the extension of royal authority. Alexander was almost certainly instrumental in the election of one of his favoured Dominicans to the see in 1264. Laurence of Argyll was followed by two other members of his order who together held the see for nearly a century.[48] Another Dominican, William Comyn (of Kilconquhar) lector of the Dominican schools of Perth, became bishop of Brechin in 1275.[49]

Even in dioceses not part of the *ecclesia Scoticana* the royal role was dominant, and it was usually Scottish clerics or candidates with Scottish connections who were preferred. In Whithorn (Galloway), subject still to the metropolitan jurisdiction of York, the Scottish king's assent was required for candidates. In the disputed election of 1253, Comyn influence (claiming to act in the king's name) secured the election of Henry, abbot of Holyrood, despite the protests of John Balliol as lord of Galloway and patron of the diocese. Henry's consecration was, however, long delayed by the Durward seizure of power in September 1255.[50] Although most of the area of the diocese of the Isles became Scottish territory following the battle of Largs, the treaty of Perth in 1266 ordained that the diocese should remain subject to Trondheim, but patronage was transferred to the king of Scots.[51] In 1275, the first vacancy to occur after the treaty, Alexander annulled the election of Gilbert, abbot of Rushen in Man, and presented a Gallovidian, Mark, to the archbishop of Trondheim for consecration.[52]

After the beginning of the king's effective personal reign a major priority of both the Scottish king and the church was a return to the usual practice of episcopal candidates travelling to the papal court for confirmation or the sending of papal letters to local scrutineers. A return to normality was in everybody's interest, and it began with Urban IV's 1263 mandate to the bishops of Brechin, Dunkeld and Ross charging them to examine the birth and attainments of Master Walter of Baltroddie, to inquire into his fitness and if they found in his favour, to consecrate him as bishop of Caithness.[53]

It was still possible for the papacy to intervene in the electoral process in unusual and unilateral ways, but on the only occasion that this happened in the adult reign of Alexander III it was done in a manner that showed a good deal of sensitivity to local conditions. In 1278 Richard, the elderly dean of Caithness, was elected to that see, but there were objections, whether from Scotland or abroad is unclear. Pope Nicholas III ordered the bishops of St Andrews and Aberdeen and the Provincial minister of the Franciscans to persuade Richard to renounce his election since he had at least one illegitimate son and was paralysed.[54] There is some irony in this mandate, for William Wishart of St Andrews, one of the delegates, was himself the father of a small family of bastard children and yet had obtained both Glasgow and St Andrews despite complaints about his moral failings.[55] Richard withdrew and a canon of St Andrews was provided instead and sent to the curia, but died before he could be consecrated. At this point the pope provided Alan St Edmund, chaplain to Hugh, cardinal of St Laurence in Lucina, who may have been a Scot and was probably a permanent bureaucrat resident at the curia. Alan returned to Scotland and took up his see, rising eventually to become chancellor of the realm in 1291.[56]

This provision may smack of the kind of exercise of papal power all too familiar from the minority, but such a judgement would be wrong. In the first instance the curia, probably acting on information from Scotland, had gently quashed the election of an aged and unsuitable member of the cathedral corporation of Caithness and had allowed the election of another local candidate. It was only when he died at the papal court that the pope exercised his right to provide, in order to avoid a longer vacancy, and the man chosen, if not a Scot, at least had Scottish connections and proven administrative abilities.

Like the rest of Western Christendom Scotland was a field ripe for the provision of foreign benefice holders. Some religious corporations in Scotland took care to obtain (or at least to claim the possession of) indulgences not to have to present foreigners or non-residents to benefices within their charge.[57] In 1263, for example, Urban IV sent a mandate to the bishop of Dunblane and archdeacon of St Andrews ordering them to make provision for two clerks, nephews of the cardinal of St Eustace, after the bishop of St Andrews had refused to make such provision, 'having sheltered himself with a certain papal indult said to have been granted him . . .', and had excommunicated the cardinal for attempting the provision.[58] The cathedral chapter of Glasgow, with four non-resident Italians amongst its nine prebends and five dignities, had in 1248 obtained the right not to present any more non-Scots until the death or resignation of existing holders,[59] although Glasgow's reserved prebends continued to be filled by other foreigners throughout the reign of Alexander.[60]

Scottish churchmen were not averse to collecting benefices them-selves, indeed the whole structure of the church depended on the holding of benefices (and their revenues) either by corporations or by individuals. This process is most clearly seen in the widespread appropriation of parish churches. A major feature of the Scottish church in the second half of the thirteenth century was the creation of vicarages, by which an appropriated church was served by a vicar for a fixed stipend, with the rest of the revenues going to the rector who held the benefice. The Wishart family, for example, were notable pluralists and were assiduous in gathering benefices ranging from parish churches to the highest offices in the land, with or without the help of the papacy. William Wishart was said to have accumulated twenty-two rectories and prebends in England and Scotland before he gained election to Glasgow.[61] Robert Wishart was not as ardent a pluralist, but his rise in the church owed much to family connections, as did the careers of other members of the family; Thomas Wishart appears as dean of Glasgow in 1286, and the bishop's son, a namesake William, had been appointed archdeacon of Teviotdale by 1288.[62]

A significant aspect of Scottish-papal relations in the reign of Alexander III concerned the various attempts to mount crusades and the financial collections necessary to support them. The period is punctuated by two general church councils, both held in Lyons. That of 1245 had been summoned primarily to preach a new crusade under the leadership of the king of France, and had ordained a levy of a twentieth on clerical incomes. In 1274 six Scottish bishops travelled to another council that passed reforming legislation, planned a new crusade and ordered a crusading tenth for six years.[63]

It was probably Bishop Bernham who brought home from the first council of Lyons word of the new crusade, and the Scots themselves were not slow to respond with fighting men.[64] They were, however, a good deal less enthusiastic when it came to the collection of crusading levies, for not only did these impositions eat into the wealth of church and laity, but their collection raised once more all kinds of questions about the internal organisation of the Scottish church and its position *vis a vis* England and the papacy. Alexander II had apparently tried to keep the collection of crusading monies in Scottish hands, and this practice was initially continued by his son. In 1250, a papal letter to the bishops of St Andrews and Aberdeen ordered them to collect legacies and offerings in Scotland for the Holy Land, and added the sinister proviso that any left over from Scottish crusaders was to go to the king of England when he set out.[65] The threat that Scottish collections would be diverted to English use remained throughout the reign.

As early as 1251 Henry III was attempting to implement these claims, and his demands became more pressing when, in the middle of the decade, crusading interest shifted away from the Holy Land to the Hohenstaufen kingdom of Sicily and Henry's attempts to find a kingdom there for his son. In the late spring of 1254 the pope issued demands for a tax of a twentieth of revenues for three years to aid the Sicilian venture, but nothing was forthcoming.[66] By the early 1260s however some collecting was being carried on in Scotland by Ivo, a Franciscan from Ayr. For several years from 1263 papal agents in London made repeated attempts to have this collection transferred from Whithorn to the Templars' House in London, but without success; indeed one messenger sent to take the money was not only refused payment but was beaten.[67] In 1263 the bishop of St Andrews was ordered to preach a crusade and collect a tenth of church revenues for five years, but these arrangements were overtaken by the arrival of Cardinal Ottoboni of Fieschli in England in 1265. Although sent initially to mediate between Henry III and his barons, he was also made legate to England, Ireland, Wales and Scotland. The new legate sent his chaplain to Scotland to ask for a licence to visit there. This was refused by the king and clergy, probably citing the clause in *Cum universi* requiring that legates be specifically deputed to come to Scotland, and an edict was issued against the legate.[68] Ottoboni's initial demand of four merks from every church and six from every cathedral was denied by the Scottish king on the advice of his clergy, who then raised 2,000 merks to take their case to the papal court.[69]

So far as the Scots were concerned Ottoboni's legatine powers were invalid, and moreover they resented the attempt to divert crusading collections to England. In 1266 the king absolutely refused to allow the Scottish tenth to be used to pay the debts of the English queen.[70] Given this background it is hardly surprising that the Scottish response to Ottoboni's preaching of a general crusade after 1267 was, in financial terms, decidedly cool, although Scots were militarily active in the resulting crusade.[71]

The Scottish church took an equally dim view of the legatine council Ottoboni held in London in 1268. The provincial council decided to send two bishops (of the second rank) and two heads of religious houses 'so that nothing which could damage or aggrieve them might be enacted in their absence'.[72] The reforming legislation of the London council was largely ignored in Scotland.

It may have been a similar desire to protect their interests that led to the large Scottish contingent at the Council of Lyons in 1274. After defying papal authority (and Cardinal Ottoboni) in such a spectacular way they needed to have a powerful presence at Lyons. The Scots were right to fear what would result from the Council's decision to mount a new crusade. No longer would collections within Scotland be gathered by Scots. This time the crusading tenth of six years was delegated to a papal bureaucrat, Master Boiamund of Vicia, a canon of Asti and chaplain to the cardinal of St Eustace. He arrived in Scotland in 1275 and announced that the collection would be based on a new, true valuation. The Scottish provincial council prevailed on him to return to Rome and ask, unsuccessfully as it turned out, that the 'old taxation' be used and that the collection be spread over seven years. Boiamund returned to Scotland and set to work.

Much work remains to be done on the details of Boiamund's collections as revealed in his still extant rolls.[73] What is clear is that Boiamund found it hard going. On the one hand there was resistance in Scotland, and on the other there were claims from the papacy that he was cooking the books. In 1282 Boiamund asked to be relieved of his duties, but this was refused. His affairs became increasingly tangled, so that in 1285 he was ordered to send his accounts to Rome. Nevertheless by 1287 Boiamund managed to collect nearly £18,000 (about one seventh of the amount collected in England).[74] Despite his limited success, Boiamund left his name in the popular consciousness of Scotland, as 'Bagimond'.[75]

It is unclear where the money collected by 'Bagimond' went. There were English demands that it should go to the crusading activities of the Lord Edward, but King Alexander was able to refuse or circumvent these claims. After his death, however, there was no strong hand to stop the sending of papal collections to England. And this fact reveals the final insoluble weakness of the Scottish church of this period: in the end its ultimate sanction against papal and other threats to its integrity lay in the strength (or otherwise) of the king and his churchmen acting together.

It is perhaps ironic that the survival of 'Bagimond's Roll' provides us with the clearest single picture of the constituent parts of the Scottish church in the reign of Alexander III, the individual parishes. Yet the mere list of names and valuations cannot begin to tell us of the reality of local church life. In this the records are almost totally silent, and yet it was in the parish that the vast bulk of the people of Scotland had their contact with the church through the services, regular or irregular, of the parish priest. Judging from the statutes of the Scottish church promulgated in this period, the proper serving of churches, such as the maintenance of buildings and their furnishings, and ensuring the decent life of the clergy, were major preoccupations. But this is only negative evidence, and cannot be used to claim that the services of the church on the local level were everywhere as black as they are painted in these reforming statutes. What they do tell us is that the hierarchy were concerned, almost to the point of obsession, to bring the teachings of Christ to the individual. This simple fact can be forgotten in the midst of evidence of pluralism, appropriation and nepotism which, because it occupies by far the bulk of the evidence that has survived, tends to make us believe that this is the whole story.

The fact is that the church was a mixture of good and bad, sacred and secular. We can obtain brief glimpses of this truth in two stories. The first is a contemporary epigram preserved in the *Chronicle of Melrose*. It was said there were three notable men in the king's dominions: Archdeacon Nicholas Moffat who always quarrelled and was never angry, William Wishart who always laughed and was never glad, and John Cheam who preached piety but never practised it.[76] Clearly these were men of ambition and ability and if we were to take this somewhat cynical passage as representing the whole truth about the church in the reign of Alexander III, it would be a very partial, not to say fractional, view. For even these 'ecclesiastical magnates' would not make the mistake of claiming that they were the entire church. The church was the body of the faithful, many of whom were doubtless as vain and grasping, as insincere and sanctimonious, as the three satirized in this epigram.

There is, however, a second piece of (admittedly later) evidence about Scottish popular spirituality in the reign of Alexander III, which may help to redress the balance. It concerns a Fife knight and St Margaret of Scotland. A few years after the ceremony of translation Sir John Wemyss, a crippled knight, had a dream in which he saw the queen, accompanied by her armed husband and three kingly sons, striding out from the great west doorway of Dunfermline Abbey towards the west. It was the third of October and at Largs that day the Norwegian army had been defeated. Sir John went to the shrine of the queen and was cured. Scotland's saints and Scotland's kings looked after their own.[77]

The age of Alexander III was one of consolidation. Professor Duncan has traced something of what this meant in royal terms through the evolution of the iconography of royal seals, from a young king surrounded by his clergy and nobility on the throne at Scone through a series of seals issued as he slowly moved towards personal government, depicting the king in majesty wearing his crown and bearing symbols of authority in his hands.[78]

This growing self-assurance was also present in the church. Something of what this meant in practical terms can be seen in the development of the cult of St Andrew during this reign. From at least the time of St Margaret herself the apostolic relics at Kilrymont had been used to foster the sense of a national church. After the refusal of metropolitan status to St Andrews by Nicholas Breakspear, Pope Adrian IV (1154–1159), the cult of the apostle became extremely important as a compensatory focus of national devotion. It is therefore to the decade of the 1160s that the earliest extant version of the St Andrew legend belongs.[79] The full legend appears by the end of the reign of Alexander III; this process of development is illustrated by stylistic changes that took place in the seals of the bishops of St Andrews. Until the accession of William Fraser in 1279 the bishops were content with conventional representations of themselves in pontificals, usually accompanied with the legend, 'Seal of [   ] bishop of the Scots'. Fraser's seal is altogether more elaborate. On one side the bishop appears in pontificals surrounded by strawberry leaves (a pun on the family name) with the legend 'Seal of William Fraser bishop of the Scots'. The other side shows Andrew being tied onto his cross of martyrdom with the bishop kneeling in adoration below and the legend 'Seal of William Fraser bishop of St Andrews'.[80]

St Andrew and Scotland have become one, with the bishop as representative and mediator. It is no accident, therefore, that the final, elaborate version of the St Andrew legend, developed during Fraser's episcopate,[81] should insist on Andrew's suzerainty over all the people of Scotland ('the Picts, Scots, Danes and Norwegians') as well as the episcopal status of St Rule who brought the apostle's relics to Kilrymont. Fraser's new episcopal seal is the prototype for the seal of the Guardians of 1286, with its royal coat of arms on one side and Andrew on his cross on the other, surrounded by the legend, 'Andrew be leader of the compatriot Scots'.[82]

The seal of the Guardians is the ultimate symbol of the new relationship forged between crown and church in the reign of Alexander III. On this seal the power of both church and state is expressed in self-assured and sophisticated forms. The metal of the seal is a common matrix for both, yet when the images of this seal are pressed into the wax they face away from each other: part of one whole, yet separate.

NOTES

1. Anderson, *Early Sources*, ii, 87, n..
2. *Chron. Pluscarden*, i, 82–83 (trans., ii, 56–57). For St Margaret and her cult see also D. MacRoberts, *St Margaret of Scotland* (Catholic Truth Society Pamphlet, n.p., n.d.).
3. Anderson, *Early Sources*, ii, 137–8 and n..
4. See G. Donaldson, 'The Rights of the Scottish Crown in Episcopal Vacancies', *SHR*, xlv (1966), 27–35.
5. Duncan, *Kingdom*, 276–8.
6. *Cum universi* survives from a copy in Roger Howden's chronicle and has been widely reprinted, including Lawrie, *Annals*, 275–6, no. cxviii. For a discussion of the bull's history since its issue, see R. Somerville, *Scotia Pontifica* (Oxford, 1982), no. 156. In the terms of *Cum Universi* the Scottish church consisted of the dioceses of St Andrews, Dunblane, Glasgow, Dunkeld, Brechin, Aberdeen, Moray, Ross and Caithness. Whithorn (Galloway) remained subject to York until 1355. The Isles and Orkney were in Norwegian territory and subject to Trondheim.
7. M. Ash, *The Administration of the Diocese of St Andrews, 1202–1328* (unpublished Ph.D. thesis, University of Newcastle upon Tyne, 1972; henceforth Ash, *St Andrews*), 19.
8. Robertson, *Concilia*, ii, 3; Patrick, *Statutes*, 1.
9. Duncan, *Kingdom*, 286.
10. See below, p. 37.
11. Hailes, *Annals*, i, 216.
12. Anderson, *Early Sources*, ii, 651. For the general circumstances surrounding this case see *Ash*, St Andrews, 62–63.
13. See below, p. 44.
14. Duncan, *Kingdom*, 293. Provincial Councils known to have been held during the reign are: 1250 Edinburgh; 1268 Perth — to excommunicate Melrose for violating the sanctuary of Stow and choose representatives to go to Ottoboni's London Council; 1273 Perth — to receive the papal encyclical announcing the Council of Lyons; 6 August 1275 Perth — to protest against Boiamund's new assessment; 19 August 1280 at the Blackfriars of Perth — to publish excommunication of Sir William Fenton, lord of Beaufort in the Aird. (Robertson, *Concilia*, lxi–lxxi and nn..)
15. For Clement and the arrival of the Dominicans in Scotland, see A. Ross, O.P., *Dogs of the Lord: The Story of the Dominican Order in Scotland* (published to coincide with an exhibition of the same name in the City Art Centre, Edinburgh, 1981).
16. *RRS: Alexander III*, no. 10 (dated 31 May 1251).

17. W. M. Mackenzie, 'A Prelude to the War of Independence', *SHR*, xxvii (1948), 105–13. The history of this attempt to create a Scottish Franciscan province is not completely clear. Mackenzie's account differs substantially from that given in Cowan and Easson, *Religious Houses*, 124.
18. Ash, *St Andrews*, 66.
19. A. A. M. Duncan, 'Documents Relating to the Priory of the Isle of May, c. 1140–1313', *PSAS*, xc (1956), 52–80.
20. Ibid., 62ff..
21. *CPL*, i, 497.
22. It was also during this reign that the shift from romanesque to gothic occurred in the building of St Andrews Cathedral, largely underwritten by Bishop Wishart. Ash, *St Andrews*, 84–85.
23. R. W. and J. Munro, *Tain Through the Centuries* (Inverness, 1966), 10, 16, 28–30. By an odd coincidence another Scottish saint was canonized in England during this period: St William of Perth, a pilgrim who had been murdered on his way to the shrine of St Thomas at Canterbury in 1208 and buried in the cathedral of St Andrew at Rochester. See Duncan, *Kingdom*, 306–7.
24. *Chron. Picts–Scots*, 183.
25. See below, pp. 39–40.
26. Dr Gunn, *The Church and Monastery of the Holy Cross of Peebles* (Peebles, 1909; henceforth Gunn, *Peebles*), 1 (paraphrased from *Chron. Fordun*, ii, 294). For the dating of the foundation see Cowan and Easson, *Religious Houses*, 109–10.
27. Gunn, *Peebles*, 5; Cowan and Easson, *Religious Houses*, 106, 109–10. Following the first house at Berwick and Dunbar, founded 1240x8, other Trinitarian houses were Scotlandwell, 1250, Houston, c. 1270 and Aberdeen x1274. (Ibid., 105–110.)
28. Duncan, *Kingdom*, 559.
29. NLS MS 15.1.18 no. 16 (printed in Robertson, *Concilia*, ii, 241–2, and trans. Patrick, *Statutes*, 211–2). For the suggested dating of this letter to the Dunfermline ceremony, see D. E. R. Watt, *A Biographical Dictionary of Scottish Graduates to A.D. 1410* (Oxford, 1977; henceforth Watt, *Dictionary*), 6, 42.
30. For a fuller discussion of this point see Ash, *St Andrews*, 47ff..
31. *CPL*, i, 270.
32. *Moray Registrum*, no. 260; Robertson, *Concilia*, ii, 242–7. See also Duncan, *Kingdom*, 289–91.
33. For Bernham's career see M. Ash, 'David Bernham, Bishop of St Andrews, 1239–1253', in *The Medieval Church of St Andrews*, ed. D. MacRoberts (Glasgow, 1976); Watt, *Dictionary*, 41–44.
34. J. Spottiswoode, *History of the Church of Scotland* (London, 1668), 44.
35. Ash, *St Andrews*, 52ff.; Watt, *Dictionary*, 225–8.
36. Ibid., 59–60. For the collegiate church of St Mary of the Rock and their participation in episcopal elections, see 'The Clergy at St Andrews', in Barrow, *Kingdom*, 212–32.
37. *CDS*, i, no. 2013; Watt, 'Minority', 11ff..

38. Anderson, *Early Sources*, ii, 586.
39. Ibid., 588–9; *CPL*, i, 350; reprinted in Theiner, *Monumenta*, no. 201.
40. Watt, 'Minority', 16.
41. Among these factional bishops were Peter Ramsay of Aberdeen (1247–56) and Albin of Brechin (1246–69), both Durwardites and already in office at the beginning of the reign. In 1250 the Durwardite Richard of Inverkeithing was provided to Dunkeld (1250–72), to be followed by Robert Stuteville in 1273. For their careers and allegiances see Watt, *Dictionary*, 460–3, 5–7, 280–2 and 527–8.
42. Ibid., 456–7.
43. Anderson, *Early Sources*, ii, 295–6.
44. *CPL*, i, 319, 320. (This second entry is printed in full in Theiner, *Monumenta*, no. 178.) The second *CPL* entry is incorrect in saying that the time limit was one year.
45. For Cheam's career see E. W. M. Balfour-Melville, 'John de Cheam, Bishop of Glasgow', *SHR*, xxvii (1948), 176–86.
46. Anderson, *Early Sources*, ii, 596 and n. 3; Watt, *Dictionary*, 96; Watt, *Fasti*, 146.
47. For these possible relationships between the Wisharts, see Watt, *Dictionary*, 585, 590.
48. Watt, *Fasti*, 26–27.
49. Comyn's surname is somewhat deceptive, for he belonged to a cadet family of the earls of Fife. He was the brother of Adam of Kilconquhar who married Marjorie countess of Carrick and died on crusade in 1270. See Watt, *Dictionary*, 107–8.
50. Watt, *Fasti*, 129.
51. *APS*, i, 420–1. The diocese of the Isles included the Isle of Man until the Great Schism in the late fourteenth century. From 1387 onwards there are two lines of bishops: the bishops of the Isles, now part of the Scottish church, and Sodor and Man, owing allegiance to York. See Watt, *Fasti*, 197.
52. Ibid., 201.
53. *CPL*, i, 379; Theiner, *Monumenta*, no. 229. For subsequent episcopal provisions along these lines see *CPL*, i, 413 — mandate to the bishops of St Andrews and Aberdeen and the abbot of Dunfermline to enquire into Laurence of Argyll, 1264; ibid., 775 — mandate to the bishops of Moray, Aberdeen and Glasgow to enquire into the fitness of Robert, dean of Dunkeld, who had been elected to that see, 1273; ibid., 446–8 — after the quashing of the election of Nicholas, abbot of Scone, 'on account of the abbot's intolerable lack of learning', Gregory X found the election of Archibald, archdeacon of Moray (although only in deacon's orders) canonical, but because he lacks evidence as to his fitness he sends a mandate to the bishops of Moray, Aberdeen and Argyll to examine the merits of Archibald, 1274; ibid., 449 — a similar mandate to the bishops of St Andrews and Aberdeen to examine master Robert Fyvie, archdeacon of Ross, elected to that see, if he is suitable they are to consecrate, but if not they are to cause another election, 1275; ibid., 450 — mandate to the

bishops of St Andrews and Dunkeld to examine the election of William Comyn (Kilconquhar) to Brechin in 1274; ibid., 466-7 — in 1282 Martin IV at first quashed the election of Henry, precentor of Aberdeen to that see because he was not in holy orders, but he was persuaded to change his mind, and ordered the bishops of St Andrews, Dunblane and Caithness to consecrate Henry after first ordaining him; ibid., 469-70 — in 1283 after the death of Hugh of Stirling, elect of Dunblane at the papal court, the pope accepted the chapter's second choice, William, dean of Dunblane; ibid., 472-3 — in 1284 William, abbot of Arbroath attempted to resign his election to the see of Dunblane at the papal court, but the pope refused to accept this and ordered the bishop of Tusculum (who rather specialised in Scottish consecrations) to proceed with his consecration.

54. Ibid., 457; Theiner, *Monumenta*, no. 270.
55. Ash, *St Andrews*, 78-79; Watt, *Dictionary*, 590.
56. Watt, *Fasti*, 59; Watt, *Dictionary*, 477; *HBC*, 174.
57. For example, Moray in 1259: *CPL*, i, 365.
58. Ibid., 414.
59. Ibid., 257.
60. See ibid., 413; Theiner, *Monumenta*, no. 239: papal mandate by Urban IV dated 9 July 1263 to the bishop of Dunblane and Peter Leti, canon of St Peter's, Rome, and resident in England, to provide Peter of the Curia, chaplain of J., cardinal of St Mary's in Cosmedin, to a prebend of Glasgow. Gregory IX (1227-41) had ordered him to be received as a canon, but the next vacant prebend had been bestowed elsewhere and Peter had been given the church of Carstairs. He is now prepared to resign this and 'to have one of the ancient prebends'.
61. See Ash, *St Andrews*, 74-77 and Watt, *Dictionary*, 590-3 for a discussion of those benefices belonging to Wishart still traceable.
62. Ash, *St Andrews*, 76; Watt, *Dictionary*, 590.
63. They were St Andrews, Glasgow, Argyll, Dunblane, Aberdeen and Ross: Ash, *St Andrews*, 79.
64. For Scottish crusading activity during the reign of Alexander III see A. Macquarrie, *Scotland and the Crusades* (Edinburgh, 1985; henceforth Macquarrie, *Crusades*), ch. 3.
65. *CPL*, i, 263.
66. See Duncan, *Kingdom*, 564.
67. *CPL*, i, 384-5, 423.
68. Macquarrie, *Crusades*, 55.
69. Robertson, *Concilia*, i, p. lxii, n. 2.
70. *CPL*, i, 432-4; Ash, *St Andrews*, 68-71.
71. Macquarrie, *Crusades*, 56ff.
72. Robertson, *Concilia*, i, p. lxii.
73. Boiamund's rolls are published in *SHS Misc.*, v, vi and x.
74. W. E. Lunt, *Financial Relations of the Papacy with England to 1327* (Cambridge, Mass., 1939), i, 341.
75. For a short discussion of Boiamund's career and methods of collecting see A. I. Dunlop's introduction, *SHS Misc.*, vi, 5-28; Ash, *St Andrews*, 80-82,

96–97; Macquarrie, *Crusades*, 63–64; Duncan, *Kingdom*, 291–2.
76. Anderson, *Early Sources*, ii, 542.
77. *Chron. Pluscarden*, i, 97 (trans., ii, 70).
78. Duncan, *Kingdom*, 555–8.
79. *Chron. Picts–Scots*, 138–40.
80. W. R. MacDonald, *Scottish Armorial Seals* (Edinburgh, 1904), nos. 943–4.
81. *Chron. Picts–Scots*, 183–93.
82. Barrow, *Bruce*, 17; W. de G. Birch, *History of Scottish Seals* (Edinburgh, 1905–7), i, 31–33 and nos. 14, 15 (illustrations).

3

ALEXANDER III — A SILVER AGE?
AN ESSAY IN
SCOTTISH MEDIEVAL ECONOMIC HISTORY

Nicholas Mayhew

Anyone who has worked on Scottish medieval economic history will be familiar with the problem of trying to build a fair amount of scattered information into a coherent unit which will reveal anything about the broader, more general development of Scotland as a whole. There are, it is true, certain general indicators of Scottish medieval prosperity and economic performance, and it is on these that this essay has to concentrate. Tax assessments, estimates of money supply, price history and demographic evidence (such as it is), can all be reviewed so the Scotland of Alexander III may be compared with earlier and later periods, and with contemporary developments elsewhere, most obviously England. The comparisons offered here are generally relative and somewhat impressionistic; one can sketch in only the broadest outline. But in a search for general economic indicators, we must not lose sight of the particular. This is important not merely because the evidence does not usually permit general conclusions, but also because even when an estimate can be made of, for instance, the total yield of the tax of 1292, or the likely money supply in 1280, that does not always give a complete picture of the fortunes of the different individuals and component groups who together made up thirteenth-century Scotland. It is therefore necessary to examine the crown, the church and the nobility, merchants and craftsmen, and to compare life in town and country, in the highlands and the lowlands. The question must be asked specifically, for whom was the age so golden?

For example, looking at the king's income, the golden peaks may come in David II's reign rather than Alexander III's. In 1264 Alexander's chamberlain, William, earl of Mar had £5,413 cash income through his hands for a year and a half,[1] but it has been powerfully argued that David II enjoyed a much stronger financial position; his chamberlain's cash receipts peaked at well over £15,000 per annum, which looks healthy even after deducting 4,000 marks for the king's ransom payments.[2] Moreover, the king's wealth may in one sense reflect the poverty of his subjects. David's sojourn in England, under Edward III among the most heavily taxed of nations, may well have taught him much about the potential profits of kingship. But from the tax-payers' point of view Alexander III's reign, especially as far as customs rates were concerned, was a period of very moderate demands compared with what was to come.[3]

The low level of thirteenth-century customs must have contributed not a little to merchant prosperity. Ancient tolls were generally set at an insignificant level, in the context of the volume and value of thirteenth-century trade, and even the new custom on wool, woolfells and hides demanded only a very modest seven per cent of the total value of the wool.[4] The merchant's social and political status, however, seem to have risen along with his fiscal contributions as the fourteenth century progressed. This merchant prominence may be discerned individually in the careers of men like John Mercer of Perth[5] who reached a position far beyond the aspirations of such major Berwick figures of the late thirteenth century as Philip Rydale or Roger Bartholomew.[6] Collectively the advance of the merchant community may be most clearly signalled by the regular summons of burgesses to parliament from the 1360s; those who paid the piper began to call the tune.[7]

Within their burghs, the power, wealth and influence of the merchant group have been contrasted with the rather more modest fortunes of craftsmen, and it has been suggested that the repression of craftsmen may lie behind a turn round of the positive thirteenth-century balance of payments to a negative fourteenth-century balance.[8] The idea of this drift into the red will be discussed below, but in fact it seems unlikely that the position of craftsmen was very much better in the thirteenth century or even in the twelfth, in which period Professor Duncan has found admission to be a burgess already very carefully regulated.[9] It may also be that the distinction between merchants and craftsmen is not a particularly helpful one. Capital was a scarcer resource than skill, and the craftsmen possessed of significant capital, the dyers and the goldsmiths, rapidly managed to enhance their status and function in trade, perhaps hiring artisans for the routine work while establishing themselves as entrepreneurs. It was trade, above all international trade, which made the biggest fortunes, and it was wealth which bought power within the burgh.

One Scottish craft of which we know something is pottery.[10] While it is true that the import of quality wares from Scarborough, France, the Low Countries and Germany increased from the late thirteenth century through the fourteenth century, this development did not take place at the expense of local Scottish pottery. From the mid twelfth century onwards (though beginning later in north-east Scotland) the local Scottish pottery industry began to flourish, driving out poorer quality imports from England. Although the quality end of the market remained in foreign hands, Scottish potters successfully supplied Scottish day to day needs. Their failure to do more than this probably lies not so much in the balance of power between Scots craftsmen and Scots merchants as in the nature of the traditional relationships between more and less developed countries, according to which the latter tend to supply raw materials while the former dominate services and finished goods.[11]

One should not however paint too 'undeveloped' or primitive a picture of the larger Scottish burghs. The monasteries recognised their economic importance and were actively increasing their investment there.[12] Also the finds evidence from excavations in Perth[13] suggests a prosperous and sophisticated town life. Aberdeen seems to have been somewhat less developed, but Berwick, if further excavated, may be expected to produce a wealth of evidence. Building methods and materials as revealed by excavation do seem to have been very basic. Wooden framework with wattle and daub walls, sometimes on a sill, and occasionally on stone, thatch and turf roofs, bare floors; all this indicates a somewhat cheerless, or at least comfortless, existence. However only small parts of these burghs have been excavated, and the documents at least suggest that much remains to be discovered. Stone houses are mentioned in documents for early fourteenth-century Aberdeen,[14] and a court roll of that date suggests a well organised society paying high rents only a little lower than those prevailing in Berwick.[15] The Berwick survey for the late 1290s, of which only a part survives, paints a picture of burgage properties with shops, cellars and solars. Burgages on Hidegate and Segate usually commanded high prices, though cheaper burgage properties were to be had in Fishergate. These cheaper properties do not appear to have been any smaller than the more expensive ones;[16] perhaps the more prosperous pursuits were reserved to specific neighbourhoods or even specific burgages. This Berwick survey does not usually mention the building materials used for the burgages, but the vacant lots, which were large and sometimes did actually contain buildings,[17] were often specifically noted as enclosed by stone walls. These open plots serve well to remind us of the many essentially rural activities which still took place within the town, in England as much as in Scotland.[18] An inquisition of 1313 speaks of forty acres in Berwick held open and pertinent to the existing burgages in addition to which were the vacant lots already mentioned, in the streets intermingled with the burgage tenements. The inquisition was told that

> the burgesses have no other place within or without their town where they can have a handful of grass or pasture or any other easement except these 40 acres, whereon all the burgesses both great and small have common pasture in open time by use and wont, and they are divided into small divisions among the burgesses, as in the time of Alexander.[19]

Under Alexander III it seems they were held freely without rent, but Edward II collected 2s an acre for them.

Berwick then, like Aberdeen, does not appear to have been overcrowded, though conditions may have been a touch more cramped in Perth.[20] But how well does thirteenth-century Perth with its impressive archaeological finds compare with late fourteenth-century Edinburgh, excavations of which have discovered imported tiled floors?[21] The comforts of life do seem more apparent in the later period.

However, the standard of living debate perhaps hinges more critically on diet than on *domus*. The archaeological evidence makes it clear that thirteenth-century Perth enjoyed its fair share of animal products; the St Ann's Lane excavations give 'a clear indication of a beef-based meat supply'.[22] Without becoming involved in the statistical complications of how to count excavated animal bones, it is clear that cattle dominated the meat supply, followed by sheep and then by pigs. No excavation has yet been able to refine the evidence of animal remains to discern any shift in eating habits over time. We have no archaeological evidence either for or against the suggestion, based on prices, that in the later middle ages more meat may have been eaten relative to grain.[23] In any case the archaeological evidence for cereal consumption is more or less impossible to quantify, and survives less obviously than animal bones.

Duncan has commented on the scarcity of ovens in noting the one mentioned in a survey of the lands of the priory of Coldingham in 1300. We may also note the commercial baker's oven mentioned in the Aberdeen 1317 court roll, which may be the same one as that excavated in St Paul Street. Another has been excavated at Perth, and we know one was built at Skipness in 1326 at a cost of 1s 8d.[24] There are therefore probably more ovens about than might appear at first sight.

Given also that domestic bread can be baked perfectly well in a pot, it may be that more bread was consumed than is sometimes thought. Some excavated features in Aberdeen, Perth, Kelso and Berwick have been linked with grain drying,[25] and wheat was of course imported through the burghs.[26] However, the real evidence for cereals, especially oats, comes from the countryside, where the overwhelming majority of the population still lived.

If one leafs through the maps of the first edition of the *Historical Atlas of Scotland*[27] from the twelfth century onwards, the concentration of almost any of the mapped items shows what has been called an 'all-too-familiar dichotomy of a well-endowed lowland region and a virtually empty highland region'.[28] As Professor Barrow goes on to point out, however, this picture can be amended, specifically regarding fairs and markets, and we must be careful not to underestimate the economic life of the highlands. Thus, although the sheriffdoms at the end of the thirteenth century were only beginning to encroach on the remoter regions, royal income derived from northern, if not highland, Scotland outweighed that from the south.[29] Similarly, Simpson's analysis of Quincy wealth laid special stress on valuable estates in remote Galloway.[30] Again, Professor E. J. Cowan has elsewhere in this volume reminded us of the contemporary concept of the fertile west.[31] When, all too briefly, the mists of the north and west lift to allow a glimpse of medieval life there, we are usually impressed by the scale of economic activity.

That said, the sources for the lowlands of the south and east are much more plentiful. Agricultural life in these regions may not have been too dissimilar to that in northern England. Livestock farming played a greater part than in southern England, but in the northern English counties and in the more densely settled regions of Scotland arable farming was attempted in even the least promising locations. In Northumberland new settlements were springing up, clearing and cultivating virgin and probably marginal land.[32] This of course is closely paralleled in Scotland by the cultivation of Lammermuir, which is probably the most investigated but by no means the only instance of marginal agriculture.[33] Let us look for example at Alexander III's estate at Wark in Tynedale which also provides evidence of thirteenth-century cultivation.[34] Although technically in England, this evidence is nonetheless admissable: as Palgrave observed, Alexander treated Tynedale as a regality, using there all his rights as sovereign, and since the climate and terrain are so similar to that prevailing in Tweeddale, it is fair to pretend, as did Alexander III, that these lands are in fact in Scotland. Included in Alexander's regalian rights was a claim to treasure trove at Wark, which the numismatist finds exciting, but the accounts for Wark and Crendon are more interesting to historians because they provide information for two comparable periods, 1264 to 1266, and 1286 to 1290.

The earliest two-year account is not as full as we might like: the cottars' rent for two years came to £10–15s–6d *cum incremento*; it would be good to know if it was the rents or the number of cottars which had increased. More detail in this early account would also make comparison with the evidence from the 1280s more meaningful. By the 1280s these cottars' rents had dwindled dramatically, but, since the overall value of the manor seems to have risen sharply, the disappearing cottars may have been entered under another category. However it is clear that the demesne was at farm throughout this period, while there appears to have been extensive assarting between 1266 and 1286. These assarts brought in a total of £17–11s–10d let at will in 1287. Those most familiar with Scottish documentary evidence are in no doubt that from the late twelfth century until the late thirteenth century at least cultivation was pushing back the frontier of waste and forest.[35]

In Scotland, however, historians have not developed a theory of Malthusian overpopulation and here the burgh and rural evidence concur.[36] The limits of extended cultivation were perhaps only reached in the immediate vicinity of the towns,[37] and climatic deterioration seems to account more successfully for the retreat from the margin of cultivation. In terms of climate, therefore, the days of Alexander III may well have been relatively golden.[38]

There are also some grounds for thinking that despite severe problems of soil acidity and altitude, in some respects Scottish agriculture may have been better placed than much English farming. It is clear that a better balance of mixed husbandry prevailed in the north.[39] Miller has found sheep in many thousands on the lands of the Umfravilles, of Newminster and Holm Cultram abbeys and on the Durham holdings in Islandshire and Norhamshire.[40] When the nunnery at Coldstream received compensation for damage by the English army in 1296 the larger part of their losses were incurred in livestock, rather than in corn.[41] The herbage, pannage and agistment met at Wark confirm the impression of active animal husbandry; Scottish wool exports have been estimated at as much as 20 per cent of the English figure, while the buoyant export trade in hides speaks of highly successful cattle raising.[42] Given that some English historians attribute the poor productivity of English agriculture largely to the shortage of fertilizer, the better Scottish balance of stock and corn farming may have been important. Moreover, the Scottish lords' limited taste for direct exploitation of demesne probably reduced landlord appropriation of the toun's manure,[43] and it is also possible that peasant cultivation of a greater proportion of the land in their own interests may have increased productivity per acre.

All this, however, is to look very determinedly on the bright side. Although successful livestock farming may have helped Scottish agriculture, the picture left by arable farming is irredeemably bleak. The dominance of oats, a hardy, but usually lower yielding crop than wheat or barley, confirms the shortness of the growing season. The labour market may have been awash with casual workers too lowly for either their jobs or even their homes to have left a mark on the record.[44] While those who held land and sold produce may have been able to benefit from gently rising thirteenth-century prices,[45] those with only their labour to sell had to market a depreciating asset. Although the size of this sub-historical proletariat can only be guessed at, the ghostly presence of this group, even more vulnerable than the subsistence farmers, must cast something of a pall over the golden landscape of Alexandrine Scotland.

No such pall hangs over the Scottish nobility who seem to have enjoyed a marked rise in their standard of living.[46] Where, all too rarely, we have figures, this impression is confirmed, but also qualified by comparison with English lords. The earl of Fife, or Roger Quincy, constable of Scotland, though both among the wealthiest of Scots, with annual Scottish incomes in the region of £400–500, rank only with middling English barons. Even the most prosperous Scottish lords appear as rather more modest fish in the English pool.

An examination of church wealth suggests that the richest areas were concentrated in the east and the lowlands. In these most prosperous zones, notably the diocese of St Andrews, Scottish wealth compared reasonably with English. Alexander Stevenson's calculations per square mile, based on the Nicholas IV tithe of 1291–2 in England and Scotland, demonstrate that mile per mile the diocese of St Andrews was wealthier than all but a handful of south-eastern English dioceses.[47] A cruder comparison of wealth based on this assessment gave a Scots total of about one fifth that of England and Wales.[48] The Anglo-Scottish ratio of 5:1 seems to be mirrored by the relative volume of English and Scots wool exports,[49] while Grant has mused on a 6:1 ratio of English to Scottish population, arable land and money supply.[50]

The relationship between the various thirteenth- and fourteenth-century assessments have been discussed by Tout,[51] and Stevenson's up-to-date study will grace the new edition of the *Historical Atlas of Scotland*.[52] Broadly speaking, Boiamund's and Bishop Halton's taxations support one another, and were both high. The old extent was significantly below the figures for the 1270s and the 1290s, but dramatically above the *Verus Valor* of 1366 with which it has been compared ever since the fourteenth century. No historian should ever venture out without his scepticism, and this is more than ever the case with the investigation of taxation records. As Nicholson notes in passing, the new assessment was completed within seven weeks;[53] we may perhaps therefore wonder how precise the valuation may have been. It is also possible that the higher rates of customs duty depressed contributions and assessments for the subsidies. Dwindling returns from repeated subsidies in England certainly argue for some cumulative tax-payer resistance. However, since these assessments constitute so large a proportion of all the evidence available to us, it would be unduly fastidious to decline to use them.

Reservations notwithstanding, the collapse in values from the old assessment to that of 1366 remains striking, and requires some sort of explanation, and whatever date is assigned to the old extent,[54] the old and the new valuations provide powerful evidence for the golden age of Alexander III. It is therefore particularly pertinent to ask why the 1366 valuation was so low.

The truth that Alexandrine prosperity was founded on a period of prolonged relative peace has the corollary that the Wars of Independence contributed to the economic crash. It has been justly pointed out that the areas of greatest war damage do not correspond with the incidence of most sharply falling values.[55] It may also be observed that although war damage was sometimes of the utmost severity, as in Berwick in 1296 or Aberdeen in 1336, the worst damage tended to be local and of short duration.[56] Berwick, despite the massacres and fires which so impressed the chroniclers, was rapidly back in business, whether on an English or Scottish basis. Aberdeen, whose 1336 coin hoards provide an example without parallel in Europe of a financial community taken totally off-guard,[57] was nonetheless rapidly back in operation as a regional seat of government for David II. Similarly the northern English counties won complete tax exemption in 1334 because of war damage, but paid as usual in 1336.

However, it would be a mistake to write off totally the deleterious economic effects of the war. The damage to business confidence, though impossible to quantify, was probably severe.[58] More tangible was the damage to Scottish trade routes. It has been shown that to minimise the costs of shipping, Scottish fourteenth-century trade was customarily carried in relatively few very large ships whose cargo values sometimes ran into thousands of pounds.[59] Scottish cargoes were therefore particularly vulnerable as they ran the gauntlet of the English coast on the long voyage to France. One obvious effect of the war was the loss of Berwick. Although to some extent perhaps off-set by the rise of Edinburgh, the loss of Scotland's premier trading burgh and port must have been a severe blow. Even if the more exaggerated estimates of Berwick's thirteenth-century wealth are set aside,[60] its disappearance from the national balance was of major significance.

Nevertheless, despite all these points calling for a more serious assessment of war damage to the economy, it must be accepted that the ravages of the Wars of Independence will not adequately account for the fallen values of the new extent.[61] An alternative explanation which has been authoritatively advanced interprets the depressed 1366 valuation in the light of severe monetary deflation.[62] The assertion that prices were falling by the early 1360s, however, is by no means proven. The information is extremely scarce, and distinctly equivocal. Although the very limited evidence for oats and barley may suggest a fall, the picture for salt, wheat, hides, coal and wax, if anything, suggests the reverse.[63] Much work remains to be done before the behaviour of prices in the fourteenth century can be described with any confidence, and the evidence is even more scarce in the thirteenth century. This writer's impression is that until Scotland left the sterling standard in 1367, Scottish prices moved broadly in line with English.[64]

Though prices remain for the moment enigmatic, a good deal more is known about money supply. Because of its possible bearing on the 1366 assessment, a fairly thorough review of the monetary position is called for. It is perfectly clear that money supply in Scotland grew impressively in the thirteenth century, especially during the reign of Alexander III.[65] Possible figures for monetary growth in England, Ireland and Scotland are set out below:

Date	England	Ireland	Scotland
c. 1247–51	c. £400,000	c. £43,000	c. £50,000–£60,000
c. 1278–84	c. £674,000	c. £60,000+	c. £130,000–£180,000+

Scotland appears to have out-performed England and Ireland, who shared roughly similar rates of monetary growth. It seems unlikely that Scotland was earning silver at a very much faster rate than England,[66] but it is possible that at this time England was spending a greater proportion of her foreign earnings than Scotland. Another possibility is that the Scottish figure for money supply in the middle of the thirteenth century is too low.

All the evidence suggests that the growth of the wool trade and the European monetary take-off which can be associated with it begins in the late twelfth century.[67] It is curious to note that in Scotland, where David I had already prepared the ground so carefully, monetary take-off should have been delayed by some fifty to sixty years. Indeed, the message of the Scottish documents is that money payments were well established by the latter part of the twelfth century.[68] Yet Scottish mint output remained relatively modest until well into the second half of the thirteenth century. Perhaps the explanation for this conflict is that while Scots mint output grew only slowly, Scottish money supply, augmented by English coin, actually grew earlier and more quickly.

It seems a reasonable assumption that at a time of Scottish recoinage, the Scots mints recoined all sterling of the old superseded type. However, it was not until 1280 that Scotland managed to stage a recoinage almost simultaneously with England. Alexander III's replacement of the Short Cross type occurred some three years after Henry III had acted in England, while William the Lion may have missed the introduction of the English Short Cross penny by as much as fifteen years. It is at least possible that the Scottish output of Long Cross pennies in the early 1250s — c. £50,000 to £60,000 — under-represents the actual quantity of coins in Scotland at that time, since coin already struck with the new English Long Cross types in the previous three years would have escaped recoinage. We cannot know how much coin may have escaped Alexander III's first recoinage in this way, but if this hypothesis is accepted it would reduce the rate of Scottish monetary growth in the second half of the century to slightly less astonishing levels, and also increase the estimate of Scotland's money supply for the first half of the century, thus bringing it more into line with everything the other historical sources tell us about thirteenth- and even twelfth-century Scottish growth. There is some support for this idea in the quite striking numbers of thirteenth-century pennies now coming to light in Scotland. The growth of Scottish medieval archaeology, and even responsible use of metal detectors, have transformed the picture of

Scottish stray finds. Thirteen years ago this writer listed twenty-two thirteenth-century finds, which was all the accumulated literature could provide; Donal Bateson is currently working on a list which will provide about thirty-five more new finds, plus five from the twelfth century. The suggestion, made in 1977, of a dramatic monetary take-off in Scotland under Alexander III may therefore be amended somewhat to admit of earlier monetary growth, though the 1280 peak remains outstanding.[69]

Scottish mint output in the first half of the fourteenth century was extremely modest — there were no general recoinages — but detailed analysis of the plentiful Scots hoards of the period suggests that Scotland's money supply shared the rapid English growth of the first decade or two of the century. The second quarter of the century in England saw a marked fall in mint output, which together with a sharp rise in overseas expenditure, principally by the government of Edward III, did cause a contraction in the money supply and brought about a perceptible dip in prices.[70] Scotland may well have also been affected by this drain on sterling, and Scottish bullionist legislation begins at this time.[71] In the third quarter of the century, however, Scots wool exports hit record levels.

Mint output figures for the Edinburgh mint survive from 1358 to 1364.[72] About £28,500 was struck, which seems a pretty impressive performance given that in a similar period (Michaelmas 1357–64) London struck £44,000 in silver. It should however be borne in mind that London also struck gold while the Scottish gold of this time was quantitatively negligible.[73] We may presume that Scottish mint output dwindled somewhat after 1364, leading to the modest weight reduction of October 1367, needed *propter raritatem pecunie de argento ad presens in regno nostro.*[74] Without totally discounting this rarity it is possible that the weight reduction was actually introduced to boost royal income rather than to supply general shortage of coin. Before the weight reduction of 1367, the king had increased his seignorage from 7d to 8d in the pound, suggesting that the reduction in royal income from the mint made itself felt first, before any general shortage in the kingdom.[75]

The increased rate of seignorage probably only made the mint less competitive and reduced output. The weight reduction of 1367, which enabled the merchant to receive more coins for his pound weight of silver, and cut seignorage back to 7d, made much better economic sense. The moneyers were able to take 11d mintage per pound, a pretty clear case of profiteering, but they still managed to pay the merchant 27s 9d for each pound of silver.[76] It seems probable that output picked up as a result of these changes. Although exact calculations are not possible, the hoards make it feasible that David II struck as much silver between 1367 and 1371 as he had between 1358 and 1367.[77] For Robert II no output figures survive, but the general impression from the finds of the second half of the fourteenth century is that Robert II's output probably continued at levels similar to those of David II.[78] Die-studies by the leading numismatists of this period, Dr Stewart and Mrs Murray, confirm and indeed strengthen this impression.[79]

The performance of the Scottish mint therefore is not in line with the assertion of a severe monetary shortage capable of halving the yield of the old assessment in the reduced circumstances of 1366. The figures are extremely rough and ready but it seems not impossible that at least £100,000 went through the Scottish mint between 1357 and 1390. Other things being equal mint output was normally very sensitive to the fortunes of the export trade, which at this time was booming.[80]

The assessment of Scottish money supply, however, depends on far more than the output of the Scottish mints. Large numbers of old English pence continued to circulate in Scotland in the second half of the fourteenth century, but a reliable estimate of what proportion of the Scottish money supply they made up must await the discovery of future hoards. The present state of our knowledge is that the earlier and larger hoards of this period tend to be dominated by English money at levels of as much as 90 per cent, while smaller and later finds are much more likely to contain large Scottish elements.[81] As time passed, especially after 1367, English money was increasingly likely to have been turned in at the mint in return for more, lighter Scottish coins, and this probability is confirmed by the stray find evidence.

We cannot then offer even an approximate figure for Scottish money supply at the time of the 1366 assessment to compare with the grand Alexandrine totals. It would certainly have been smaller than in 1280, but despite the bullionist legislation[82] and the unquestioned deepening of the European later medieval monetary shortage,[83] it does not seem to have been sufficiently reduced by 1366 to explain the low *Verus Valor*. But to make even this judgement we need not only better money supply data, but also some kind of a handle on Scottish population after the Black Death.

Money supply per head of the population must have risen sharply in England after the plague, and this factor may have contributed to the buoyant prices noted in England for the third quarter of the fourteenth century. Some kind of assessment of the severity of the plague in Scotland is essential, both for its own sake and for its bearing on prices and the monetary thesis as advanced to explain the *Verus Valor.* Scarcity of evidence, however, has prevented the investigation of the Black Death and its effects in Scotland. In general terms it has been noted that the chronicles are surprisingly silent about the plague, and apart from the oft-cited twenty-four canons of the priory of St Andrews who died in 1349,[84] statistical evidence is very hard to come by. Logically it is reasonable to assume that a dispersed settlement pattern may have reduced the impact of bubonic plague in Scotland.

In the absence of hard figures for Scotland it is perhaps permissible to look for comparative data from those English regions whose scattered settlement and hardy climate might also be thought to have limited the ravages of disease. Detailed evidence of mortality among beneficed clergy of the diocese of York survives.[85] This evidence, specifically that for the archdeaconry of Cleveland, which provides comparative data from three deaneries of differing geographical character, confirms the suspicion that high moorland was less severely affected by the plague. Nevertheless, even in relatively lightly affected areas, such as the moorland deanery of Cleveland, in 1349–50 there was still a mortality rate of 21.42 per cent.[86] In the York archdeaconry the relatively healthy upland district of Craven still scored 26.92 per cent.

Thus while it may be assumed that plague was less severe in Scotland than England, the York upland figures suggest that Scotland may still have suffered a 20–25 per cent fall in population, compared with the English mortality of 33–50 per cent. A fall in population of this magnitude would not only offset any effects of dwindling money supply, but might go some way towards explaining the low 1366 assessment figure in its own right. Tax assessments, closely based on tithes and rents, are always extremely sensitive to population change. Historical geographers working on medieval England have little doubt that the distribution of population was closely related to that of taxed wealth.[87] It seems a reasonable assumption that plague in Scotland in 1349–50 and 1361–2 was a major factor in the reduced assessments of 1366. It may of course be legitimately pointed out that the largest falls in the 1366 assessments took place in the west and north, where one might imagine the incidence of plague to have been less severe. However, replacement tenants and workers were perhaps also scarce in these areas, while we know in any case that the highland landlords were reluctant to accept any assessment at all in 1366, but were more co-operative for Robert II in 1373.[88]

Thus if it is true that the low *Valor* of 1366 chiefly represents fewer people being taxed rather than a fall in living standards, it seems possible that conditions in the third quarter of the fourteenth century, at least for those who survived the plague, were very good. This was the golden age of the English labourer, and it is difficult to escape the conclusion that in Scotland too, for the mass of working people, the arithmetic of prices and wages worked out less harshly in 1360 than in 1260.

In some respects, therefore, it has been argued that for many of its people, Scotland after the plague and while at peace with England has a better claim to be a golden age than it does under Alexander III. Similarly, although space does not permit a thorough review of the age of David I, it is clear that much thirteenth-century growth was built on foundations laid down by him. Moreover, the economic achievements of Alexander's reign are common to the whole century and not restricted to the third quarter. Having laid aside the golden spectacles, however, one may be left in a more objective position to single out the areas of greatest achievement in the thirteenth century. It was indeed a period of prolonged relative peace which fostered a growing population who brought more land than ever before into cultivation. It was a period of great trading prosperity, founded chiefly on wool, which stimulated and sustained the development of town life, drew Scotland into the mainstream of European trade and won for Scotland a bigger share of growing European silver supplies. This growing money supply, though partly off-set by rising prices, stimulated economic life; without the silver boom, economic prospects for what has been called above the sub-historical proletariat would have been much more limited. And it is because of this monetary boom, and as a reminder that in some respects Alexander's reign was good but less than golden, that it is appropriate to speak of a Silver Age of Alexander III.

NOTES

1. *ER*, i, p. xlvii.
2. Nicolson, *Scotland*, 177. The comparison should not be pushed too far without an attempt to allow for legitimate royal expenditure at sheriff and bailie level.

3. The low taxation of the 13th. century in Scotland can perhaps best be seen as one of the benefits of prolonged peace. There was, however, some early taxation, particularly during the less settled reign of William the Lion, who received aids in 1189 and 1211 (*ER*, i, p. xc), and it may be that some taxation took place which has left no clear record. In the late thirteenth century assessments were levied as contributions to the crusades.

4. A. W. K. Stevenson, *Trade Between Scotland and the Low Countries in the Late Middle Ages* (unpublished PhD thesis, University of Aberdeen, 1982; henceforth Stevenson, *Trade*), 152, estimates the custom at 7% of the basic price from the producer, and only 3% or 4% of the final sale price in Flanders. Dr Stevenson's work has been a starting point for many of the questions raised in this essay, though he would not always agree with its conclusions.

5. *ER*, ii, p. xlii, n. 4.

6. The scale of activity of these Berwick men may be guessed at from the surviving snippets of information. See, for example, the lawsuit of Marjory Moigne, widow of William Goldsmith, and Master Roger Bartholomew. Here we read of debts of £180 and 200 marks, and of personal cash holdings of £60, and cash payments of 80 marks. (Stevenson, *Documents*, under 1292). For a fuller assessment of merchant business see J. Donnelly, 'Thomas of Coldingham, Merchant and Burgess of Berwick upon Tweed (died 1316)', *SHR*, lix (1980), 105–25, though by then Berwick was in English hands.

7. James Campbell, 'England, Scotland and the Hundred Years War in the Fourteenth Century' (henceforth Campbell, 'England, Scotland') in *Europe in the Late Middle Ages*, edd. J. R. Hale, J. R. L. Highfield & B. Smalley (London, 1965), 184–216, at 204.

8. Stevenson, *Trade*, 7, 10, 273–4; Nicholson, *Scotland*, 16.

9. Duncan, *Kingdom*, 484–5.

10. This paragraph is based chiefly on *Excavations in the Medieval Burgh of Aberdeen 1973–81*, ed. J. C. Murray (Society of Antiquaries of Scotland, Monograph Series no. 2, 1982; henceforth Murray, *Excavations*), 122–6, and the pottery from Kelso Abbey discussed by George Haggarty in Christopher J. Tabraham, 'Excavations at Kelso Abbey', *PSAS*, cxiv (1984), 365–404, at 396–7.

11. It seems possible that the Scottish domestic weaving trade may have been similar to the local pottery industry, aiming at the lower end of the market. I am grateful to Dr A. Grant for calling the weavers to my attention. The ability of Scottish wool growers to increase the provision of wool for export rapidly at short notice argues that at other times when foreign demand was not so strong a portion of the clip was regularly taken up by Scots weavers. These views on the nature of Scottish weaving and pottery are endorsed and substantiated by Elizabeth Ewan, *The Burgesses of Fourteenth-Century Scotland: A Social History* (unpublished PhD thesis, University of Edinburgh, 1984), which confirms the notion of an active domestic trade. Similarly Dr Ewan, in common with Dr E. Torrie (especially for Dunfermline) and Dr M. Lynch ('Whatever Happened to the Medieval

Burgh?', *Scottish Economic and Social History*, iv (1984), 5–20, at 12–13), does not accept the notion of a body of depressed craftsmen distinct from a more buoyant merchant community.

12. Wendy B. Stevenson, 'The Monastic Presence in the Scottish Burghs in the Twelfth and Thirteenth Centuries', *SHR*, lx (1981), 97–118.
13. *Excavations in the Medieval Burgh of Perth, 1979–81*, ed. Philip Holdsworth (Society of Antiquaries of Scotland, Monograph Series no. 5, 1988).
14. *Aberdeen Burgh Recs.*, 11.
15. The evidence is insufficient for accurate comparison of specific tenements.
16. The burgages were not measured, although the vacant lots were. One *vacua placea* in Fishergate, however, which contained an acre and a half, used to be a burgage. For this Berwick survey see Stevenson, *Documents*, no. ccccxviii.
17. Cellars and solars are recorded on vacant lots, but in the centre or on the corner of the plot, not on the frontage.
18. For England see R. H. Hilton, *The English Peasantry in the Later Middle Ages* (Oxford, 1975), especially 'The Small Town as a Part of Peasant Society', 76–94. For Scotland, *Aberdeen Burgh Recs.*, p. xliii.
19. J. Scott, *History of Berwick-upon-Tweed* (London, 1888; henceforth Scott, *Berwick*), 434–5.
20. Was Perth a crowded exception because of its town walls? Duncan, *Kingdom*, 474 suggests the walls may date from the mid-13th. century.
21. J. Schofield, 'Excavations South of Edinburgh High Street, 1973–4', *PSAS*, cvii (1975–6), 155–241, at 170–80, reports on a stone house with timber frame, garderobe, and tiled floor. The tiles may be of early 15th.-century date. Tiles were apparently imported from the Netherlands as ballast (ibid., 213).
22. Lisbeth M. Thoms, 'Trial Excavation at St Ann's Lane, Perth', *PSAS*, cxii (1982), 437–56, at 457. The bone report is by Hodgson and Jones.
23. Grant, *Independence*, 79, 82, notes how livestock became cheaper relative to grain after the plague.
24. Duncan, *Kingdom*, 354. This Coldingham oven was valued at 3s. per annum. For the Aberdeen ovens see *Aberdeen Burgh Recs.*, 14, and Murray, *Excavations*, 53, 81. Murray notes that all the burgesses had the right to a bread oven. The Perth oven is reported in Linda Blanchard, 'Kirk Close — A Backland Excavation', in *Town Houses and Structures in Medieval Scotland — A Seminar*, edd. Anne Turner Simpson and Sylvia Stevenson (Scottish Burgh Survey, 1980), 32–8, at 37. For the oven at Skipness, see *ER*, i, 56.
25. For Aberdeen and Perth see the sources cited in n. 24. For Berwick see J. R. Hunter, 'Medieval Berwick-upon-Tweed' (henceforth Hunter, 'Medieval Berwick'), *Archaeologia Aeliana* (series 5), x (1982), 67–124, at 78. I am grateful to W. Windram for information about the recently excavated corn drying kiln in Roxburgh Street, Kelso.
26. Duncan, *Kingdom*, 323.

27. *Historical Atlas.*
28. G. W. S. Barrow, 'The Sources for the History of the Highlands in the Middle Ages', in *The Middle Ages in the Highlands*, ed. Loraine Maclean (Inverness Field Club, 1981), 11–22, at 11–12.
29. *SHS Misc.*, ii, 25.
30. Simpson, *Quincy*, 81.
31. See above, pp. 124–5.
32. Robert Newton, *The Northumbrian Landscape* (London, 1972), 89–90.
33. M. L. Parry, 'Secular Climatic Change and Marginal Agriculture', *Transactions of the Institute of British Geographers*, lxiv (1975), 1–13, at 5–11.
34. For Wark (or Werk) see *ER*, i, pp. xlvi, 23; Palgrave, *Docs. Hist. Scot.*, i, pp. vii, 3–14; Stevenson, *Documents*, 1–3, 36–39, 59–61, 122–3, 192–8; *CDS*, ii, no. 53.
35. Duncan, *Kingdom*, 366.
36. R. A. Dodgshon, 'Medieval Settlement and Colonisation' (henceforth Dodgshon, 'Medieval Settlement') in *The Making of the Scottish Countryside*, edd. M. L. Parry and T. R. Slater (London, 1980), 45–68, at 48, cites legislation of Alexander II in 1214 compelling bondmen and landowners to cultivate land (*APS* i, 397).
37. Duncan, *Kingdom*, 367.
38. M. L. Parry, n. 33 above, and *Climatic Change, Agriculture and Settlement* (Folkestone, 1978). Stevenson, *Trade*, 22–23, summarised Parry's work carefully, but his comments on the relative performance of wheat, barley and oat prices are flawed by his failure to distinguish between prices for oats and oatmeal. Climatologists seem pretty unanimous about the deterioration from c. 1300. See also H. H. Lamb, *Climate: Present, Past and Future* (London, 1977), and E. le Roy Ladurie, *Times of Feast, Times of Famine: A History of Climate Since the Year 1000* (in translation, London, 1971).
39. Dodgshon, 'Medieval Settlement', 48, cites complaints from the year 1209 of livestock ousting arable (*APS*, i, 397, 382), rather than of a shortage of livestock.
40. E. Miller, 'Farming in Northern England During the Twelfth and Thirteenth Centuries', *Northern History*, xi (1976 for 1975), 1–17, especially 11–12.
41. Stevenson, *Documents*, 32–35.
42. Grant, *Independence*, 62; Stevenson, *Trade*, 18–19. This is actually a 14th-century figure.
43. Duncan, *Kingdom*, 339–48 on limited labour services, 425 on the trend towards farming. As already noted the demesnes at Wark and Grendon were at farm, and the 'Ministers' Accounts of Norhamshire and Islandshire, 1261–2' (R. B. Pugh, *Northern History*, xi (1976 for 1975), 17–26) show demesnes at farm there. The Norham demesne had been totally at farm in 1183: *The Victoria History of the County of Durham*, i (London, 1905), Bolden Book, 259–342, at 332. On manure, see Alexander Fenton, 'Early Manuring Techniques', in *Farming Practice in British Prehistory*, ed.

Roger Mercer (Edinburgh, 1981), 210–17. Fertilising options were a good deal more varied than is sometimes assumed, and need to be seen in the whole context of field, hearth and byre.

44. Duncan, *Kingdom*, 346.
45. Rising prices and the attempt to profit by them may perhaps be inferred from the fact that Kelso thought it worthwhile to enshrine in the rental of c. 1300 their right to buy beer from the brewers of Holden at a fixed price of 1d for a gallon and a half (*Kelso Liber*, 462). It is suggested below that Scotland had much in common with 13th-century English monetary and price history.
46. For the fortunes of the nobility, see Duncan, *Kingdom*, 426–7 and 438–43. For Quincy wealth see Simpson, *Quincy*, 78–81. Simpson also notes especially the wealth of Alexander the Steward and John Balliol (father of King John), at 214–16.
47. Stevenson, *Trade*, 245 and n. 2, 264–5.
48. Tout, in his introduction to *Register of John de Halton, Bishop of Carlisle*, edd. W. N. Thompson and T. F. Tout (Canterbury and York Society, 1913), p. xv.
49. Stevenson, *Trade*, 18–19.
50. Grant, *Independence*, 72–73.
51. See n. 48.
52. A revised and greatly expanded edition of the *Historical Atlas* is due for publication in 1990.
53. Nicholson, *Scotland*, 175.
54. Tout, op. cit., p. xii suggests 1256. Stevenson, *Trade*, 256 (n. 46), dates the old extent before 1267 and perhaps as early as 1201.
55. Ranald Nicholson, 'Scottish Monetary Problems in the Fourteenth and Fifteenth Centuries' (henceforth Nicholson, 'Monetary Problems'), in *Coinage in Medieval Scotland 1100–1600*, ed. D. M. Metcalf (British Archaeological Reports, vl; Oxford, 1977; henceforth Metcalf, *Coinage*), 103–14, at 104.
56. Grant, *Independence*, 61, quotes Froissart's memorable comment on the sack of Lothian in 1385; 'the people of the country made light of it, saying that with six or eight stakes they could soon have new houses'.
57. N. J. Mayhew, 'The Aberdeen Upperkirkgate Hoard of 1886', *British Numismatic Journal* (henceforth *BNJ*), vl (1975), 33–50, at 36.
58. The Scottish Wars of Independence left behind an extraordinary number of coin hoards, and hardly a year goes by without new finds being added to that number. This hoarding of capital which might otherwise have been available for production, investment or expenditure is a vivid illustration of war's damaging effect on business confidence.
59. Stevenson, *Trade*, 165–73; Campbell, 'England, Scotland', 212 (for the 1380s), citing *CPR, 1381–5*, 83–84.
60. *ER*, i, p. lxxxiii notes the assignment of the Berwick customs in 1286 to a Gascon wine merchant for a debt of £2197. The original source (*Foedera*, i, 787) makes it clear that the assignment was not for a single year, but until the debt was settled. *Pro quibus ipsi Johanni custumam suam de*

Berewyk specialites obligavit, quousque esset sibi de dicta pecunia seu debito satisfactum. George Burnett's footnote in *ER*, however, warning that we cannot assume from this that the Berwick customs amounted to so much has been ignored by many. Scott, *Berwick*, 14 in particular may have been responsible for misleading Margaret Ellison, 'An Archaeological Survey of Berwick-upon-Tweed' in *Archaeology in the North*, edd. P. A. G. Clack and P. F. Gosling (Durham, 1976), 150 and Hunter, 'Medieval Berwick', 82.

61. It may be noted that after the first bout of the wars, at least, burgh rentals in the 1320s and 1330s were rising. *ER*, i, p. lxxxviii.
62. Nicholson, *Scotland*, 175, and also Nicholson, 'Monetary Problems', 104. This is the line followed by Stevenson, *Trade*, 9–10, 256.
63. These comments are based on an analysis of prices taken from *ER*, i and ii.
64. English prices of course were buoyant for a quarter of a century after the Black Death.
65. N. J. Mayhew, 'Money in Scotland in the Thirteenth Century', (henceforth Mayhew, 'Money') in Metcalf, *Coinage*, 85–102. The money supply estimates were based chiefly on the work of Dr I. Stewart, 'The Volume of Early Scottish Coinage', ibid., 65–72. Recent work on the contemporary Irish mint output suggests that estimates of the size of Alexander III's 1280 coinage may even have erred slightly on the low side. See N. J. Mayhew, 'Irregularities in the Irish Mint Accounts 1279–1284' in *Later Medieval Mints: Organization, Administration and Techniques*, edd. N. J. Mayhew and Peter Spufford (British Archaeological Reports, International Series, 389; Oxford, 1988), especially n. 36.
66. Scotland may, however, have benefited from the Anglo-Flemish embargo of the 1270s.
67. T. H. Lloyd, *The English Wool Trade in the Middle Ages* (Cambridge, 1977), 6; P. D. A. Harvey, 'The English Trade in Wool and Cloth, 1150–1250: Some Problems and Suggestions', in *Produzione, Commercio e Consumo dei Panni di Lana* (Florence, 1976), 369–75, at 372. For Scotland particularly, see Stevenson, *Trade*, 2–3.
68. W. W. Scott, 'The Use of Money in Scotland 1124–1230', *SHR*, lviii (1979), 105–31, at 106.
69. Mayhew, 'Money', 101–2.
70. N. J. Mayhew, 'Numismatic Evidence and Falling Prices in the Fourteenth Century', *Economic History Review*, (2nd series), xxvii (1974), 1–5.
71. Grant, *Independence*, 77; *ER*, i, p. cxxxvi, for the 1331 customs duty of 12d in the pound on hard cash (*sicca pecunia*) exported.
72. R. W. Cochran-Patrick, *The Records of the Coinage of Scotland*, i (Edinburgh, 1870, henceforth Cochran-Patrick, *Coinage*), 3–5.
73. The Scots figures included a partial recoinage, which the London figures for 1357–64 do not. However, as noted above, the occurrence of a major recoinage in England some years before a similar event in Scotland may have resulted in some of the coin in Scotland being drawn south for recoinage.
74. Cochran-Patrick, *Coinage*, 1–2.

75. Ibid., 5. The 8d rate was in force for only the last month of Tor's account ending December 1364. Presumably the new 8d rate continued until the 1367 weight reduction, but this is not certain.
76. Ibid., 1–2. The English figures in force since 1361 were: Seignorage 3d, Mintage 7d, Merchant received 24s 2d. Total number of pennies to the pound 300. (See N. J. Mayhew's chapter in *The History of the Mint*, ed. C. E. Challis (forthcoming).) The Scottish figures after 1367 were: Seignorage 7d, Warden 1d, Mintage 11d, Merchant 27s 9d. Total number of pennies to the pound 352.
77. This is very much a rule of thumb calculation. It involves regarding all the Robert II head coins of David II as post-1367 (which was not the case), and then comparing the numbers of David II coins pre- and post-1367 in the finds. Unfortunately the finds do not all tell the same story, and few hoards are amenable to such an approach, but for what it is worth the rough figures are:

Hoard	1357–67	Robert II head struck by David II, c. 1367–71
Balleny (groats)	5	14
Tranent (all denominations)	31	16
Knockagh (groats and half-groats)	3	2
Craigie (groats and half-groats)	4	21
Aberdour (all denominations)	33	8
	76	61

In fact there are some grounds for excluding Aberdour, which would suggest that later David II coins may have outnumbered earlier ones. Dr Stewart's die studies would support such a possibility. See n. 79 below.
78. The best single summary of the available hoard evidence is provided by the invaluable appendix to W. A. Seaby and B. H. I. H. Stewart, 'A Fourteenth-Century Hoard of Scottish Groats from Balleny Townland, Co. Down' (henceforth Seaby & Stewart, 'Scottish Groats'), *BNJ*, xxxiii (1964), 94–106.
79. Dr Stewart has identified 64 David II Edinburgh groat dies pre-1367 and 83 post-. Moreover, statistical analysis suggests that the pre-1367 figure is much nearer the total number of dies originally used than the post-1367 figure when many more new dies probably remain to be discovered. Mrs Murray has recorded 78 groat dies for Robert II and estimates that they will have struck about 89% of the total groat output. I am most grateful to them both for this information so generously shared. The figures suggest that the impressive Edinburgh mint performance of 1358–64, for which we have documentary evidence, was sustained and even surpassed later in the reigns of David II and Robert II.
80. T. H. Lloyd, 'Overseas Trade and the English Money Supply in the Fourteenth Century', in *Edwardian Monetary Affairs 1279–1344*, ed. N. J. Mayhew, (British Archaeological Reports, xxxvi; Oxford, 1977), 96–124.
81. Seaby and Stewart, 'Scottish Groats', 96.
82. Cochran-Patrick, *Coinage*, 2–3, 8.

83. J. Day, 'The Great Bullion Famine of the Fifteenth Century', *Past and Present*, lxxix (1978), 3–54.
84. *Chron. Bower*, ii, 347; Nicholson, *Scotland*, 149.
85. A. Hamilton Thompson, 'The Pestilences of the Fourteenth Century in the Diocese of York', *Archaeological Journal*, vii (1914), 97–154.
86. Percentage death rates for the whole of the archdeaconry of Cleveland (of which the deanery of Cleveland was but a part) were as follows:

1347–9	*1349–50*	*1350*	*1361–2*	*1369*
1.19	33.74	0.00	12.37	11.61

Ibid., 130, 133.
87. R. E. Glasscock in *A New Historical Geography of England before 1600*, ed. M. C. Darby (Cambridge, 1976), 144; also R. A. Donkin, ibid., 81.
88. Nicholson, *Scotland*, 178, 188.

4

SCOTS LAW UNDER ALEXANDER III

Hector L. MacQueen[1]

Later medieval writers on Scottish history sing the praises of Alexander III as a just king and lawmaker. Andrew Wyntoun says that

> Be justys he gave and eqwte
> Till ilke man, that his suld be.
> . . .
> He gert chasty mysdoarys,
> As lauch wald be thare manerys.
> The lawch he gert be kepyd welle
> In all his kynryk ilka delle.[2]

'In his days', comments Walter Bower, 'justice flourished everywhere in the realm'; elsewhere he narrates how every year the king would tour through his kingdom, accompanied by his justiciar to administer justice to all.[3] Both writers give instances of the king's judgements in individual cases: the dissension in 1269 between the earl of Atholl and John Comyn over the latter's erection of a castle at Blair which the king settled with his council is mentioned by Bower, while Wyntoun gives an account of the plea between William Comyn and Walter Stewart over the earldom of Menteith in 1285 where the king gave his 'delyverans fynale' with the aid of his council at Scone.[4] They also record the king's legislative activities. Wyntoun tells how the king caused all men who had oxen to set them to ploughing:

> Swa wes corne in [his] land enwche;
> Swa then begowth and efftyr lang
> Off land wes mesure, ane oxgang.
> . . .
> A pluch off land efftyr that
> To nowmyr off oxyn mesuryd gat.[5]

Bower, here adding to Fordun, mentions three enactments of Alexander III: the first a solution to the problem of unemployment (all those

74

without possessions or a trade must each day dig a piece of ground seven feet square); the second a provision that in the train of every prelate and magnate there should only be a certain small number of horses because a multitude of unnecessary horses destroyed the sustenance of the poor; and the third a measure to stop exports, necessary, we are told, to ensure that they were not lost at sea. This measure compelled foreign merchants to come to Scotland if they wished Scottish goods and thus placed upon them the risk of the hazards of the sea. It was apparently a law difficult to enforce but nonetheless, according to Bower, very successful; it gave the king and his kingdom such a reputation abroad that some Lombards offered to build a city at Queensferry or on Cramond Island in order to exploit its wealth.[6]

It is difficult to accept at least some of these supposed enactments as being derived from anything other than the fertile imaginations of Wyntoun and Bower. This scepticism is reinforced by their complete absence from the manuscripts of the laws and statutes of Scotland which were being compiled at the same time as the works of the historians. It is a striking fact that the reign of Alexander III was apparently not one hallowed by the legal as distinct from the historical tradition of the later middle ages. When Scottish lawyers of the period gathered together those parts of their law which had been reduced to writing and ascribed them to the legislative activities of earlier kings, they did not, so far as we can tell, find anything which they could attribute to Alexander III. Much of their material was thought to belong to a remoter past: it had been promulgated, or so the lawyers said, by kings like Malcolm Mackenneth, David I, William I or Alexander II, the father and immediate predecessor of Alexander III. In none of the surviving lawyers' collections, even those later ones which attribute legislation to kings of the fourteenth century, is there any reference to laws given by Alexander III.[7] When in the last quarter of the sixteenth century Sir James Balfour of Pittendreich and Sir John Skene of Curriehill began to collect and, in Skene's case, to publish the old Scottish laws, they could find nothing described as legislation of Alexander III in their sources. So in Skene's *Regiam Majestatem*, published in 1609, the Statutes of Alexander II are followed by those of Robert I.[8] Similarly in the nineteenth century, when the next great attempt to arrange and publish the 'auld lawes' was made by Thomas Thomson and Cosmo Innes in the first volume of the *Acts of the Parliaments of Scotland*, no legislative acts of Alexander III could be found and the editors had to content themselves for his reign with treaties agreed to by the king and his council together with a few bits and pieces culled from cartularies and other sources showing the king settling disputes *in colloquio* or in the *curia regis*.[9]

It has been only in the twentieth century that the years between 1249 and 1286 have come to be seen as of real significance in the legal history of Scotland. This was largely the result of the work of one man, the late Lord Cooper of Culross. Despite holding high political and judicial offices throughout what was also his most productive period as a legal historian (he was successively Lord Advocate, Lord Justice Clerk and Lord President of the Court of Session between 1935 and 1955, during which time he published all his significant work), he was able to develop a particular view of the character of the law of thirteenth-century Scotland which remained standard for many years.[10] As finally presented in the Stair Society's *Introduction to Scottish Legal History,*[11] Cooper's thesis was that in the course of the century the law of Scotland developed under three main influences: the common law of England, the canon law and the feudal law. By the reign of Alexander III there had emerged a system which Cooper called the Scoto-Norman law and which was a distinctive blend of these three influences. Its starting point had been in borrowing from the law of twelfth-century England; but in the thirteenth century English law became increasingly complex and Scots lawyers began to turn elsewhere for a model for the development of their law. The relative weakness of the secular judicial machine meant that already much business which would have been conducted in the royal courts in England was dealt with in Scotland by the ecclesiastical courts. Hence, in Cooper's words:

By the middle of the thirteenth century Scottish lawyers were already deeply imbued with the methods of the *Curia Romana* and the Romano-Canonical procedure and had thereby become habituated to the civilian idiom of legal thinking and to a habit of mind which led to reasoning from principles to instances, to reliance upon syllogisms rather than precedents, and to concentration not upon remedies but on rights and duties. Such characteristics have been typical of Scots law throughout its later history and persist strongly to this day. Under such influences it would only be natural that from the time of Alexander III onwards the Scottish lawyers, nearly all of whom were then ecclesiastics, would view with instinctive distaste the later trend of English developments and particularly the empirical effort to contrive a new tool for every job, to use that tool only for that job, and to circumvent occasional obstacles by legal fictions. The Scottish aim would rather be to use the smallest number of tools for the largest number of jobs, to abstract the general from the particular, and to avoid excessive technicality and needless elaboration.[12]

This picture of thirteenth-century legal development, which in some elements derived more from what Cooper thought was the essential character of modern Scots law than from detailed analysis of the historical evidence,[13] has been vitally, perhaps fatally, affected in two respects by the work of Professor Duncan and Professor Barrow. Professor Duncan's attack concerned the date of *Regiam Majestatem*.[14] Lord Cooper had produced an edition of this central text of medieval Scots law and put its composition at c. 1230. It was based on the late twelfth-century English text known as *Glanvill* with additions drawn from Romano-Canonical sources and some native material which was attributed elsewhere to the legislative activities of the Scottish kings of the twelfth and early thirteenth centuries. None of this legislation was later in date than 1230 and so, in Cooper's view, *Regiam* was

> compiled by an unknown ecclesiastic about the time of Alexander II, depicting more or less accurately the phase of development which had been reached about 1230, that is, before Scoto-Norman Law had begun to diverge notably from Anglo-Norman Law.[15]

But, as Professor Duncan pointed out, the description of this native material as legislation of any king before 1300 cannot be taken at face value. It comes from the lawyers' collections already mentioned, the earliest of which, the Berne MS, can be dated c. 1270 and the remainder of which are of fourteenth-century or later date. When we find that Berne and the next earliest manuscript, the Ayr MS, contain this native material but do not assign it to any specific period or king, then it is apparent that many of the attributions can only have been made round about the beginning of the fourteenth century or later. There is no mechanism for dating this material, therefore, other than internal evidence; given this, its appearance in *Regiam* tells us nothing about the date of the work's composition and in particular Lord Cooper's conclusions could be seen to be without any foundation. Professor Duncan went on to argue that *Regiam* must have been put together after 1318 and before 1400 because it does contain undoubted legislative material of the earlier date and the earliest manuscript version is of the fourteenth century.[16]

Professor Barrow's article on the Scottish justiciar tackled the question of the weakness of the secular judicial structure and concluded that at any rate the justiciary was 'a principal institution within the framework of Scottish royal government' in the twelfth and thirteenth centuries, responsible *inter alia* for a wide range of judicial functions, both civil and criminal.[17] For the purpose of the justiciarship the country was divided into regions bearing some relation to the older kingdoms which now made up the realm of Scotland. The basic division was between the regions of Lothian (roughly, Scotland south of Forth) and Scotia (Scotland north of Forth) but there was also a justiciar of Galloway from time to time. Probably twice in the year, in the spring and early autumn, the justiciars went on circuit, or on ayre, one to each region, and held courts at the *caput* of each of the sheriffdoms within their jurisdiction. (Incidentally this in part verifies what is said about justiciars by Bower.) They were not 'professional' full-time judges comparable in any way with the English justices but were 'without legal training, laymen rather than clergy, noblemen rather than of middle rank, and enjoying office by something akin to hereditary succession'.[18] Nevertheless, as Professor Barrow is able to show:

> A study of the office as it was actually exercised in a period so formative for the historical Scottish kingdom ought at least to put us on our guard against hasty condemnations of the native secular legal machinery. It is not self-evident that the institutions at the disposal of the Scottish state for administering justice during the period from David I to John Balliol were inadequate for the purposes for which they were designed.[19]

There has been no comparable study of other secular courts in the period before 1300, although Haddington's transcripts of the sheriffs' accounts for the 1260s certainly show that the sheriff courts, like those of the justiciars, were a steady source of income for the king, presumably implying regular judicial activity there too.[20] Other sources enable us to catch glimpses of these and the baronial and burghal courts at work,[21] while they also show the king's council, sometimes said to be meeting as a *colloquium*, exercising judicial functions.[22] There are hints, particularly in the treatise produced perhaps for John Balliol and known as 'The Scottish King's Household', that a formal hierarchy of courts existed, ranging upwards from the local courts through those of the justiciars to the king himself.[23] Although trial by combat and compurgation were still known and in use,[24] most cases in these courts were determined either by their suitors as a body under the presidency of the judge or, more often, by an assize, a smaller group made up of those good and faithful elder men who best knew the verity of the matter under dispute.[25]

Given all this, it may reasonably be asked what becomes of the Scoto-Norman legal system described by Lord Cooper. In particular, if the manual of Scoto-Norman law before it had diverged from Anglo-Norman law was written as an account of contemporary law in the fourteenth century, then it would seem probable that the divergence from English models, if any there was, did not take place in the second half of the thirteenth century. Further, if there were active secular judges operating under royal authority, was it necessarily the case that late thirteenth-century litigants preferred to take their business before the ecclesiastical courts, or that their lawyers thought in the terms suggested by Lord Cooper, of right rather than of remedy? The present trend amongst historians aware of the flaws in Cooper's thesis seems to be to go back to a dictum of the great English legal historian, F. W. Maitland, who remarked that although English law 'had no power north of the Tweed . . . we may doubt whether a man who crossed the river felt that he had passed from the land of one law to the land of another' and continued 'It seems clear enough from abundant evidence that, at the outbreak of the war of independence, the law of Scotland . . . was closely akin to English law'.[26]

In some important respects — for example, the itinerant justiciars, the use of the jury in the presentment of criminals and to decide disputes, the basic principles of landownership and much of the written burgh law — there can be no doubt that Maitland's English observer would almost certainly have recognised a good deal of Scots law as a version of the law and practice in his own country. Most of all, perhaps, he would have been struck by the way that in Scotland as in England it was possible to raise an action by going to the king's chancery and buying a writ or brieve which commanded that a dispute be tried by a particular officer. Typically the procedure following upon the use of a brieve involved the officer putting the issue it contained to a jury. Many of these brieves were available *de cursu*, that is, in stereotyped forms, with names for each, and for a small fee.[27] Form and name were often demonstrably drawn from English models, especially with regard to the brieves by which dispossessed persons might recover their lands, the brieves of right, mortancestor and novel dissasine.[28] In this area too there was a rule that one in possession of land could only be removed by action begun by brieve.[29] As Alexander Macdonald of Islay informed Edward I (of all people) in 1296, on this point the laws of Scotland and of England were the same.[30]

On the other hand it is clear that the borrowing from England had been neither slavish nor complete and that even in fields where it had taken place the institution or rule might proceed on a path of development quite distinct from its English source.[31] So for example there were no Scottish equivalents to the writs of entry, probably because the complex jurisdictional and other factors which led to their emergence in England did not apply in Scotland; instead the brieve of right was modified in form and covered a wider range of situations than its English equivalent.[32] Further, our notional observer would surely have agreed with Cooper that changes in English law and its administration during the period of Alexander III's reign had created some other significant differences between the two systems. The ever-increasing amount of litigation in the English royal courts had led to the emergence of three centralised courts — the Exchequer, the Common Bench and the King's Bench — and of a laicised legal profession practising before them. *Magna Carta* and legislation — the Provisions of Merton (1236) and of Marlborough (1267) and the great body of Edwardian legislation from the first Statute of Westminster in 1275 to *Quia Emptores* in 1290 — had helped to transform the substance of the law, while it had also been given an articulated form in texts such as *Bracton, Britton,* and *Fleta.*[33] Nothing that happened in Scotland during the reign of Alexander III could parallel these changes in the administrative structure and content of English law.

Some of the other points made by Cooper still seem valid, especially the extent to which the church courts in fact exercised jurisdiction in Scotland and the impact which this had on the secular law. Thanks to the researches of Professor Donaldson and Dr Ollivant in particular, we now know a good deal more about the exercise by the church of its jurisdiction in medieval Scotland. As was the case all over western Europe, the church successfully claimed an exclusive jurisdiction over matters pertaining to the sacraments, such as marriage and its concomitants, legitimacy and divorce.[34] But it is far from clear that its courts enjoyed a practical monopoly over all forms of civil legal business. There is some evidence for a conflict between ecclesiastical and secular authorities over jurisdiction, especially with regard to questions about land.[35] On that particular point more often than not the king's courts won out and the fourteenth-century registers contain a form for a brieve of prohibition forbidding the hearing of cases concerning lay tenements in the courts Christian, suggesting that this was an area where conflict often arose.[36] Nevertheless, there were still cases about the ownership of lands before church courts in the reign of Alexander III where, even though laymen were involved, no-one seems to have argued that the tribunal was inappropriate.[37] This does not mean that the secular rules were ineffective or unused, only that for one reason or another the parties to these particular cases had chosen not to invoke them. In general this rather *laissez faire* approach of letting the parties decide which forum to use, subject to a few basic rules if they could not agree, seems characteristic of the period in Scotland. Thus in questions of contract and defamation, for example, there appears to have been a free choice, with the decision perhaps depending on what precisely the individual raising the action wanted to achieve through it. It is important to recognise that his choice does not seem to have fallen invariably upon the ecclesiastical alternative.[38]

Another critical point to note is the way in which the canon law provided an essential prop to the secular law of landownership through its definitions of marriage and legitimacy, both questions central to the descent of lands. As David Sellar has shown, the canonical norms were at variance with the customary practices in much of Scotland;[39] but the king's courts gave effect to the former rather than the latter so that the canonical norms were woven into the fabric of the secular law. Of course this was not only true of Scotland, but the impact of canon law on secular law was not everywhere the same. For example, the canonical rule of legitimation by subsequent marriage seems to have been accepted in relation to the inheritance of lands in Scotland, whereas in England it prompted a famously negative baronial response and the rule formed no part of medieval English land law.[40] The impact of the church's lawyers on practice in the secular courts should not be underestimated either; although, so far as is known, no churchman acted as a justiciar or a sheriff during the thirteenth century, such men were often amongst those present in court as suitors, while others were probably also there as advocates for the parties and perhaps even as assessors who as *jurisperiti* would assist the court in its deliberations.[41] Much work remains to be done on the precise effects upon secular law of the operations within it of the canon lawyers, but we need have no doubt that in many and various ways it was of very great significance.

One further factor which Cooper certainly ignored was the Celtic element in Scots law. Yet it was still clearly of significance in the thirteenth and later centuries, as David Sellar has argued in his recent O'Donnell lecture.[42] Alexander III was himself the descendant of a Celtic royal house; at his inauguration in 1249 he had listened to a recitation of his genealogy by a sennachie, while seven women would dance and sing before him when he progressed through Strathearn, this latter being a custom which, as Professor Barrow remarks, was 'an entertainment . . . quite in keeping with the progress of a Celtic chief'.[43] All over the country there were officers connected with the administration of justice, like the *judices* and the mairs, whose institutional origins were clearly Celtic and ancient.[44] Their system was being gradually overlaid by the sheriffdoms which were the product of the Anglo-Norman intrusion of the twelfth and early thirteenth century, but even in 1286 the process was far from complete.[45] But again the evidence does not suggest that the old native system was being destroyed or displaced as a matter of deliberate policy; rather it was being assimilated, so that the *judex* became the dempster of the new courts and the mairs their executive officers to make arrests, serve summonses and carry out judgements. These were not new functions for these men; rather old functions were made to serve in new surroundings.

As Professor Barrow has shown, thirteenth-century contemporaries certainly regarded Scotland as having its own laws and customs, distinct from those of England.[46] To the evidence which he cites we may add the 1277 plea of Llywelwyn ap Gruffydd, prince of Wales, to the effect that every province under the dominion of the English crown — England, Gascony, Ireland and Scotland — had its own laws and customs, a fact enlarging rather than diminishing the authority of the English king.[47] There are also some references to the 'common law' of the kingdom, in particular one in a royal administrative brieve of 1264 which speaks of 'the usage throughout our kingdom of Scotland according to ancient approved custom and by the common law'.[48] The recently published records of the 'Great Cause' also frequently mention the laws and customs of Scotland, sometimes distinguishing them from the law of England. Thus John Balliol asked that the cause be determined 'according to the Scots law and customs',[49] while Robert Bruce, who, to begin with, based his claim upon 'the natural law by which kings reign', argued that succession to the Scottish throne should not be settled by any custom used between subjects or tenants of the Scots realm, and that in any case there was no usage in the Scots realm regarding this matter.[50] Balliol replied that the matter should not be settled by 'imperial laws', since Scotland was held of the English crown and of no empire. To decide by the imperial laws in the English king's court would be in prejudice of his crown.[51] Balliol later affirmed that his claim should be dealt with 'according to the laws and usages of the realms of Scotland and England', so that he appears to have taken the line that the two were identical, perhaps covering Bruce's argument that there was no specifically Scottish custom governing the issue.[52]

It is the response to these arguments of the president of the court deciding the Great Cause, King Edward I of England, that is particularly interesting here, for he clearly recognised that Scots and English law might be different. First he asked the court by which laws and customs he should judge, and, if there were no laws to be found, or if the laws were different in England and Scotland, how he should proceed. The court replied that he should judge by the laws of his kingdom and that, if there were none, he could make a new law.[53] Later Edward again asked whether he ought to proceed by the imperial laws, by the laws and customs of the English realm, or by those of the Scottish realm, and he was told that he should apply the laws of England.[54] Edward then asked the Scottish members of the court what law to apply, emphasising his position as feudal superior and stating that he should give judgement 'according to the laws of the Scots and English realms where they both agree'. What was the position if 'the laws of England and Scotland in this case are different and opposite'? The Scottish auditors replied that if 'in the Scots realm . . . an express law may be had the same law suffices and ought to suffice'.[55]

This is not the place for a detailed analysis of the jurisdictional twists of the Great Cause or of the legal rights of the parties to it. But it is manifest that all the participants took account of the existence of a distinct Scots law which might, but need not, be different from the law of England. No simple assumption of identity between the two laws was made and the final judgement was expressed to be in accordance with both laws. Moreover it seems that the English government continued to respect the law of Scotland after the conclusion of the Great Cause. In 1292 Roger Bartholomew lodged an appeal from the court of the Guardians of the Scottish kingdom to that of Edward I; the king sought advice as to Scots law before reaching judgement.[56] Again, when John Comyn, earl of Buchan, made a claim under 'the law and usage of Scotland' before Edward and his council, the king sought information on the relevant 'Scots law and custom'.[57] Nor can it be said that there was any attempt during this period to assimilate Scots law with English. So for example when the burgesses of Berwick sought the extension of the English 'statute for merchants' to Scotland, Edward and his council referred the matter to the parliament to be held at Scone by the lieutenant for the consent of the Scots magnates.[58] It is true that in 1305 Edward instituted an inquiry into the laws of King David and their amendments and additions, intending to 'reform and amend the laws and customs which are clearly displeasing to God and to reason';[59] but again this seems to recognise the historic independence of Scots law rather than to be a prelude to its wholesale abolition.[60]

It is of course clear that many of these references to Scots law are only in general terms and that the emphasis placed on its existence and independence was a consequence of the unique political situation of the 1290s. The existence and independence of Scots law was bound up with the national identity and political independence of Scotland itself. This can be seen in other sources for the period, for example in the provision of the 1290 treaty of Birgham that if Scotland and England should be united through the marriage of the child queen Margaret to the heir of Edward I then 'no-one of the Scots realm shall have to answer outwith the same realm for contracts made or delicts committed in the same realm or in any case against the laws and customs of the realm just as they have hitherto been reasonably observed'.[61] The whole issue of the validity of appeals from the Scottish courts to King Edward's court was also plainly political in character;[62] at the same time, however, it shows how important the seemingly technical questions of laws and jurisdiction were to the contemporary sense of national identity.[63] If, however, we are to be able to regard these statements about an independent Scots law as more than mere political rhetoric, then we have to carry out a much more detailed investigation of all the evidence about it than has been done to date.[64]

What then is the evidence for the actual content of these Scots laws and customs in the reign of Alexander III? As has already been remarked, there is unfortunately now very little material with which an answer to this question can be attempted. Certainly at the end of the thirteenth century there was a good deal of written law in existence, even though there was no *Regiam Majestatem*. In 1291 a roll of 'the old statutes of the Scottish kingdom' was held in the king's treasury at Edinburgh;[65] perhaps it was the same roll which was inventoried for Edward I a year later as containing 'the statutes of King Malcolm and of King David'.[66] (This shows incidentally that the tradition ascribing laws to Malcolm Mackenneth (most probably) and David I had been established before 1300.) The 1292 inventory also mentions two rolls of the 'laws and assizes of the Scottish kingdom and of the laws and customs of the Scottish burghs and of certain statutes issued by the Scottish kings', as well as a copy of the March Laws.[67] This last was certainly the group of laws declared by and written down after a mixed inquest of Scots and English knights meeting at the border in 1249,[68] while the burgh laws may well have been a text of the *Leges Quatuor Burgorum*.[69] As to the assizes and statutes we can but guess, although presumably they did include authentic legislative acts such as are known to have been promulgated by the Scottish kings from the time of David I onward.[70]

The 1292 inventory also reveals that some records of judicial proceedings were held in the king's treasury. For example, it refers to 'a great roll containing [*inter alia*] pleas in all of which judgement was respited or which were amicably terminated and also various concords and agreements concerning controversies between magnates and other men of the realm and also inquests of purprestures and perambulations', as well as to 'ninety three small rolls, schedules and memoranda of various inquests, perambulations and extents of land' and 'two pleas, contained in two schedules, in which judgement was rendered in the king's presence'.[71] The inventory testifies to the capacity of law to generate record, even though it looks as though the treasury held only material bearing directly on the king's interests as feudal superior and on his own personal judicial activities. There is no mention of the justiciary rolls which were certainly in existence in the reign of Alexander III, of which some at least may have been held centrally;[72] nor is there reference to records of any other courts, although it is highly probable that these were made and kept on a regular basis, if only to permit the kind of detailed accounting to the king which we can see the sheriffs making in the Haddington transcripts of the exchequer rolls. Presumably such records were held locally in most if not all cases.

Thus, while once there was a good deal in writing by which we might have investigated the state of Scots law in the thirteenth century, now, so far as the practice of the courts is concerned, we are left only with those chance records of individual cases drawn up by or on behalf of one of the parties involved and then preserved in surviving private muniments or cartularies. This evidence can be made to yield much; but it is no real substitute for continuous records of the kind available from contemporary England. As for the legislation and other texts, there is only one precious survival, the Berne MS which is now held in the Scottish Record Office.[73] Written throughout in a uniform hand, the greater part of the manuscript is in fact taken up by English material: a text of *Glanvill*, a register of the writs used in the courts running in the name of Henry King of England Lord of Ireland and Duke of Aquitaine, and a copy of the 1267 Statute of Marlborough. These items and some marginalia help date the manuscript to the last years of the reign of Henry II (1216–1272). The manuscript also contains the March Laws of 1249. It is only in the last few folios that purely Scottish material can be found. First come what are called the *leges Scocie*, twenty-two fairly miscellaneous chapters, some of which purport to be royal legislation. Then comes another collection headed *Leges et consuetudines quatuor burgorum, Edinburg, Rokisburg, Berwic, Strivelin, constitute per dominum David regem Scocie.* This comprises fifty chapters of the much longer work containing the burgh laws mentioned above; the text breaks off in mid-chapter at the end of the last surviving folio, suggesting that the manuscript is now incomplete. So it is probable that the manuscript continued with the remainder of the *Leges Quatuor Burgorum*; and it is legitimate to speculate that it contained further Scottish material.[74]

What are we to make of this curious collection? A first point is that the English material — *Glanvill*, a register of writs, some statutes — is what one would expect to find in the collection of an English lawyer of the mid-thirteenth century.[75] Forty years ago Lord Cooper argued from internal evidence that the manuscript was indeed the working library of a lawyer who had an extensive practice in the north and east of England and who also had clients amongst the members of the Anglo-Scottish nobility — that is, those who held land on both sides of the border. He drew particular attention to an apparent link with John Balliol I and his wife Devorguilla.[76] Although, as Cooper himself conceded, 'in all this there is a good deal of imaginative conjecture',[77] more recent work on the Anglo-Scottish nobility of this period has shown the existence in their households of clerks who carried out legal work for them in both England and Scotland and who might therefore have required knowledge of and access to both systems of law.[78] Cooper's suggestion of a specific Balliol connection may gain support from the fact that three chapters of the *leges Scocie* relate to Galloway: Devorguilla Balliol had brought her husband extensive property mainly in the east of that province. It is also interesting to note that the first John Balliol was sheriff of Cumberland from 1248 to 1255 as was his brother Eustace from 1261 to 1265; in this office both would have had an important role in the administration of march law.[79] But Balliol links will not account for the presence of the *Leges Quatuor Burgorum*, which was the most important collection of burgh laws in Scotland; if Berne represents a working library, then presumably its compiler's clients included others who had Scottish burghal connections.

Perhaps the greatest interest in the Scottish material attaches to the *leges Scocie*. Many of its twenty-two chapters deal with crime: laws relating to stolen goods and the enforcement of obligations of warrandice in relation thereto, or to slaughter and other injuries to the person and the compensation payable for these wrongs. Four chapters deal with jurisdiction and procedure in the seignorial, shrieval and justiciary courts. Finally, as already noted, three of the chapters relate to Galloway, all of them appearing to be judgements of the *judices* of that province, in one case acting with the *judices* of Scotia. Many of the other chapters proclaim themselves to be assizes, statutes or constitutions, sometimes with other references to known events which permit assignation to a particular date. Without exception, these references point to the reign of William I (1165–1214).[80] There are also some indirect hints in the texts: for example, the very first of the laws refers to and affirms a preceding constitution of King David, much in the style which we know to have been used in authentic twelfth-century legislation.[81] Sometimes external evidence allows us to fix dates for other chapters. A statement of the English chronicler Roger of Howden strongly suggests that chapter sixteen is to be dated 1197.[82] Two of the Galloway chapters seem to belong to the period from 1185 when Roland son of Uchtred recovered Galloway and brought the province within William's sway. One records a judgement 'in the court of the lord king before Roland son of Uchtred'; it seems probable that this took place between 1187 and 1189.[83] The other, also a report of a judgement, may possibly be dated 1186.[84] The third Galloway chapter is probably of later date, though not as late as 1228, the date suggested by the editors of *APS*.[85] Overall, we seem usually to end up in the reign of William. It can also be said that some of the otherwise undateable laws have a distinctly antiquated air even for the late thirteenth century, and their provenance may well go beyond the reign of William; for instance, it has been said that the final chapter, comprising the so-called *Leges inter Brettos et Scotos*, was probably originally composed c. 1100.[86] Another chapter defines 'burthensak', certainly a jurisdictional term used in twelfth-century charters but found only rarely in the reign of Alexander III.[87]

All this raises questions, however, for the hypothesis that Berne is a working lawyer's library. To what extent was this largely elderly material in the *leges Scocie* current in the time of Alexander III? It is notorious that the compilers of medieval legal manuscripts frequently merely copied what they found written down elsewhere without much regard to its status as law used in practice. Thus the fact that many of the *leges* also appear in the miscellaneous collection bound in at the beginning of the early fourteenth-century Ayr MS, and in *Regiam Majestatem*,[88] proves only that their respective compilers probably drew on the same sources or ones closely related to those used by the writer of Berne, not that the laws were in force when each was at work. In order to establish that proposition, we need independent evidence, contemporaneous or later, for the operation of that law. For the thirteenth century, of course, it is precisely that kind of evidence which is lacking and it is virtually impossible to determine, for example, how far laws about fishing rights, or about when one might travel abroad at night, such as are found in the *leges*,[89] were ever enforced in practice, even though they are stated to be legislative acts of the king.

However some of the chapters can be related to other evidence in such a way as to suggest something about late thirteenth-century Scots law, if not perhaps to permit categorical statements on particular points. The statements in chapter fifteen, that suitors should come to the sheriff court held every forty days, but that they need only come to the pleas of the justiciar *ex precepto regis*, is at least consistent with other evidence of early practice in this connection and there seems no reason to suppose that it is not an accurate description of how things stood in the thirteenth century.[90] More difficult to assess is the first chapter which, as already remarked, purports to affirm a preceding statute of David I.[91] It contains various provisions about the calling of warrantors by the defender when it is alleged that goods are stolen. The goods are to be held at particular unnamed places. The accused is to be allowed various periods of time for the arrival of his warrantor, their length depending on where in Scotland the warrantor is to be found. If the warrantor does not come, his lord will answer. If the warrantor dwells in Moray, Ross, Caithness or 'Argyll pertaining to Moray', then the accused should apply to the sheriff of Inverness who will send the king's sergeants with him to see that all is dealt with justly according to the assize of the land and the king. If the warrantor dwells in 'Argyll pertaining to Scotia', the accused may apply to the earl of Atholl or the abbot of Glendochart to send witnesses with him; similarly, if the warrantor dwells in Kintyre or Cowal, then the accused may apply to the earl of Menteith for the same privileges.

Lord Cooper thought it unlikely that this scheme could ever have been operative;[92] but the provision of witnesses for the men of his earldom is referred to in a late thirteenth-century charter of Malcolm, earl of Lennox, and it is probable that this should be linked with the service of 'bode and witnessman' found in contemporary northern England, where lords seem to have had officers whose functions included the witnessing of the service of summonses, the making of arrests and the performance of transactions.[93] Thus the first chapter of Berne may mean that the officers of the sheriff of Inverness and the lords mentioned would testify to the transaction between the warrantor and the accused or to the proper calling of the former to fulfil his obligation. The reference to the abbot of Glendochart is particularly interesting in this respect. In his *Celtic Scotland*, W. F. Skene pointed out that the Columban abbey of St Fillan in Glendochart had passed into the hands of a lay abbot, and its lands into secular possession, but that there still survived as late as the fifteenth century an officer who had custody of the staff of St Fillan and 'a certain jurisdiction which bears an obvious relation to that possessed . . . by the abbot of Glendochart' under this law.[94] That jurisdiction, which was later discussed in detail by W. C. Dickinson,[95] involved the pursuit of stolen goods and may well have also included a witnessing function. This officer must have been operating in the reign of Alexander III and his later appearances therefore give a little support to the connection of the Berne chapter with current law in the thirteenth century.

If this be so, then some of the other chapters dealing with stolen goods and warrandice also gain credibility, since they clearly have some links with chapter one. There is a notably northern and western bias to the chapter; this is also reflected in chapter two, which deals with all those warrantors who dwell in Galloway and '*ultra*' Forth and who are called by persons accused in Scotia.[96] In context, '*ultra*' must mean on the other side of the Forth from Scotia, that is, to the south of the river. Such warrantors are to be convened at Stirling. Chapter seventeen also lists the places to which warrantors should come, which may well be the same as the unidentified places mentioned in chapter one where goods alleged to be stolen should be held pending the arrival of the warrantor.[97] Again all the districts mentioned are in Scotia. The remaining chapters on warrandice lack this explicit Scotia connection but seem to work along similar lines. Taken as a whole, they suggest a system of rules comparable with those which had quite recently prevailed in England and which could still be found in Ireland and Wales.[98]

The chapters on compensation for slaughter and other wrongs also tie in quite well with what is known of later medieval practice in Scotland. The final chapter, which unlike all the others is in French, refers to different kinds of payment, exigible at varying rates dependent on the nature of the injury and the status of the victim, and called *cro, galanas* and *gelchach* or *kelchin*.[99] A Latin version of these rules found its way into *Regiam Majestatem*, which also mentions *cro* and *galanas* in another of its chapters.[100] *Cro* also turns up as *croy* in legislation of 1432[101] so it seems likely that although, as already mentioned, the chapter may have had very early origins it would still have been comprehensible in Alexander III's Scotland. Chapter eleven of the *leges Scocie* also explains what the *wergild* of a thief is in Scotia.[102] This and the other terms mentioned are all familiar from Anglo-Saxon, Irish and Welsh sources, where they are used to describe the compensation payments which will settle a dispute or feud, either between an injured person and his assailant or between the kindred of a deceased and his slayer. The researches of Jenny Wormald in particular have revealed how a form of this 'justice of the feud' continued to operate in Scotland until early modern times and it is certain that its history goes back well beyond the days of Alexander III.[103]

Wormald stresses the extra-legal nature of this system but draws attention to the fact that it was also incorporated into the legal structure in what became the remedy of assythment.[104] It is not difficult to see why judicial participation might have been required. Suppose that an accused denied that he had committed the wrong, as with the Bissets in the case of the death of the earl of Atholl in 1242.[105] In such cases the accusation or the denial would have to be proved, by the parties' bodies or their oaths or the oaths of their neighbours. The amount of the assythment might be settled on a purely private basis but again, where there was dispute about the matter, then resort to law would be necessary. Moreover, the king and other lords had an interest in the system to protect and their courts and officers were an instrument to this end. The Berne chapter gives the payments due to the king, earl or thane if someone is slain within their 'peace', so that potentially a killer was liable both to the kin of his victim and to the holder of any peace which the homicide might have broken. The rights of the kin and of the wider community were thus closely linked. The twelfth and thirteenth centuries saw an increasing force in the concept of the king's peace reflected in the elaboration of the 'pleas of the crown' and the development of a procedure of presentment of criminals by inquests of local communities prior to the justice ayres.[106] In this way the king's special interest in particular breaches of his peace was clarified and the role of the community at large in prosecution became a more formal element in the system. These changes are evidenced in some of the *leges Scocie*. Thus in the chapter which seems to represent an 1197 statute, it is provided that the magnates and prelates have been sworn to assist the king to take *vindicta* of wrongdoers, while they themselves will not take *pecunia* from the accused whereby justice is not done.[107] Another chapter speaks of how the king will have full right of groups of relatives who themselves vengefully slay the killers of members of their kindred 'as far as they were fully breakers of his peace'.[108] Lastly, in the chapter containing the statute of 1180, it is provided that the magnates and prelates are not to hold their courts except when the king's sheriff or his sergeants are present to see that they are conducted rightly. This is linked with a reservation of the pleas of the crown.[109]

Coupled with the chapters on the private compensation system, these laws suggest an increasing emphasis from the end of the twelfth century on the rights of the king which is reflected in the later action of assythment. As Robert Black and Christopher Gane have shown, by the early modern period the perpetrator of a criminal act was liable to punishment at the hands of the king and his officers but might (normally in return for payment) obtain a remission or pardon. In the older terminology, he bought back the king's peace. This did not however elide a continuing responsibility to compensate the victim or, in the case of homicide, his kin, although, where assythment had been paid and a letter of slains granted by the recipients, a pardon was virtually automatic.[110] There is a clear continuity between assythment and the earlier compensation systems, and it seems highly likely that the balance between the interests of the king and the kin which it manifests had been struck after the twelfth-century legislation recorded in the *leges Scocie*. Outwith the *leges* there are only the slightest hints of this system in the later thirteenth century but they are just enough for a conclusion that so far as the king's role was concerned its chapters did bear some relation to current law. The exchequer rolls make it clear that the courts of the justiciar and the sheriff produced an income for the king by virtue of the fines and escheats arising from convictions and give one or two specific instances: for example, that of the son of Gilaverianus, farmer of the Cumbraes, who was held by the sheriff of Ayr as a pledge for a fine of eighty cows due to the king from his father [111] (Incidentally, this reference shows that the quantification of fines in cows or other animals as specified in the *leges Scocie* was by no means obsolete in our period.) Equally, the sheriff's accounts show that fines might be remitted and it would appear from an entry in the 1292 inventory of the Scottish records that this could be done by royal letters.[112] There is also a reference in the accounts to the beheading of one unfortunate individual, demonstrating that not all were able to make peace with the king.[113] Finally the well-known inquest into the death of Adam the miller, which determined that Richard had killed him in self-defence and that Adam was a known thief, suggests a procedure comparable to that used in contemporary England, to determine whether or not a homicide deserved a pardon from the king.[114]

As to the system of compensation payments to the victim or his kin, there is no direct evidence in the sources for the period other than the *leges Scocie*. But much may be read into the brief with which Edward I entrusted his Scottish law commission in 1305, to amend the law of Scotland where it was plainly contrary to God and reason, and the fact that at the same time he felt able to abolish the laws of the Scots and the Bretts without further ado.[115] Presumably their contrariety to divine law and reason required no investigation. The language immediately recalls the earlier activities of the same Edward and his lieutenants in Ireland and Wales. In 1277 he had declared that 'the laws which the Irish use are detestable to God and so contrary to all law that they ought not to be deemed laws',[116] while in the immediately succeeding years, aided and abetted by his archbishop of Canterbury, John Pecham, he had begun to apply similar yardsticks to the native laws of Wales.[117] In both countries a principal target for this condemnation was the system of compounding for homicide rather than inflicting punishment upon the wrongdoer.[118] Whether or not the 'laws of the Scots and the Bretts' are represented by the final chapter of the *leges Scocie*,[119] it seems likely that in 1305 the precedents of a quarter century before were being recalled in response to the existence in Scotland of just such another system.

It is difficult if not impossible to show that the *leges Scocie* were law under Alexander III but it does seem that they can be used to illustrate something of the development of Scots law in the twelfth and thirteenth centuries. In particular their evidence supports the view that the character of the law was much more archaic and complex than suggested by Maitland and Cooper. There is a mixture of elements: primarily legislative in character, the *leges* nevertheless incorporate elements which we can recognise as coming from the world as it was before the coming of Anglo-Norman feudal practices and the elaboration of the canon law. If the *leges Scocie* embody genuine twelfth-century legislation, then we can see that royal policy did not disfavour these elements but sought to use them in the creation of generally applicable rules. Moreover, some at least of these laws bear a clear relation to rules which certainly formed part of later medieval law. Thus there is not in Scotland any evidence to support a theory that at any given moment in the thirteenth century one or other element was so dominant that the law can be characterised by words like 'Celtic' or 'Anglo/Scoto-Norman'. All these elements were embraced within a changing law and legal system.

The stages of development under Alexander III can probably be recovered only in the broadest of terms, but it is interesting and suggestive to draw comparisons and contrasts with the position in Ireland and Wales at the same period. The Anglo-Normans invaded Ireland just as the reforms of Henry II initiated the changes which were to bring about the common law of thirteenth-century England. By the beginning of the thirteenth century Ireland had its own justiciar and the writs of right, mort d'ancestor and novel disseisin, amongst others, were in use there. One of the earliest surviving registers of English writs is a collection which may have been sent to Ireland as early as 1210. But by and large only the Anglo-Norman settlers and their descendants automatically enjoyed the benefits of English law; if a native Irishman raised a claim under that law he could be met with 'the exception of Irishry' and his action would fall. Some Irishmen received the privilege of using English law by grant and from 1277 to 1280 there was an attempt inspired by the church to purchase it for all the Irish. This failed and for the remainder of the middle ages the Anglo-Irish law co-existed with the purely native system, each exercising some influence on the other's development and, in some areas, mingling within particular jurisdictions.[120] In Wales too the use of English law with its writs and assizes as imposed by the Statute of Wales in 1284 reflected the hard facts of conquest. The native Welsh, like the native Irish, had no right to use English law except by grant, with the result that Welsh law survived the events of 1284 and continued on into the sixteenth century. But it is important to note that even before 1284 there had been movements within Wales itself seeking the replacement of the law of Hywel Dda with 'the law of twelve' (i.e. the jury), presumably under the influence of the English example.[121] Perhaps this was affected by what was happening in the marcher lordships held by Anglo-Norman barons from the twelfth century where, although the English king's writ did not run, the assizes of novel disseisin and mort d'ancestor were in use from early in the thirteenth century. Feudal practices and English procedures interacted with Welsh customs to produce what was termed 'the law of the march', which also continued to have its own independent existence and character until the sixteenth century.[122]

In Ireland and Wales the law drew on diverse sources, native and English, and in each case created its own distinctive character. In Scotland there was no military conquest by the Anglo-Normans and no jurisdictional subjugation to the English king's writs, courts or statutes. The Norman intrusion upon Scottish society, brought about primarily through royal patronage, also occurred and had been consolidated well before the legal reforms of Henry II began to take effect in England. But like the burgesses and the men of the religious orders also introduced under royal patronage in the course of the twelfth century, the Anglo-Norman knights brought with them customs of tenure and other special privileges already familiar in England and elsewhere in western Europe. These rights and claims did not always fit readily with the existing structures of society and law and the incomers would certainly have expected kings who by and large shared their ways of thinking to make provision for their protection and enforcement by way of new institutions. Moreover, together with the king, they employed the powerful instrument of writing to define and record their rights, especially to land, in terms which became standardised as time went on. As writing was used more and more for purposes of record, so these formulae were adapted and applied to all manner of transactions concerning land. Native society began to claim the privileges and adopt the new customs of landholding, expressing rights in the convenient written formulae; equally its customs were received and adapted by the incomers. It may be that the recording in French of the compensation tariffs found in the Berne MS is part of this process. Loyalty to the king, continuity of settlement, intermarriage and passage of time gave a sense of common identity and brought about the integration of the various elements of society as the kingdom of the Scots, meaning that in the secular sphere there was no distinction between the king's subjects: all were under his governance and equally all were under his law. There was no conflict between old 'Celtic' law on the one hand and new 'feudal' law on the other, and no institutionalised form of apartheid similar to the exceptions of Irishry and Welshry to ensure that Anglo-Norman and older native laws followed separate paths of development.

But throughout western Europe the thirteenth century was a critical period in the way people thought about law and what might be done with it.[123] Although the collective knowledge of the various communities which made up society had always been important in European legal systems, now it came to be increasingly formalised and seen as the only way in which justice might truly be done within the limits of human capacity. The decline of combat as a method of proof and the attack on the ordeal by the fourth Lateran council in 1215 are symptoms of this change. Within the British Isles England led the way in the development of the jury in judicial proceedings and it was the natural model for others seeking to achieve the same end. In Scotland the close similarity of land tenures made English law in this area a particularly appropriate source for borrowing, notably with regard to those rules and actions which protected security of tenure and inheritance using the assize. But this was not all that lay behind this kind of legal transplantation. There was a rejection of old custom in favour of the new. In 1285 Robert Bruce, earl of the mainly Celtic province of Carrick, and his wife Marjorie made a grant to the local tenants of Melrose Abbey that, because they claimed *legem Anglicanam*, no longer should they be troubled by his sergeants accusing them of crimes in the earl's court.[124] The precise meaning of this is not completely clear; its chief interest for present purposes lies in the apparent contrast of existing custom with English law. It may properly be linked with the petition made twenty years later to Edward I by the community of Galloway against the 'strange and tortious' custom of lords' sergeants having powers to make accusations and compel people to answer them.[125] In that petition, and in the grant of 1285, perhaps we can see the emergence in Scotland of concepts of law and justice against which some of the Celtic and other more ancient elements of the laws and customs of the kingdom seemed irrational, immoral and barbarous by contrast with the more enlightened state of affairs in England. But it is submitted that the process of eliminating these archaic features from the legal mainstream, as opposed to adapting and amending them, had barely begun under Alexander III.

NOTES

1. I am grateful to my colleagues John Cairns and David Sellar for helpful comments on earlier drafts of this chapter.
2. *Chron. Wyntoun* (Laing), ii, 265.
3. *Chron. Bower*, ii, 129–30.
4. Ibid., 110; *Chron. Wyntoun* (Laing), ii, 263.
5. Ibid., 265–6.
6. *Chron. Bower*, ii, 129–30. I take Bower's *insula Leneri prope Crawmond* to be Cramond Island in the Firth of Forth.
7. See the 'Notice of the Principal Manuscript Collections of the Ancient Laws of Scotland' in *APS*, i, 175–210. Other legal MSS have since been discovered but they too lack legislation of Alexander III.
8. *Regiam Majestatem*, ed. J. Skene (Edinburgh, 1609), part II, fos. 28v–29r. The table of 'auld lawes' in *The Practicks of Sir James Balfour of Pittendreich*, ed. P. G. B. McNeill (Stair Society, 1952–3), i, p. ci, reveals no references to legislation of Alexander III. Other early modern legislative collections, like Henryson's 'Black Acts' (1566), Skene's *Lawes and Acts* (1597) and Glendook's *Acts* (1681) all start at 1424.
9. *APS*, i, 21, 43–44, 419–28.
10. The most important of these works are *Select Scottish Cases of the Thirteenth Century* (Edinburgh, 1944), *The Register of Brieves 1286–1386* (Stair Society, 1946), and *Regiam Majestatem and Quoniam Attachiamenta* (Stair Society, 1947). Henceforth these will be cited as respectively Cooper, *Cases, Reg. Brieves*, and Cooper, *Regiam*. Many of his relevant articles are gathered in his *Selected Papers* (Edinburgh, 1957, henceforth Cooper, *Papers*).
11. 'From David I to Bruce 1124–1329', in *Introduction to Scottish Legal History* (Stair Society, 1958, henceforth *ISLH*), 1–17.
12. Ibid., 15.
13. For Cooper's views on the modern Scottish legal system, which throw interesting sidelights on his interpretation of medieval legal history, see Cooper, *Papers*, 26ff., 58ff., 172ff., 201ff. and 244ff..
14. A. A. M. Duncan, '*Regiam Majestatem*: a Reconsideration' (henceforth Duncan, '*Regiam*'), *Juridical Review*, vi (1961), 199–217.
15. Cooper, 'From David I to Bruce 1124–1329', *ISLH*, 7.
16. For a recent suggestion, unsupported by any evidence, that *Regiam* should be attributed to the reign of Alexander III, see two works by D. M. Walker: *The Scottish Jurists* (Edinburgh, 1985), 11–18 and *A Legal History of Scotland*, i (Edinburgh, 1988), 114–17.
17. G. W. S. Barrow, 'The Scottish Justiciar in the Twelfth and Thirteenth Centuries', *Juridical Review*, xvi (1971), 97–148, reprinted in Barrow, *Kingdom*, 83–138.
18. Barrow, *Kingdom*, 122.
19. Ibid., 136.
20. See *ER*, i, 1–34 for frequent mention of the issues of sheriff and justiciary courts.

21. See e.g. *APS*, i, 95-102, *CDS*, i, nos. 2193, 2677, 2679, 2680, and Cooper, *Cases*, 55-92. See also references cited in Professor Dickinson's introductions to *Fife Court Bk.* and *Aberdeen Burgh Recs.*

22. See *APS*, i, 425-8 and the cases cited above, n. 4.

23. The treatise was edited by Mary Bateson and printed in *SHS Misc.*, ii, 3-42. The relevant passages are at 36-37.

24. G. Neilson, *Trial by Combat* (Glasgow, 1890), 75-146. The ordeal may have been abolished in 1230 (*APS*, i, 400, c. 6): see further R. Bartlett, *Trial by Fire and Water: the Medieval Judicial Ordeal* (Oxford, 1986), 127-39.

25. I. D. Willock, *The Origin and Development of the Jury in Scotland* (Stair Society, 1966), 3-37.

26. F. Pollock and F. W. Maitland, *The History of English Law Before the Time of Edward I* (2nd. edn. Cambridge, 1896; henceforth Pollock and Maitland), i, 222-3; and see Barrow, *Anglo-Norman Era*, 118-20; Keith Stringer, 'The Charters of David, Earl of Huntingdon and Lord of Garioch: a Study in Anglo-Scottish Diplomatic' (henceforth Stringer, 'Charters of David'), in Stringer, *Nobility Essays*, 72-101 at 96; and J. H. Baker, *An Introduction to English Legal History* (2nd. edn. London, 1979; henceforth Baker, *Introduction*), 31. But see now also W. D. H. Sellar, 'The Common Law of Scotland and the Common Law of England' (henceforth Sellar, 'Common Law'), in *The British Isles 1100-1500*, ed. R. R. Davies (Edinburgh, 1988), 82-99.

27. For brieves *de cursu* and a contrast with brieves *de gratia*, see *SHS Misc.*, ii, 31-32; Stevenson, *Documents*, 169; Stones and Simpson, *Edward I*, ii, 97; *RRS*, vi, no. 306. For discussion of fees, see *RRS*, v, 213-14.

28. See H. L. MacQueen, 'The Brieve of Right in Scots Law', *Journal of Legal History*, iii (1982), 52-70, and idem, 'Dissasine and Mortancestor in Scots Law', ibid., iv (1983), 21-49.

29. H. L. MacQueen, 'The Brieve of Right in Scots Law', 61-62.

30. PRO, SC 1/18/47, printed by A. A. M. Duncan and J. G. Dunbar in *SHR*, 1 (1971), at 15-16.

31. See especially Sellar, 'Common Law', 87-88.

32. See H. L. MacQueen, 'The Brieve of Right Revisited', in *The Political Context of Law*, edd. R. Eales and D. Sullivan (London and Ronceverte, 1987), 17-25. For writs of entry see R. C. Palmer, 'The Origins of Property in England', *Law and History Review*, iii (1985), 1-50, and literature cited therein.

33. A convenient account of this transformation is still T. F. T. Plucknett, *Concise History of the Common Law* (5th. edn. London, 1956), 22-31. See also his *The Legislation of Edward I* (Oxford, 1962), but cf. P. A. Brand, 'Legal Change in the Later Thirteenth Century: Statutory and Judicial Remodelling of the Action of Replevin', *American Journal of Legal History*, xxxi (1987), 43-55, and M. Prestwich, *Edward I* (London, 1988), 267-97.

34. G. Donaldson, 'The Church Courts', in *ISLH*, 363-73; S. D. Ollivant, *The Court of the Official in Pre-Reformation Scotland* (Stair Society,

1982). For a legitimacy dispute between two laymen in an ecclesiastical court in 1251 see Cooper, *Cases*, 61–65.

35. Cooper, *Papers*, 81–87; Barrow, *Kingdom*, 90–92.
36. *Reg. Brieves*, 46, 55; *Formulary E*, nos. 4–7.
37. See Cooper, *Cases*, 70–71, 78, 89; P. G. Stein, 'Roman Law in Scotland', *Ius Romanum Medii Aevi* (Milan, 1968), part 5, 13b, 25–28.
38. Cp. Barrow, *Kingdom*, 92. See further Cooper, *Cases*, 68, 86; also *Arbroath Liber*, i, no. 293 for an agreement in 1286 between a churchman and a layman to submit to the jurisdiction of the justiciar of Scotia.
39. W. D. H. Sellar, 'Marriage, Divorce and Concubinage in Gaelic Scotland', *TGSI*, li (1978–80), 464–93.
40. A. E. Anton, 'Parent and Child', in *ISLH*, 116–29 at 117–18; Baker, *Introduction*, 400–1. On the church's influence on the law of heritable property see J. Goody, *The Development of the Family and Marriage in Europe* (Cambridge, 1983), ch. 6, and G. Duby, *The Knight, the Lady and the Priest* (London, 1984).
41. The best known example of a late 13th.-century cleric who was involved in law proceedings which may have included the purely secular is Adam Urry, for whom see *Chron. Lanercost*, 124. See also Barrow, *Kingdom*, 99–100, 135 and n..
42. W. D. H. Sellar, 'Celtic Law and Scots Law: Survival and Integration' (henceforth Sellar, 'Celtic Law'), *Scottish Studies*, xxix (1989), 1–27. The lecture was delivered at Edinburgh on 9th. May 1985. I am grateful to Mr. Sellar for allowing me to read his lecture in typescript in advance of publication.
43. Barrow, *Bruce*, 5.
44. *Fife Court Bk.*, pp. lxii–ix; W. C. Dickinson, 'The Toschederach', *Juridical Review*, liii (1941), 85–109; idem, 'Surdit de Sergaunt', *SHR*, xxxix (1960), 170–5; Barrow, *Kingdom*, 69–82; Sellar, 'Celtic Law', 3–11.
45. The sheriffdom system did not cover the whole country by 1286, particularly in the north and west: see *Fife Court Bk.*, appendix D.
46. Barrow, *Kingdom*, 89 and n..
47. *The Welsh Assize Roll 1277–1284*, ed. J. Conway Davies (Cardiff, 1940), 266.
48. *Melrose Liber*, i, no. 309. See also Stevenson, *Documents*, 168–9; *SHS Misc.*, ii, 37; and Sellar, 'Common Law', 86.
49. Stones and Simpson, *Edward I*, ii, 140.
50. Ibid., 167.
51. Ibid., 179.
52. Ibid., 183. For another comment, see Sellar, 'Common Law', 86–87.
53. Stones and Simpson, *Edward I*, ii, 198–9.
54. Ibid., 212.
55. Ibid., 214–15.
56. Stevenson, *Documents*, 385–6.
57. *Memoranda de Parliamento: Records of the Parliament Holden at Westminster . . . (1305)*, ed. F. W. Maitland (Rolls Series, 1893; henceforth *Memoranda de Parliamento (1305)*), 228–9.

58. Ibid., 178–9. The statute in question may have been the 1285 Statute of Merchants, or, less probably, the *Carta Mercatoria* of 1303.

59. *APS*, i, 122; Stones, *Relations*, [125].

60. Note, however, that in 1307 a parliament at Carlisle laid down a statute about the rents and dues uplifted from their British houses by foreign abbeys which was to have effect in England, Ireland, Wales and Scotland: see *Statutes of the Realm* (Rec. Comm., 1810–28), i, 150–2, *Rot. Parl.*, i, 217–18 and *Statutes Ordinances and Acts of the Parliament of Ireland: King John to Henry V*, ed. H. F. Berry (Dublin, 1907), 240. See also H. G. Richardson and G. O. Sayles, *The English Parliament in the Middle Ages* (London, 1981), no. xii, 425–37. It is unlikely that the statute ever took effect in Scotland.

61. Stevenson, *Documents*, 168–9.

62. See Barrow, *Bruce*, 54–60.

63. On law and national identity in the middle ages see R. C. van Caenegem, *The Birth of the Common Law* (2nd. edn., Cambridge, 1988), 97–98 and R. R. Davies, 'Law and National Identity in Thirteenth Century Wales', in *Welsh Society and Nationhood*, edd. R. R. Davies *et al* (Cardiff, 1984), 51–69.

64. Walker, *A Legal History of Scotland* (above, n. 16), published since this chapter was completed, does not carry us very far forward.

65. *APS*, i, 112.

66. Ibid., 117.

67. Ibid., 114–15.

68. See ibid., 414.

69. Ibid., 333–56. For discussion of the *Leges Burgorum* see H. L. MacQueen and W. J. Windram, 'Laws and Courts in the Burghs', in *The Scottish Medieval Town*, edd. M. Lynch *et al* (Edinburgh, 1988), 208–27.

70. See references to legislation in *RRS*, i, nos. 233 and 258, and in *RRS*, ii, nos. 406, 442 and 475; also discussion in *APS*, i, 53 and Barrow, *Kingdom*, 73 and n.. The acts of Alexander II printed in *APS*, i, 397–404 have usually been taken as authentic. See Duncan, *Kingdom*, 185–6, 200–3, 539–41.

71. *APS*, i, 114–15.

72. See *Arbroath Liber*, i, nos. 227, 230 and 294 and Barrow, *Kingdom*, 99, 117.

73. SRO, PA 5/1, described in *APS*, i, 177–8.

74. Might it have included a recension of the *Leges Forestarum*, for example? See J. Gilbert, *Hunting and Hunting Reserves in Medieval Scotland* (Edinburgh, 1979), 243–7.

75. *Early Registers of Writs*, ed. G. D. G. Hall (Selden Society, 1970), introduction, p. xviii.

76. Cooper, *Papers*, 161–71.

77. Ibid., 170.

78. Simpson, 'The *Familia* of Roger de Quincy', 110–12; Stringer, 'Charters of David', 78.

79. Stell, 'The Balliol Family', 151–2, 155–6 and 159; G. Neilson, 'The

March Laws', in *Miscellany*, i, (Stair Society, 1970), 1–77 at 24.

80. Cc. 7, 8 and 12, respectively printed in *APS*, i, 374 (cc. 11 and 12) and 376 (c. 16). See also *APS*, i, 282–3. The texts in Berne do not correspond exactly with the printed ones, which have been collated with other MSS. With regard to these and other chapters I have relied on the Berne text alone.

81. C. 1 is printed as part of *APS*, i, 372, c. 3. See references at n. 70 above.

82. Anderson, *Scottish Annals*, 318. C. 16 is printed in *APS*, i, 377, c. 20.

83. C. 21 (*APS*, i, 378, c. 23); Duncan, *Kingdom*, 186 and n..

84. C. 19 (slightly different from *APS*, i, 378, c. 23); Duncan, *Kingdom*, 185.

85. C. 20, dated 1228 in *APS*, i, 398, c. 3. See also ibid., 285, but cf. Duncan, *Kingdom*, 529.

86. C. 22, the French text printed in *APS*, i, 663–5. See K. H. Jackson, 'The Britons of Southern Scotland', *Antiquity*, xxix (1955), 77–88 at 88 and Duncan, *Kingdom*, 107–8.

87. C. 9 (part of *APS*, i, 375, c. 13). See Barrow, *Anglo-Norman Era*, 199, for early references; the only example from the reign of Alexander III known to me is *Kelso Liber*, ii, no. 474 (1271).

88. See Duncan, '*Regiam*', 209, for a table.

89. Cc. 6 and 7 (printed in *APS*, i, 374, cc. 10 and 11).

90. See *Fife Court Bk.*, introduction, p. xiii, for the sheriff court; *Ordo Justiciarie*, c. 5 (*APS*, i, 706) for the justiciar. See also *RRS*, v, 56–59, and *Pitfirrane Writs* no. 24 for the precept of a justiciar to a sheriff to summon suitors to his ayre in 1435.

91. See above, n. 81.

92. Cooper, *Regiam*, 86, 89.

93. Fraser, *Lennox*, ii, no. 210; R. Stewart-Brown, *The Serjeants of the Peace in Medieval England and Wales* (Manchester, 1936), 82–86; Barrow, *Anglo-Norman Era*, 160–1.

94. Skene, *Celtic Scotland*, ii, 406–7.

95. W. C. Dickinson, 'The Toschederach' (see above, n. 44); see also Sellar, 'Celtic Law', 9–11.

96. C. 2 is the final part of *APS*, i, 372, c. 3.

97. C. 17 is *APS*, i, 373, c. 4.

98. The remaining chapters are 3–5, 12–14 and 18, printed in *APS*, i, 373, cc. 5–7; 376, cc. 16–18; and 737, c. 1. Cp. Pollock and Maitland, ii, 157–9.

99. See above, n. 86.

100. See the edition of *Regiam Majestatem* by Thomson and Innes: *APS*, i, 640–1 and 637. See also Cooper, *Regiam*, 275–8 and 269.

101. *APS*, ii, 21, c. 5. See further Sellar, 'Celtic Law', 11.

102. Printed in *APS*, i, 375, c. 14.

103. See generally, J. Wormald, 'Bloodfeud, Kindred and Government in Early Modern Scotland' (henceforth Wormald, 'Bloodfeud'), *Past and Present*, no. lxxxvii (1980), 54–97 and comparative references there given.

104. Ibid., 66.

105. Duncan, *Kingdom*, 544–6.

106. Barrow, *Kingdom*, 110–13; Duncan, *Kingdom*, 201–4, 206–8, 546–7; Wormald, 'Bloodfeud', 57–66.
107. C. 16 (*APS*, i, 377, c. 20); see n. 82 above. Duncan, *Kingdom*, 201, translates *vindicta* as 'compensation'; I see no reason for not giving it its more literal sense of 'vengeance' — the king avenges the affront to his peace, although of course he *may* be bought off by the offender.
108. C. 10 (part of *APS*, i, 375, c. 15).
109. C. 8 (part of *APS*, i, 374, c. 12).
110. R. Black, 'A Historical Survey of Delictual Liability in Scotland for Personal Injuries and Death', *Comparative and International Law Journal of South Africa*, viii (1975), 46–70; C. H. W. Gane, 'The Effect of a Pardon in Scots Law', *Juridical Review*, xxv (1980), 18–46.
111. *ER*, i, 5. See also ibid., 4–5.
112. *APS*, i, 117.
113. *ER*, i, 4.
114. *APS*, i, 97–98. For England see T. A. Green, *Verdict According to Conscience* (Chicago, 1985), 28–64.
115. *APS*, i, 122; Stones, *Relations*, [125].
116. *Foedera*, i, part ii, 540, quoted in A. J. Otway-Ruthven, 'The Request of the Irish for English Law 1277–80', *Irish Historical Studies*, vi (1949), 261–70 at 262.
117. See R. R. Davies, 'The Twilight of Welsh Law 1284–1536' (henceforth Davies, 'Twilight'), *History*, li (1966), 143–64, especially at 143 and 147.
118. For Ireland see K. Nicholls, *Gaelic and Gaelicised Ireland in the Middle Ages* (Dublin, 1972), 53–57 and R. Frame, *Colonial Ireland 1169–1369* (Dublin, 1981), 106–7; for Wales, R. R. Davies, 'The Survival of the Bloodfeud in Medieval Wales', *History*, liv (1969), 338–57; cf. L. B. Smith, 'The Statute of Wales 1284' (henceforth Smith, 'Statute'), *Welsh History Review*, x (1980–81), 127–54 at 151–2.
119. There are some difficulties, as Mr William Windram has pointed out to me. The text is first identified as the *Leges inter Brettos et Scotos* by Sir John Skene in his edition of *Regiam* (see fo. 103). It is unlikely that he knew of Edward's ordinance, which was first published much later in 1661: W. Ryley, *Placita Parlementaria* (London, 1661), 503–8.
120. G. J. Hand, 'English Law in Ireland 1172–1351', *Northern Ireland Legal Quarterly*, xxiii (1972), 393–419 is a useful survey with references to other literature. See also two articles by G. Mac Niocaill: 'The Contact of Irish and Common Law', ibid., 16–23, and 'The Interaction of Laws', in *The English in Medieval Ireland* (Royal Irish Academy, Dublin, 1984), 105–17, and K. Nicholls, 'Anglo-French Ireland and After', *Peritia*, i (1982), 370–403 at 374–7. On the early Irish register see P. A. Brand, 'Ireland and the Literature of the Early Common Law', *Irish Jurist*, xvi (1981), 95–113. The exception of Irishry accounts for the case of Henry the Scot (who claimed English law in Ireland), discussed in Barrow, *Anglo-Norman Era*, 119, Sellar, 'Common Law', 87, and Walker, *A Legal History of Scotland*, i, 90.

121. See R. R. Davies, *Conquest, Coexistence and Change: Wales 1063–1415* (Oxford, 1987), 419–25, as well as Davies, 'Twilight' and Smith, 'Statute', both *passim*.
122. See R. R. Davies, 'The Law of the March', *Welsh History Review*, v (1970–1), 1–30 and *idem*, *Lordship and Society in the March of Wales 1282–1400* (Oxford, 1978), 160–8.
123. Stimulating reading on this theme can be found in S. F. C. Milsom, 'Law and Fact in Legal Development', *University of Toronto Law Journal*, xvii (1967), 1–19; M. T. Clanchy, 'Remembering the Past and the Good Old Law', *History*, lv (1970), 165–76; and S. Reynolds, *Kingdoms and Communities in Western Europe 900–1300* (Oxford, 1984), 12–66.
124. *Melrose Liber*, i, no. 316. Dr P. A. Brand has suggested to me that the *lex Anglicana* (i.e. English *written* law) in question may have been clause 38 of *Magna Carta*, which provided that no bailiff should put someone to his law by a simple complaint but should lead faithful witnesses to it. See J. C. Holt, *Magna Carta* (Cambridge, 1965), 226, 326–7. For other views see Barrow, *Anglo-Norman Era*, 119, Sellar, 'Common Law', 87, and Walker, *A Legal History of Scotland*, i, 90.
125. *Memoranda de Parliamento (1305)*, 171–2.

5

NORWEGIAN SUNSET – SCOTTISH DAWN:
HAKON IV AND ALEXANDER III

Edward J. Cowan

There are several striking parallels in the careers of Alexander III and Hakon IV. Both succeeded as minors, their minorities potentially calamitous so far as the well being of their respective kingdoms was concerned. Both had to contend with, and overcome, factious nobilities. Both pursued aggressive expansionist policies and both, in later tradition, presided over 'golden ages'. The fledgling kingship of Alexander was to be severely tested when Hakon, in his sixtieth year, personally led his great fleet into the Minch, an action which hindsight has imbued with more than a hint of the elegiac. 'The culmination of the Middle Ages in Norway is embodied in the figure of Haakon Haakonsson. The ripe summer of Norwegian medieval civilization, and the first rich colours of its autumn, are reflected in the personality of the king who sailed with that mighty armada to his death in the west.'[1] A similar ambience suffuses the poetry embedded in Sturla Thordarsson's *Hakon's Saga* where Hakon's impressive naval campaign is transformed into a Viking expedition on the grand scale:

> Valkyrie lanterns
> To bulwarks made fast,
> Smote the bright heavens
> With gleam of red gold;
> The host of the king
> As it skimmed o'er the main
> Was just like lightning
> Springing from the sea.[2]

Over five centuries later the same events inspired the prentice works of one of Ayrshire's native sons who was later to leave his mark upon the New World as well as the Old. John Galt's execrable 'Gothic poem' on 'The Battle of Largs' warned Hakon to avoid the fate which awaited him in the west:

> Nor fatten Scotland's meagre sod
> With Norway's best and bravest blood,

but in vain:

> Thus while green Largo's breezy shore
> Tumultuous strife deform'd with gore,
> Deep in their dark eternal den
> the Sisters spun the fates of men.[3]

Galt was mistaken, as were many subsequent Scottish historians, in detecting a Norwegian defeat at Largs; neither the saga nor the medieval Scottish sources distinguish it as such. Nonetheless, as will be suggested below, the expedition of 1263 is to be regarded as a complete failure verging upon unmitigated disaster. This argument will be developed from a critical evaluation of *Hakon's Saga* in an attempt to demonstrate its strengths and weaknesses as a source. Few, if any, Scottish historians have bothered to read this extremely tedious saga in its entirety; yet its author, Sturla Thordarsson, is recognised as one of the most gifted sagamen to emerge from the literary glories of thirteenth-century Iceland. Why did he produce such a dismal piece of literature on this occasion?

Dull though it may be, the saga sheds considerable light upon the policies pursued by both the Alexanders in the west; indeed it comes closest to articulating the Hebridean point of view during the troubled thirteenth century. The saga tradition preserves a useful reminder that the strife in the Hebrides was part of a wider Atlantic problem which, in turn, was bound up with the vexed question of the role of kingship. Viewed in this context the cession of the Hebrides in 1266 represented a much greater and more profound setback than the failure of 1263.

Although this period has been investigated by some of Scotland's finest historical talent[4] there is a grave flaw in Alexandrian historiography which seldom questions those twin essentials espoused by so many medievalists — strong centralised monarchy and the consolidation of the kingdom. That same historiography has a tendency to simultaneously applaud both Alexander's resistance to the imperialistic overtures of Henry III and Edward I, and his own domination of the Hebrides. If it is often protested that History is the version of the conqueror, the conquered are still too often ignored. There is little point in undertaking yet another rehearsal of the minutiae of the expedition of 1263; Munch's account in *Det Norske Folks Historie* has not, so far, been superseded, though it can be supplemented.[5] It is doubtful if Dr Watt would be as confident about the overmighty subject today as he was in 1971.[6] Professor Barrow's excellent chapter in *Kingship and Unity* on 'The Winning of the West' for good or ill, connotes images of palefaces and natives, not to mention a shoot-out at Largs. There was even a Marshal Vigleikr on hand who took time out during the expedition to mosey a little in a cave on the west side of Arran's Holy Isle where he scratched out his name in runes.[7]

The Western metaphor is appropriate. Both Scotland and Norway harboured frontier societies where the heroic code prevailed, at least in the minds of the sagamen who, writing in an age when significant individual action seemed less possible, attempted to enshrine these values as they committed the saga texts to vellum. An entire way of life was under threat and colourful characters abounded; some of these, like Eyvind Foul-breath or Thorvald Mound-shitter, briefly enliven the dead pages of *Hakon's Saga*. It is worth considering the author of this piece — Sturla Thordarsson.

Sturla belonged to the powerful and prominent Icelandic family which gave its name to the 'Age of the Sturlungs'. This period of strife extended, as did the Sturlungs themselves, from the late twelfth to the late thirteenth century.[8] Sturla's uncle was the great Snorri Sturluson author of *Heimskringla, The Prose Edda* and *Egil's Saga*, one of the most brilliant writers and historians to be produced anywhere in the medieval world. Both Snorri and Sturla spent a large part of their lives opposing Norwegian imperialist ambitions, specifically those of Hakon IV. In an endeavour to secure Icelandic recognition of Norwegian sovereignty Hakon played rival Icelandic chieftains against one another. In 1241 Snorri was to die at the hands of his own son-in-law, slaughtered like an animal in the cellar of his own house. It fell to Sturla to chronicle those events in his *Sturlunga Saga* and in *Hakon's Saga*.[9] He may also have been the author of the magnificent *Grettir's Saga*[10] and if so, his dichotomous hero Grettir may be seen as a reflection of the profound tensions and ambiguities present within Sturla's own being as he became engulfed in the struggle which would bring about the demise of the Old Icelandic Commonwealth. If Snorri had been known to vacillate Sturla was consistent in his opposition to King Hakon. It was therefore an extremely unfortunate, if not hazardous, circumstance when Sturla was driven out of Iceland by his enemies in 1263 and forced to seek shelter in Norway.

Sturla Thordarsson's reputation as both a great teller of sagas and as a poet of distinction preceded him. His own saga tells of how he met with a very cool reception from Hakon's son, Magnus who had been crowned in 1261, and who was currently tending the kingdom while his father indulged in his heroic enterprise in the Hebrides.[11] It was not long, however, before Sturla was entertaining some members of the royal retinue by telling them the saga of Huld the giantess 'better and more knowledgeably than any of them had ever heard it before . . . a good story very well told'. The queen was curious but Magnus told her to pay no attention and to go to sleep. Next day she requested the saga and Sturla obliged, 'speaking for a great part of the day'.[12] Magnus 'made no comment but only smiled slightly'. Having thus broken down the royal defences through the endless appeal of story Sturla announced that he had composed poems about Magnus and Hakon. The queen was favourably impressed by the Magnus poem. 'Are you sure you clearly understand it?', responded her husband thus revealing his sensitivity to the idea that the scald or bard in Sturla might be mocking him. In the event Magnus declared himself well satisfied with a poem about Hakon. 'To my way of thinking you recite better than the Pope himself', doubtless a compliment to Sturla's facility for language. Magnus then offered the Icelander hospitality but warned him that he would have to answer in person to King Hakon when he returned from his expedition. 'Soon after', says *Sturlunga Saga*, 'Magnus commissioned him with the highly responsible task of composing the saga of his father according to his own account and the reports of the wisest men'. While Sturla was engaged upon his composition word arrived that Hakon had died in Orkney.[13] An internal reference indicates that he was still working on the project in October 1265;[14] it therefore took him over two years to complete it. Soon thereafter Sturla returned home; on a subsequent visit to Norway he was appointed Lawman of all Iceland. He also composed *Magnus Saga* of which only a fragment now survives. He died in 1284.

In writing *Hakon's Saga* Sturla was essentially commissioned with the official biography of the king. Magnus himself was closely involved in the process, communicating his version of events, and it may be reasonably inferred that the intervention of the patron interfered with Sturla's artistic freedom.[15] He was in the ironic situation of producing the biography of a man he detested, who had caused the deaths of Snorri and other kinsmen and who had ended the exhilarating experiment of the Icelandic Commonwealth.[16] Another problem may have been that as the members of Hakon's expedition returned to

Norway they provided Sturla with a superabundance of information. There was precedent for this. After the battle of Nissa in 1062 'there was a tremendous amount of talk and storytelling about the battle, for everyone who had taken part in it felt he had something worth telling about it'.[17] In this section of the saga, however, Sturla seems to have enjoyed much greater freedom to organise his material. Magnus, after all, had no first hand experience of the Scottish campaign; he was as much at the mercy of informants as was Sturla. The author's hostility towards his subject, and the interference of the patron, alike combine to account for the tedium of the bulk of the saga. There is some compensation, however, for both author and audience, in the last sixteen of the saga's three hundred and thirty-three chapters, when Sturla effectively orchestrates his material to convey the essential hollowness of Hakon's achievement.

In describing Hakon's deathbed Sturla reinforced a point of which his audience would doubtless be aware. At first Hakon listened to readings from Latin works but as the language became confusing he demanded the lives of the saints in Old Norse followed by 'the tale of the kings from Halfdan the Black, and so on of all the kings of Norway, one after the other . . . When the tale of the kings was read down to Sverrir then he had them read *Sverrir's Saga*. It was read both night and day whenever he was awake . . . Near mid-night the reading of *Sverrir's Saga* was completed. But just past mid-night Almighty God called king Hakon from this world's life'.[18] In this passage Sturla stressed that Hakon was the successor of King Sverre (1184–1202) whose saga provided a fitting conclusion to *Heimskringla*, Snorri Sturluson's great compilation which treated of Norway and her kings all the way from legendary and prehistoric times down to the reign of Magnus Erlingsson in the twelfth century. The events of Hakon's personal history, in the mind of the sagaman, transcended the king's own times, woven as they were into the tapestry of the Norwegian cosmos.

The full elaboration of this point requires a further paper. Briefly, what might be described as the Sturlung tradition in Icelandic historiography recognised kingship as a suspect institution while kings themselves were perceived as potentially, and often demonstrably, corrupt in the execution of office; kings were regarded as tyrannical, whimsical and oppressive but perhaps also essential. True to the saga tradition the earlier part of Hakon's career was rooted in chaos, surrounded as he was by the rival factions who appear in English translation as the Birchshanks, Croziermen, Tattercoats and Ribbalds. Such were the rigours of his youthful experience that he had earned the soubriquet of 'old' almost before he had escaped his teens. His claims were first debated at a great conference in Bergen in 1223 — 'never had a better choice come together in the king of Norway's realm'. From this impressive and crucial assembly Hakon emerged triumphant.[19] It is noteworthy that the year after this memorable gathering a delegation from the Hebrides approached with 'many letters concerning the needs of their lands'.[20] Though described as *Sudreyingar*, Hebrideans, they were clearly regarded as part of the fabric of the Norwegian *natio*.[21]

After the killing of Duke Skuli, his father-in-law and rival, Hakon went from strength to strength. He became a monarch of European stature who was cultivated by the emperor, who was offered command of the French fleet during the Crusades, whose daughter's hand was sought by Alexander Nevsky and later given to a prince of Castille, and who sent falcons to the Sultan of Tunis.[22] Nearer home Hakon consolidated his kingdom, brought Sweden and Denmark to heel and extended his sway over both Iceland and distant Greenland. Sturla rejoiced that on the very eve of the Hebridean campaign Hakon was the first king to rule over the Arctic Circle:

> North it pleases you to stretch
> Your hand upon the frozen world
> Under the lode-star far away
> Polar men will therefore rejoice
> No other lord but you has ever
> Held sway among those icy regions
> Now people sing your praises further
> Than ever shines the glorious sun.[23]

As an Icelander (and a one time activist) Sturla was clearly in sympathy with the plight of the Hebridean chiefs. There are stray references throughout *Hakon's Saga* to the fortunes of Iceland as her people responded to Norway's imperialistic overtures. Icelanders always retained an interest in the Gaelic west since there was a significant Celtic component in the original Icelandic settlement of the ninth and tenth centuries. Hauk Erlendsson, who produced a version of *Landnamabok*, was not the only celto-maniac in Iceland.[24] Several sagas dwell upon Celtic origins while Alfred Smyth has recently made the interesting, and convincing, suggestion that the Celts were involved in every successive penetration westwards to Iceland, Greenland and the North American continent.[25] Yet Icelanders were also ambivalent about the Celtic peoples. The typical Celt in the sagas is treacherous, vacillating, violent, dangerous and, except in one respect, unpredictable. It is a general rule that if a person with a Celtic pedigree is introduced into a saga that person will generate maximum trouble and mayhem and will eventually come to a bad end. The Celts shared the same characteristics as the thrall class in Iceland, the despised slaves among whose ranks there was an undue preponderance of Celtic stock. The attributes of a debased class in society were transferred to an entire people.[26] As the prisoner of literary convention Sturla had no choice but to depict the Hebrideans as somewhat unstable and volatile. But at heart Sturla empathised with those men in the Western Isles who were fighting the same battle against Scotland and Norway as the Icelanders had been waging against King Hakon. A similar story of struggle for survival against truly formidable odds had already been told in *Orkneyinga Saga*. The kings of Scotland and Norway had exploited the rivalries between different contenders for the earldom of Orkney to their own advantage. The Norwegians played off powerful Icelandic chieftains against one another to the point of manipulating rivals within the same family, as had happened in Orkney. Similarly Norway and Scotland exploited the rivalries between claimants to the kingdom of Man and the Isles both within and outwith the MacSorley kindred — the descendants of the great Somerled — in the twelfth and thirteenth centuries. The problem was well expressed in *Konnungs Skuggja*, the *King's Mirror*, a tract which was written during Hakon's reign:

> The petty kings, having rent the realm asunder will quickly divide the loyalty of the people who inhabit the land, both of the rich and the poor and each of these lords will then try to draw friends about him as many as he can . . . Soon immorality begins to multiply, for God shows his wrath in this way that where the boundaries of the territories of the chiefs touch, he places a moving wheel on a restless axle. After that each one forgets all brotherly love and kinship is wrecked.[27]

The moving wheel on the restless axle is a brilliant pivotal image which is as appropriate whether it refers to Iceland, the Hebrides or Orkney; all shared a common Atlantic problem.[28]

Due to Sturla's sympathies *Hakon's Saga* provides the closest approximation to what might be called the Hebridean point of view in the conflict between Scotland and Norway. A letter of 1262 in the *Diplomatarium Norvegicum* refers to Alexander III's 'unjust treatment of the Norwegians in Scotland'.[29] Sturla might have retorted that it was ever thus, there being little discernible difference in the policies adopted by both the Alexanders. In 1244 Alexander II, 'a great chief and sufficiently ambitious', sent envoys to Norway asking whether Hakon would surrender the Hebrides which King Magnus Barelegs had won 'with some unfairness'. Insult was added to injury when silver was proferred. It is evident that whatever they meant by 'unfairness' the Scots never denied the reality of the treaty between Magnus and Edgar in 1098. As has been elsewhere suggested corroboration for the existence of the treaty, or agreement, may be found in the unusual transaction involving the translation of the bones of Donald Ban to Iona in 1099, an act to be interpreted, perhaps, as one of compensatory aggression, designed to signify that the Scots had not totally abandoned sovereign and territorial claims in the west.[30]

The brief reign of Magnus Barfótr, so nicknamed because he 'wore the clothes which were customary in the British Islands' sporting bare legs, a short kirtle and an outer garment,[31] is comparatively well documented. He is mentioned in a number of British sources while several versions of his saga are extant.[32] To judge from surviving manuscripts there was considerable interest in Magnus during the reign of King Hakon, doubtless engendered by the two's shared aggressive expansionism. Magnus appears in the *Agríp* written towards the end of the twelfth century, a summarised History which in turn drew upon the *Historia de Antiquitate Regum Norwegiensium* composed by Theoderic, a monk of Nidarhólmr in Iceland.[33] Another important source is the poem *Noregs Konunga Tal* (Succession of the Kings of Norway) which was composed in honour of Jón Loptsson of Oddi (also in Iceland) around 1190. Jón's mother was an illegitimate daughter of King Magnus but Jón, in turn, was the foster father of Snorri Sturluson who thus could be expected to have drawn upon traditional accounts preserved by the family in composing his own version of *Magnus Saga* in the *Heimskringla*. The poem not only demonstrated Jón's descent from Magnus but is also drew upon the now lost work of one of Iceland's greatest historians, Saemundr the Learned (1056–1133), a contemporary of Magnus and, as it happens, Jón Loptsson's paternal grandfather.[34] Through Jón, Snorri was thus exceptionally well placed to imbibe information about this colourful king who, he relates, was also known as Magnus the Tall or *Styrjaldr Magnus* — the turbulent or warlike. Such was the impact of this short-lived ruler that he permanently entered the Gaelic oral tradition.[35] The great Icelandic historian Grimur

Thorkelin in the 1780s claimed to have collected stories about Magnus's expedition to Ireland from 'an old man who can repeat them and an infinity of traditions on smaller subjects'.[36]

In short, if Snorri romanticised Magnus's career, there is little reason to suppose that he totally fabricated it. The poetry of the skald, Bjorn Cripple-hand who accompanied the expedition, indicates that the Norwegians, at the level of the royal household, made a close acquaintance with the Hebrides for the first time; no sagas dealing with the period before Magnus display such a detailed knowledge of Hebridean topography:

> Harried on Skye he who
> hungry ravens battens.
> Their teeth on Tiree reddened
> tawny wolves on corpses.
> Grieved there Greenland's ruler
> girls in Shetland Isles —
> high up in Scotland harried
> he who Mull's people frightened.[37]

The sagamen can hardly be blamed if they were vague about the name of the Scottish king in 1098 since the regnal succession is somewhat confused at this point. Most important of all, *Orkneyinga Saga* may preserve a fragment of the actual treaty in the legalistic-looking phraseology of *Skotakonungr vill gefa honum eyjar allar, þaer er liggja fyrir vestan Skotland ik fara maetti stjórnfǫstu skipi milli ok meginlands* — 'the Scottish king will let him have all the islands off the west coast separated by water navigable by a ship with the rudder set' — terminology which was clearly designed to define an island despite the claim that Magnus had his galley hauled across Kintyre.[38]

Norwegian sovereignty, however, was to prove neither very apparent nor very real.[39] Hebridean history in the twelfth and thirteenth centuries is as complex, intricate and elusive as a Celtic artistic motif with tendrils snaking out to Ireland, England, the Northern Isles and occasionally Norway, but that history is above all obscure because large chunks of the pattern have been obliterated by the fragmentary nature of the historical evidence. What is not in doubt is that the kingdom of Man and the Isles was effectively partitioned when Somerled appeared on the scene: 'he did not cease (until) he cleared the western side of Scotland of the Lochlannaich, except the islands of the Norwegians called Innsigall; and he gained victory over his enemies in every field of battle'.[40] Following the great naval battle, in 1156, between Somerled and Godred, king of Man the two 'divided the kingdom of the Isles between them; and from that day to this there has existed a division in the kingdom. The ruin of the kingdom of the Isles began from the time the sons of Somerled gained possession of it'.[41] The MacSorley Saga was well under way; it would outlast both Hakon and Alexander III to conclude in the carnage of the sixteenth and seventeenth centuries, but the shorter version can be viewed as almost exactly parallel to *Sturlunga Saga* in plot and course, internecine feud and external manipulation, until the kingdom of Man and the Isles and the Icelandic Commonwealth alike succumbed to the seemingly inexorable forces of History in the mid 1260s.

Contemporaneously the Scottish Crown was advancing towards the Minch. Already, by the reign of David I the Stewarts had been granted estates on the Clyde coast as a bulwark against the wild Scots of the Inner Hebrides.[42] It is thus dramatically, as well as historically, appropriate that Somerled should have been killed at Renfrew in 1164 while the final battle for the Hebrides should have been fought at Largs since both places are within the Stewart lordship. As *Clanranald* states of Somerled's fatal campaign: 'his own people assert that it was not to make war against the king that he went on that expedition, but to obtain peace, for he did more in subduing the king's enemies than any war he waged against him',[43] thus implying that Somerled was guiltless of 'wicked rebellion'[44] and was merely trying to defend himself against a rival, and upstart, kindred, namely the Stewarts. In the mind of the Gael crown loyalty was not incompatible with hostility towards crown servants; for centuries he would nurture the notion that if he could obtain the ear of the king all would be well.[45] Somerled's efforts were in vain since within a generation of his death Bute had passed into Stewart hands.[46]

By the point at which the Hebrideans are first noted in *Hakon's Saga* the last of Somerled's sons had been killed. Angus with three of his own sons was slain in 1210, a year of 'warfare in the Hebrides', reinforced by a bunch of disaffected Norwegians anachronistically embarking upon a Viking expedition,[47] though doubtless compounded because members of the MacSorley kindred were fighting with the claimants to Man as well as with one another. It is a possibility that the Reginald, *Konge aff Möen* who accompanied Godfrey, *Konge paa Manö* to seek reconciliation with the king of Norway during the first decade of the thirteenth century was Reginald, son of Somerled rather than Reginald,

THE MACSORLEYS

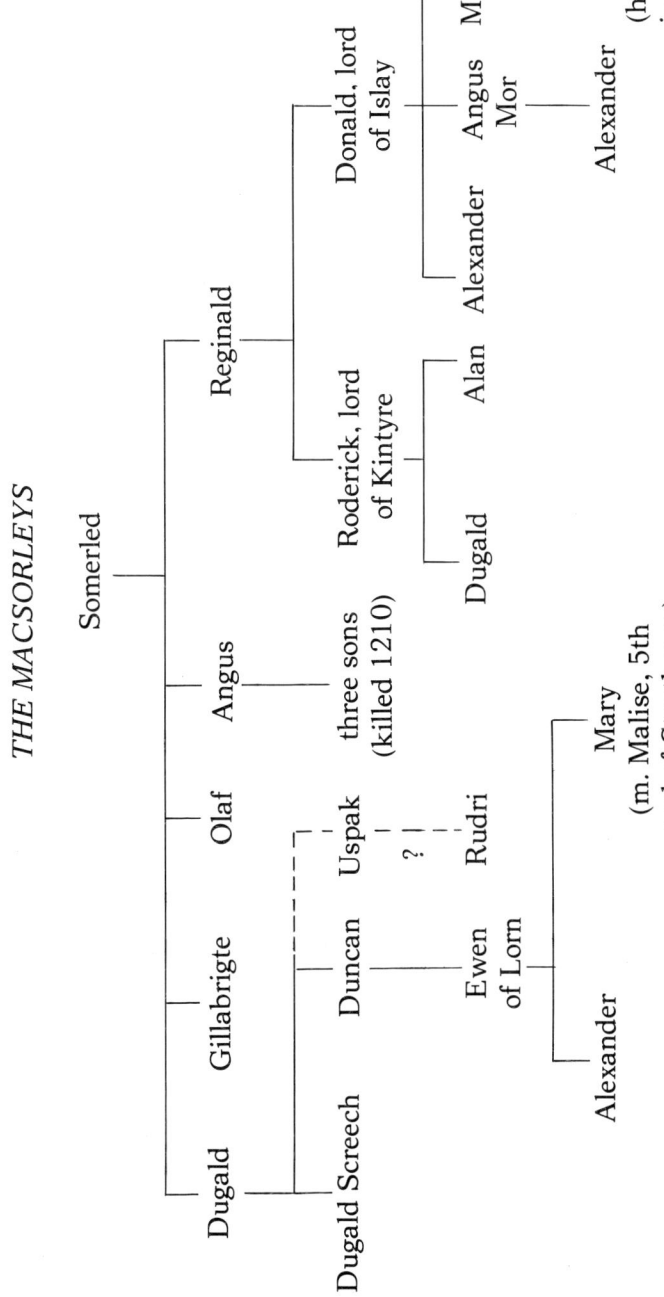

Note: According to Durham's *Liber Vitae*, Dugald son of Somerled had two other sons named Olaf and Ranald.

king of Man. If this was indeed the individual who endowed Saddell Abbey in Kintyre and who styled himself *dominus de Inchegal* in a grant to Paisley[48] he possibly disappeared in the strife of 1210. Two years later his sons, Roderick and Donald were plundering Derry alongside Thomas mac Uhtred of the Galloway family.[49]

Alexander II led an expedition to Argyll in 1221–2 which clearly resulted in the consolidation of his hold upon the area and the displacement of Roderick mac Somerled in Kintyre in favour of his brother Donald or possibly of Donald's sons.[50] The perception that Alexander was now poised to launch an attack on the Hebrides prompted the Hebridean delegation which appealed to Hakon in 1224 on 'the needs of their lands'. Hakon had more than enough distractions in his own kingdom during the next few years, but he was forced to act in 1228–9 when he received reports that Alan of Galloway, 'the greatest warrior in that time', was harrying Man and the Isles. Even more disconcerting was the news that the MacSorleys had seized the opportunity to prove 'unfaithful to Hakon'. Specifically mentioned were Dugald Screech and Duncan, the grandsons of Somerled. The saga mentions a third brother, Uspak, and another kinsman named Somerled; all four were exploiting the situation to their own advantage.[51] Alan maintained such pressure throughout the year that Olaf of Man was driven to seek help at the Norwegian court reporting Alan's proud boast that it was as easy to cross from Scotland to Norway as in the opposite direction, though as the saga drily remarks, *en þat var maelt, eigi gört* — 'that was said not done'.[52] Hakon had, in any case, anticipated Olaf's plight by despatching Uspak, royally favoured with the name Uspak-Hakon, to the west. The *Chronicle of Man*, an often confused source, confusingly calls this individual Uspak son of Ogmund. If this information is disregarded, there is no reason why Dugald mac Somerled could not have had a son named Uspak. Somerled himself bore a Scandinavian name. On the other hand name changes are not uncommon in the sagas; since this individual spent some considerable time in Norway he could have acquired a new name there even if he had a different title in the Hebrides. Hakon would hardly have taken the chance of alienating the MacSorleys if Uspak did not have some blood claim to the kingship of the Isles which all would recognise. Noteworthy is the information provided by Sturla that the Norwegians who accompanied Uspak did not trust the Hebrideans, shrewdly refusing, as would anyone with a shred of common sense in a Hebridean context during the next half millennium, an invitation to a feast. In due course the Norwegians fell upon the MacSorleys though Uspak was not involved; Somerled was killed and Dugald placed in fetters while Duncan, who enjoyed Uspak's protection, was allowed to escape. The force went on, significantly, to attack Bute, though success in winning the Stewart stronghold was clouded by Uspak's subsequent death.[53]

Sturla's account appears to infer that the MacSorleys, Uspak apart, were supporting Alan of Galloway who was doubtless acting at the prompting of King Alexander. When Alan died in 1234 the impetus went out of Scottish designs on the Hebrides, though if the grandfather of the future Robert I is to be believed Alexander was planning a Hebridean campaign in 1238.[54] Instead the king resorted to diplomatic missions throughout the 1240s, further alienating Hakon with each successive offer. Although the endemic problems of the kingdom of Man continued to surface from time to time the silence of saga and chronicle alike would suggest a period of almost twenty years of comparative peace in the Hebrides. When next the saga parts Atlantic mists it reveals a new generation of MacSorleys. 1248 found Ewen, or John, of Lorn and Dugald mac Roderick in Bergen, to request the kingship of the north isles (of the Hebrides) from King Hakon. Following the tragic drowning of Harald of Man and his young bride Cecilia, daughter of Hakon, off the coast of Shetland, Hakon granted Ewen the title; a year later Dugald was similarly favoured on the well tested Norwegian monarchical principle of divide and dominate. Harald's accident could not have happened at a better time so far as the MacSorleys were concerned. By marrying his daughter to the king of Man Hakon was surely signifying a strong presence in the islands and indicating that he would tolerate no further nonsense from Somerled's descendants. Ewen, based at Dunstaffnage, held territories extending as far as the Treshnish Islands; Dugald can reasonably be dubbed lord of Garmoran while the sons of Donald mac Reginald can be described as the Islay branch of the kindred.[55] As indicated above, Donald's brood also held lands of the king of Scots in Kintyre. However, unfolding developments were to demonstrate that while divided territories, or even titles, might favour monarchs, divided allegiances do not.

In preparation for what would prove his final assault on the Hebrides Alexander demanded a meeting with Ewen who agreed only on condition that four Scottish earls would pledge for his safety. The king insisted that Ewen surrender Cairnburg in the Treshnish Islands and three other castles which he held from King Hakon in return for 'a far greater realm in Scotland and along with it his support and friendship'. When

Ewen refused to break his allegiance to Hakon he was angrily informed that no man could serve two masters, to which he retorted that he could if the two were not enemies.[56] Both *Hakon's Saga* and the *Chronica* of Matthew Paris coincide in depicting Alexander II as the unjust aggressor in 1249. Matthew, hardly an unbiased commentator at best, had actually visited Norway the previous year when he could well have met Ewen, thus colouring his view of events.[57] He portrays Alexander as a wise, modest and peaceful ruler who went off the rails at the end by attempting to disinherit 'an innocent man', Ewen of Lorn. By this unjust act the king displayed a perversity 'whereby he incurred the displeasure of God and of St Columba'; in short he died at Kerrera.[58]

Hakon's Saga preserves Alexander's dream on the eve of his death and this may well represent genuine Hebridean tradition.

> When king Alexander lay in Kerrera Sound, he dreamed a dream: and he thought that three men came to him. He thought that one wore royal apparel; this man was very frowning and red-faced and stout in figure. The second man seemed to him tall, and slender, and youthful; the fairest of men, and nobly dressed. The third was by far the largest in figure, and the most frowning, of them all. He was very bald in front. He spoke to the king and asked whether he intended to go plundering in the Hebrides. He thought he answered that such was certain. The dream-man bade him turn back, and said to him that they would not hear of anything else.

> The king told his dream; and men begged him to turn back, but he would not do that. And a short time after he fell ill and died . . . The Hebrideans say that these men who appeared to the king in his sleep must have been St Olaf, king of Norway; and St Magnus Earl of Orkney; and St Columba.[59]

The message was clearly, 'woe unto those who attack St Columba', and Alexander II ignored the portents at his peril. More importantly the message of the dream medium is that the king of Scots is the one causing strife in the Western Isles.

Innocent or otherwise Ewen was severely weakened by Alexander's campaign. On his deathbed the king granted the church of St Bride, in the heart of Lorn, to the see of Argyll. The charter, significantly, was witnessed by Clement, bishop of Dunblane.[60] Matthew Paris claimed that Alexander had acted against Ewen through 'the vehement promptings of a certain indiscreet bishop of Strathearn'. That same Clement had been entrusted with filling the vacant see of Argyll, an action which Ewen may be presumed to have blocked,[61] for the very good reason that the church militant fully supported royal interference.

Contemporaneously the church was taking exactly the same stance in Iceland; it clearly favoured the suppression of the independent Atlantic lordships. Just as Clement urged Alexander against Ewen, the Norwegian bishops supported Hakon against the Icelanders. Even more disastrous from Ewen's point of view were the secular consequences; a royal bailiff in Argyll is on record in 1250.[62] That same year Ewen attempted to force his claim as king of the Isles upon Man while 1253 found him associated with Hakon, campaigning against Denmark.[63] Both activities presumably indicate displacement from his mainland Scottish territories. He was restored to his lordship, and as it turned out, to his Scottish allegiance, by the coup of 1255, thus deriving permanent advantage from the demise of the Comyns. Ewen, in common with the rest of the disaffected baronage, was to enter Alexander's peace by making reparation to Henry III of England or, alternatively, in the event of invasion by a foreign prince. As has been indicated,[64] that foreign prince could have been none other than King Hakon who was thus widely believed to be preparing for retaliatory action against the Scottish crown. Ewen essentially entered the protection of the English king in what should perhaps be regarded as the first of a series of alliances between the lords of the Isles and English monarchs which would persist through the fourteenth century and the treaty of Westminster-Ardtornish. He paid a hefty annual-rent for his lands while he enjoyed the surety of powerful magnates such as Mar, Fife and Strathearn.[65]

When Alexander III effectively adopted the reins of power following the death of Walter Comyn, earl of Menteith, in 1258[66] he thus inherited a legacy of Norwegian hostility. Diplomatic overtures were once again attempted when an unnamed archdeacon and a knight whom Sturla calls Sir Missel, were despatched to Bergen. They put to sea shortly after their arrival and were forcibly taken back to spend the winter in Norway because their behaviour had been incompatible with that of envoys.[67] Professor Duncan has suggested that the unusual Missel should be read as 'Frisel' which would make that individual a Fraser,[68] but it is possible that the Norwegian form of the name resulted in metathesis from Malise. The powerful Strathearn family perhaps even supplies a possible candidate for ambassador Missel in Malise, laird of Rossie, who is known to have been knighted before 1247 and who was the sixth son of Earl Gilbert.[69] Whoever he was, Sir Missel was adequately compensated for his unplanned residence in Norway, by attending the spectacular coronation of Hakon's son, Magnus. After the failure of the embassy Alexander followed his father's practice by initiating raids on Skye, led on this occasion by the earl of Ross and Kiarnak Makamal's son,[70] an action which Hakon interpreted as a declaration of intent to take over the whole of the Hebrides. Hakon's response was to summon levies and provisions for the summer of 1263 'to avenge the warfare that the Scots had made on his dominions'.[71]

In a most interesting document of November 15, 1262 Henry III acknowledged receipt of a recent letter from Hakon and thanked him for liberating the two Scots envoys. Henry was satisfied that Hakon did not intend to invade Scotland or to excite war, the English king declaring that he recommended peace between the two powers and that he had requested Alexander to make amends for any injuries done to Hakon.[72] According to Powicke, Henry, as late as 1263, was trying to dissuade Alexander from undertaking an expedition to the Isles,[73] which suggests that Henry believed Hakon's assurances of peaceful intentions. Brøgger thought that Ross's attack on Skye was in unfortunate contrast to the friendly negotiations carried on through Henry III,[74] but this is to miss the point. Henry was clearly concerned to maintain what little remained of his rapidly evaporating influence upon Alexander and the kingdom of the Scots. It might even be suspected that Henry and his advisors were sufficiently devious to be wilfully blind to the implications of the situation in 1263. When the arrival of Hakon's fleet in the Outer Isles was reported it was claimed that it was not known where it was bound,[75] a matter of which few Scots could have been in doubt; it is not impossible that Henry harboured some notion that Scotland's defeat might prove England's opportunity.[76] Alexander may not have fully realised the danger in which he was potentially placing his kingdom by tempting the wrath of Hakon but he enjoyed the inestimable boon of youth and the physical advantage of the North Sea. If Hakon was to hold the Isles he must come to Alexander.

Meanwhile Alexander took steps to defend his kingdom; the thoroughness of his preparations is impressive. The castle at New Ayr was refortified and weapons were deposited there although the burgesses of Ayr refused to garrison the castle and soldiers had to be hired to replace them. Compensation was paid to those whose cattle were taken to feed the garrison. There is an account for the building of two galleys and for the manufacture of oars. Payments were made to those who guarded the ships for twenty-three weeks as well as to spies who followed the movements of the Norwegian fleet. Although Alexander evidently anticipated an attack on the Stewart lordship he could not be certain of where Hakon would land and thus took the precaution of also fortifying Wigtown, Inverness and Stirling as well as Inverurie where a garrison was maintained for six months, payment once again being made for cattle. Hostages were taken from Skye, Kintyre and Caithness.[77] Clearly a lengthy campaign was considered possible.

Two days' sailing brought Hakon's mighty fleet to Shetland where he lay in Bressay Sound for two weeks.[78] When he arrived in Orkney he received unwelcome reports that Ewen of Lorn had repudiated his allegiance and had turned to the king of Scots but Hakon 'would not believe that before he had proved it'. It was August before the fleet reached Skye where Hakon was joined by King Magnus of Man and King Dugald of the Isles. The latter had foiled yet another planned Scottish expedition to the Isles in the summer of 1263 by spreading the news that the arrival of the Norwegian fleet was imminent. Knowing of Ewen's change of heart he presumably had already determined to fix his colours to the Norwegian mast. Alternatively he may have been genuinely persuaded that the future lay with Hakon:

> Terror went forth from the steerer of brine-deer
> All over the wave-washed shores of the west,
> At which time those outlawed unruly chieftains
> Brought to king Hakon, the queller of robbers,
> Their helmeted heads, as a token of peace,
> Bowing before him and doing him homage.

From Skye the entire fleet, now some one hundred and twenty ships strong, proceeded to Kerrera. From there a detachment of fifty ships under the command of Magnus and Dugald was despatched to harry Tarbert in Kintyre with the objective, clearly, of securing the allegiance of Angus Mór and Murchaid, the sons of Donald of Islay. This branch of the MacSorley kindred had displayed leanings towards the Scots ever since Alexander II's campaign of 1222. In the 1240s Angus granted the church of Kilkerran in Kintyre to Paisley 'for the salvation of the soul of my lord Alexander, illustrious king of Scots'; among the witnesses was Robert Bruce, earl of Carrick. One further indication of Angus's pro-Scottish tendency was that he named his eldest son Alexander.[79] That his loyalty was not above question is signified by the bond of the barons of Argyll in 1256 promising loyalty in the event that the lord of Islay should change his allegiance.[80] That same year Henry III ordered his bailiffs in Ireland to refrain from receiving Angus 'or other malefactors of the kingdom of Scotland' for a period of seven years, a mandate reinforced in 1260.[81] That Alexander III doubted Kintyre loyalty is attested by his taking of hostages from the area. The sheriff of Forfar expended twenty-one shillings for the maintenance of the son of Murchaid for twenty four weeks, while the sheriff of Ayr for six months supported the son of Angus together with his nurse and a female attendant.[82] The Kintyre raiding party experienced fierce resistance before Murchaid (Margrad in the saga), soon followed by Angus, submitted to Hakon who promised to seek atonement for their action in the event of a settlement with the Scots. The Kintyre men were in a wretched situation and provide a neat illustration of the perils of split allegiance. They had to provide Hakon with hostages and, despite swearing allegiance to him, a fine of one thousand cattle was levied from their estates. Angus surrendered Islay in return for a regrant:

> To the serpent's treasure spoiler,
> To Hakon squanderer of gold,
> Angus surrendered the isle of Islay
> As plunder to the warlike king.

The castle of Dunaverty, at the south end of Kintyre, was also surrendered to Hakon by a nameless individual who may have been yet another MacSorley.

According to Sturla many of the Hebridean chiefs 'did Hakon a bad turn in this business'. Not the least of these was Ewen of Lorn who attended the king at Gigha to proclaim his adherence to Alexander from whom he held 'a greater realm' than he did from Hakon; he begged Hakon to grant his Hebridean holdings to someone else. Hakon detained Ewen, attempting to sway his allegiance, until the fleet reached Holy Island in Arran. There the two parted on good terms, Ewen, the recipient of royal gifts, promising to exert his best efforts to secure peace between the two kings and to visit Hakon if required to do so. Ewen, however, was now irrevocably committed to the Scottish cause.

From Kerrera Hakon had also sent fifteen ships to attack Bute. Accompanying this force was 'a ship-captain whose name was Rudri — he was thought to have a claim to Bute'. For earlier raids on the island he had been outlawed by the king of Scots. He and his two brothers swore allegiance to Hakon. After the castle on Bute had surrendered Rudri viciously slaughtered nine of the garrison and he went on the rampage on the mainland. Rudri's pedigree is not recorded, though the plausible suggestion that he could have been a son of Uspak, the conqueror of Bute in 1230, is attractive.[83] If so he exploited the situation in 1263 to settle private scores.

The first overtures for negotiation came from the Scots while Hakon lay off Arran, but a series of ambassadorial exchanges achieved nothing: the Scots 'spun out matters more and more and set their faces against the making of peace at all; for the summer was passing away and the weather was taking a turn for the worse'. Hakon offered the final option of serious negotiation or the alternative of battle, at the prospect of which latter, Alexander declared himself undaunted.

Hakon's response appears inexplicable unless he was attempting to draw part of Alexander's force away from the vicinity of Ayr to the east of Scotland. He sent sixty ships — half of his fleet — up Loch Long and across the portage at Arrochar to harry the shores of Loch Lomond. The detachment was commanded by Magnus of Man, king Dugald and his brother Alan, and by Angus and Murchaid. They wasted the 'well-tilled' islands of the loch and burned the whole district around it. Sturla was impressed as they

> Drew boats over dry land
> For many a length;
> Those warriors undaunted
> They wasted with war-gales
> The islands thick-peopled
> On Lomond's broad loch.

Alan penetrated *mjök um pvert Skotland ok drap Margan mann* — 'almost across Scotland and slew many men'. An item in the exchequer rolls suggests that Alan was resisted from Stirling Castle — *in expensis hominium vigilancium in castro tempore quo rex Norvegie fuit in partibus istis xxxv s. vi d.* In addition to the sum paid for lookouts at the time the king of Norway was in the area, fourteen shillings and eightpence was expended upon the cleaning of weapons.[84] Norwegian and Scottish enterprise was indeed impressive.

The Loch Lomond episode perhaps provides a key of a kind to the entire expedition. By raiding the area, as the saga says, the force was wasting the territories of the earldom of Lennox; it omits to mention the equally salient point that by venturing further east the pillagers were encroaching upon the earldom of Menteith. Walter Comyn, earl of Menteith was the single most powerful noble in Scotland in the period 1249–58.[85] He was succeeded in the earldom by the son of Walter the Steward of Scotland, also Walter, who in 1263 was sheriff of Ayr.

Maldowen of Lennox had married Elizabeth, daughter of Walter the Steward and was thus a brother-in-law of Walter Stewart, earl of Menteith.[86] Throughout the abortive diplomatic negotiations of 1263 Alexander III refused to discuss the disposition of Bute, Arran and the Cumbraes, which were almost certainly in Stewart hands. The struggle against the Stewart lordship initiated by Somerled was thus still very much in progress.

Stewart tentacles, however, were also being fastened upon the area west of the Clyde estuary. Walter the Steward and Malcolm, son of the earl of Lennox, witnessed a grant of lands in Glassary to Paisley.[87] In 1262 Walter, earl of Menteith confirmed a charter granting to Paisley the patronage of St Colmanel and the chapel of St Columba near Skipness Castle.[88] The Stewarts were thus consolidating their hold upon Kintyre and Knapdale, perhaps compounding rights anciently enjoyed by the earls of Menteith over Cowal and Kintyre.[89] Somerled's perception that the Stewarts constituted the spearhead of crown advances against the Gaelic west had thus been considerably reinforced by 1263 and, in the event, Hakon's forces not only concentrated upon the old Stewart heartland but also directed their attention towards the islands of the Clyde as well as the Kintyre peninsula and, if the suggestion be accepted, towards the Stewart earldom of Menteith and its close ally, the earldom of Lennox. The Stewarts, furthermore, appear to have been closely allied to the powerful Strathearn family whose earldom neighboured Menteith. Ewen of Lorn was merely acknowledging political reality when he married his daughter, Mary to Malise, fifth earl of Strathearn.[90] If the finer nuances of these subtle, and not so subtle, relationships escaped Hakon, there can be little doubt that Dugald, Alan, Angus and Murchaid knew exactly what they were doing when they carried their torches east of Loch Lomond.

The equinoctial storms of the dying days of September created havoc with Norwegian ships in Loch Long as well as with those in the Firth of Clyde. The engagement at Largs on October 2 decided nothing. Afterwards Hakon remained a few nights at Lamlash before beginning a leisurely progress northwards through the Isles. At Kerrera he rewarded the faithful. He granted the lands of Ewen to Dugald and Alan, to Rudri he allotted Bute and to Murchaid, Arran; Angus already enjoyed the possession of Islay. The last beams of the Norwegian sunset bathed the MacSorleys in their fading light while Hakon returned to Orkney and his deathbed.

Sturla reported that in the expedition of 1263 Hakon achieved all that he had set out to do, but it is quite evident from his account that the campaign was a failure. 'During the summer the king had many sleepless nights and much anxiety; he was often put upon and had little peace from his men'.[91] Almost everything he advocated was rejected by his followers from the sensible suggestion that he divide his force in Orkney in order to send part of his fleet to attack the Moray Firth area, to the question of accepting the invitation of Irish envoys to winter in the Emerald Isle, and the final return to Norway of a large part of the fleet without the king or his express permission. The season was already late before the expedition was under way and then it was plagued by delay. The ruthlessness and single-mindedness requisite for any medieval king were not apparent. His treatment of Ewen of Lorn was incomprehensibly mild. When, on the return voyage, nine defenceless Norwegians were slaughtered by the Caithness men, he set free the hostages who should have suffered death as instant retaliation. Earlier in his career he had brought Denmark and Sweden to heel by a strong show of force in the shape of an awesome armada appearing off their respective coasts; if he planned a similar impression and consequence in Scotland, he miscalculated. If many of Hakon's actions and responses appear attractive it must not be forgotten that he had himself been raised in a hard school and much of his behaviour in 1263 would appear out of character. Indeed it would not be difficult to believe that throughout the campaign Hakon was already suffering from the disease which was to kill him in Orkney. In this section of the saga we may suspect that Sturla enjoyed sweet revenge upon the king who had been his enemy throughout most of his life. In the Hebrides Hakon suffered the first real setback of a spectacular career.

There is no need to rehearse here the negotiations which culminated in the treaty of Perth of 1266.[92] Yet viewed in the wider context Hakon's defeat was even more momentous. Hakon the Old was the successor to Sverre, the greatest absolutist hitherto known to Norway. Sverre was in many ways a remarkable king who fought his way to the Norwegian throne from obscure origins in the Faeroes. During his reign there was an ecclesiastical crisis in the course of which he elevated the divine right of kingship against an ever more aggressive church. Sverre in his own saga which he commissioned, and in a remarkable document known as the *anecdoton Sverreri*, was concerned to define the powers of monarchy. The following quotation, from the latter document, refers specifically to immediate trouble with the clergy, but the secular implications are inescapable:

It is a great charge and special command that all Christian men be taught to be faithful and obedient to the rulers of the world. Let not men think that they may easily be released from what an earthly king ordains. Who is so great a man that he will not render full homage to his king, when the very Son of God, paid tribute, and rendered full homage to an earthly king . . . The salvation of a man's soul is at stake when he does not observe complete loyalty, kingly worship, and a right obedience; for kingly rule is created by God's command, and not after man's ordinance, and no man obtains kingly rule except by divine dispensation. A king would not be more powerful or mightier than others if God had not set him higher than others in His service; for in his kingly rule he serves God and not himself.[93]

Hakon co-operated with the church in advancing his own claims in Iceland. It was said that 'there would be better peace in that country if one man had most power'.[94] In 1247 Cardinal William thought it unjust 'that Iceland was not subject to some king like all the others in the world',[95] ominous words indeed for the Icelanders. But if Hakon was not above exploiting ecclesiastical support for his own purposes, he was as anxious as Sverre had been in his famous address to teach the church its place. The *King's Mirror*, which was written in the 1240s, spells this out:

(The king) is so highly honoured and exalted upon earth that all must bend and bow before him as before God. So great is his power that he may dispose as he likes of the lives of all who live in his kingdom; he lets him live whom he wills and causes him to be slain he wills.[96]

There is much further discussion of the point in the tract just as ecclesiastical affairs take up a great deal of space in *Hakon's Saga*. Hakon was an absolutist, and a very successful one, up until the setback in the Firth of Clyde. No kings in the Middle Ages were permitted to alienate any part of their kingdoms;[97] absolutists did not for a moment consider the remote possibility. The treaty of Perth is unthinkable if Hakon had lived. Even so it was a bitter blow and an adequate symbol of Norway's setting sun. The matter still rankled in 1281, for when Eric of Norway married Alexander's daughter, Margaret he paid 14,000 marks 'principally for the sake of the marriage contract (i.e. as dowry), but accessorily in order to buy back his rights to the islands'.[98]

The two Alexanders were as intent as was Hakon upon the creation of a strong centralised monarchy. The point has been strangely overlooked, but in their eyes the rulers of the Hebrides were themselves experiencing something of a golden age in the first half of the thirteenth century. The evidence survives in the fabric of the astounding distribution of early stone castles in the area so helpfully mapped and described by the Royal Commission on Ancient and Historical Monuments of Scotland. If more ecclesiastical evidence had survived the testimony of the stones might be even more impressive than it is. Of castles which fell within the MacSorley lordships the following were all in existence by 1263 and the fabric survives to prove it — Dunstaffnage, Dunollie, Achadun, Castle Coeffin, Cairnburg, Duart, Ardtornish, Aros, Castle Tioram, Mingarry and Dunaverty. Other early castles are Skipness, Tarbert, Caisteal na Nighinn Ruaidhe (Kilmelford), Fraoch Eilean (Loch Awe), Innis Chonnell, Castle Rarey, Castle Sween, Dunoon and Duntrune. Many others such as Dunyveg and Dunakin should almost certainly be added to the list. There is also a respectable amount of ecclesiastical architecture surviving from the period.[99] Just how this energetic tradition in castle building developed will probably never be known, but the surviving evidence clearly reflects the wealth of the islands and the west coast. It is worth recalling that right through until the reign of James VI, contrary to modern preconceptions, the area embraced by the Hebrides was considered to be wealthy.[100] Quite apart from the military threat posed by the castles, MacSorley power must have appeared from the perspective of the Alexanders to have been much more monolithic than in fact it was. The prospect was looming of a self-sustaining kingdom, well defended and well provided, extending all the way from Man to the Butt of Lewis and encompassing a considerable chunk of the western seaboard. The lords of the Isles could be perceived as embodying a threat to the very kingdom of Scotland.

A recent study[101] finds that absolutism, despotism or tyranny develop as monarchs attempt to destroy the kinship system. So central is this idea to the numerous societies which the author surveys that he is able to assert that 'so close was the connection between the breakdown of the kinship system and the rise of the state that the state may be defined as that form of society in which non-kinship forms of social cohesion are as important as kinship forms'.[102] Alexander III and Hakon of Norway may thus be seen, in the last resort, to have been engaged upon a similar, possibly an identical, enterprise, in attempting to tame the Hebrideans. Norway's advantage is indicated by *Hakon's Saga* when Sir Missel attends the coronation of king Magnus in 1261. 'During the mass, the knight Missel stood above in the choir and wondered greatly at the proceeding of the consecration: because it is not the custom to crown kings in Scotland'.[103] This was the sad reality faced by Alexander III, yet the evidence, such as it is, suggests that the absence of unction did not deter him. In launching his attacks upon the Hebrides, Alexander conformed to the modern model of crown versus kin, as well as to the pattern of kingship described by Snorri Sturluson in *Heimskringla*.

The campaign of 1263 and the subsequent cession of the Isles in the treaty of Perth thus have a significance which transcends their own decade. It could be contended that Alexander's victory drove the first great nail into the coffin of the western *Gaidhealtachd*, that it was a significant part of the inexorable historical process which would persist through the reigns of the later Stewarts to the aftermath of the Jacobite risings and the Clearances. As Sir James Fergusson observed, Alexander II 'was the last Scottish king against whose power . . . regions of the country tried to assert their independence'.[104] Despite the well-attested, and with hindsight the ironic, fact that a Gaelic speaking *seanachaidh* graced his inauguration ceremony, Alexander III was perhaps the first Scottish king to launch a successful offensive against one considerable section of his Gaelic subjects. Although his father had anticipated him in this endeavour Alexander was certainly not the last Scottish monarch to pursue this particular enterprise. If the campaign of 1263 did indeed launch a golden age then the victory was qualified and the tarnish was on the gold. History was to demonstrate that in acquiring the Hebrides Scotland had created her Afghanistan.

NOTES

1. A. W. Brøgger, *Ancient Emigrants: A History of the Norse Settlements of Scotland* (Oxford, 1929; henceforth, Brøgger, *Ancient Emigrants*), 177.
2. *Icelandic Sagas* (Rolls Series, 4 vols., 1887–1894), ii (Icelandic Text): *Hakonar Saga and a Fragment of Magnus Saga with appendices*, ed. Gudbrand Vigfusson (London, 1887); in translation, *HS*. Both texts have been consulted throughout. Dasent's translation leaves much to be desired and I have modified it in many places. *HS*, 344.
3. *The Collected Poems of John Galt 1779–1839*, ed. Hamilton B. Timothy (London, Ontario, 1969, 1982), i, 1–28. Galt's effusion was written in 1804 but he sensibly suppressed its publication. He must have based his poem on the ground-breaking translation by Rev. James Johnstone, *The Norwegian Account of Haco's Expedition Against Scotland A.D. MCCLXIII* (Copenhagen, 1782). On Johnstone, and Galt's context see

Edward J. Cowan, 'Icelandic Studies in Eighteenth and Nineteenth Century Scotland' (henceforth Cowan, 'Icelandic Studies'), *Studia Islandica*, xxxi (Reykjavik, 1972), 109–51. Galt claimed that his poem was inspired by John Pinkerton, *A Dissertation on the Origin and Progress of the Scythians or Goths* (London, 1787) and by Bishop Percy's translation of Paul Henri Mallett, *Introduction a l'histoire de Dannemarc* (Copenhagen, 1755), which appeared in English in 1770. See J. Galt, *Autobiography* (London, 1833), 56–58.

4. A. A. M. Duncan and A. L. Brown, 'Argyll and the Isles in the Earlier Middle Ages' (henceforth Duncan and Brown, 'Argyll and the Isles'), *PSAS*, xc (1959), 190–220. See also Duncan, *Kingdom*, 576–83; Barrow, *Kingship and Unity*, 115–21. See also *Orkney Miscellany*, v (Kirkwall, 1973) *King Hakon Commemorative Number*, for articles by Knut Helle, E. F. Halvorsen, Per Sveaas Anderson, Eric Linklater and Hermann Pálsson; Knut Helle, 'Trade and Shipping Between Norway and England in the Reign of Hakon Hakonsson', *Sjofartshistorisk Arbok* (Bergen, 1967) and three articles by Narve Bjorgo: 'Skaldekveda; Hakonar Saga', *Maal og Minne* (1967), 'Hakon Hakonssons ettermaele', *Syn og Segn* (1968) and 'Hakonar Saga og Boglunga Sogur', *Maal og Minne* (1968). Magnus Magnusson, *Hakon the Old — Hakon Who?* (Largs and District Historical Society, 1982) is disappointing. While a title such as 'The Old and the Who' might be thought neatly to encapsulate much modern television programming it does not make for good history. To be fair, however, Magnusson is one of the few popular or academic writers who has tried to allocate due space to Scotland — see *Viking Expansion Westwards* (London, 1979), ch. 2, and *Vikings* (London, 1980), 248–66.

5. See *The Norwegian Invasion of Scotland in 1263: A Translation from Det Norske Folks Historie by P. A. Munch* (Glasgow, 1862).

6. Watt, 'Minority'.

7. Aslak Liestol, 'Runes', in *The Northern and the Western Isles in the Viking World*, edd. Alexander Fenton and Hermann Pálsson (Edinburgh, 1984; henceforth Fenton and Pálsson, *Isles*), 237.

8. Einar Ol. Sveinsson, *The Age of the Sturlungs: Icelandic Civilization in the Thirteenth Century: Islandica,* xxxvi (Ithaca, 1953); Jon Johanneson, *A History of the Old Icelandic Commonwealth* (University of Manitoba, 1974), 'The Death Throes of the Commonwealth', 222–87.

9. *Sturlunga Saga*, trans. Julia H. McGrew (New York, 1970, 1974; henceforth *Sturlunga Saga*). See the useful introductions in both volumes.

10. Paul Schach, *Icelandic Sagas* (Boston, 1984), 124. For an excellent translation which does justice to this great saga see *Grettir's Saga*, trans. Denton Fox and Hermann Pálsson (Toronto, 1974).

11. For this and what follows see *Sturlunga Saga*, ii, 489 ff..

12. This is one of the very few references in the saga literature on how long it might have taken to recite a saga. For a discussion of this passage see Carol J. Glover, *The Medieval Saga* (Ithaca and London, 1982), 194–5 and nn..

13. This conflicts with Vigfusson's dating which seems to imply that Sturla knew of Hakon's death before he began to compose the saga (*HS*, ii, pp. ix–x).

14. *HS*, 282.

15. The role of patronage in Icelandic literature deserves further investigation, but see A. B. Taylor, 'Orkneyinga Saga: Patronage and Authorship', in *Proceedings of the First International Saga Conference*, edd. P. G. Foote, H. Pálsson and D. Slay (London, 1973), 396–410.

16. These and other points are highlighted by Hermann Pálsson in 'Hakonar Saga: Portrait of a King' in *Orkney Miscellany*, v (1973), 49–56.

17. *King Harald's Saga*, trans. Magnus Magnusson and Hermann Pálsson (Harmondsworth, 1966), 120.

18. *HS*, 366–7.

19. Ibid., 78–80.

20. Ibid., 89–90.

21. They continued to be so regarded. References to 'Norwegians in the Hebrides' in English royal correspondence are to persons who could just as well be described as Hebrideans. See, e.g., Brøgger, *Ancient Emigrants*, 169 n..

22. *HS*, 277, 314, 317, 338.

23. Ibid., 334.

24. *Islensk Fornrit, Islendingabok Landnamabok*, ed. Jacob Benediktsson (2 vols, Reykjavik, 1968), i, pp. lxxx–lxxxi. Sturla Thordarsson also produced a version of Landnamabok — the *Sturlubok*. For an English translation see *The Book of Settlements — Landnamabok*, trans. Hermann Pálsson and Paul Edwards (University of Manitoba, 1972).

25. Alfred P. Smyth, *Warlords and Holy Men: Scotland A.D. 80–1000* (London, 1984), 170–4.

26. See William Sayers, 'Kjartan's Choice: The Irish Disconnection in the Sagas of Icelanders', *Journal of Scandinavian Canadian Studies*, iii (1988), 89–114.

27. *The King's Mirror*, trans. L. M. Larson (New York, 1917; henceforth *King's Mirror*), 199. Text: *Konge Speilet*, edd. R. Keyser, P. A. Munch, C. R. Unger (Christiana, 1848).

28. Edward J. Cowan, 'Caithness in the Sagas', in *Caithness: A Cultural Crossroads*, ed. John R. Baldwin (Edinburgh, 1982), 25–44.

29. *Diplom. Norv.*, xix, 272, quoted in Brøgger, *Ancient Emigrants*, 169.

30. Edward J. Cowan, 'The Scottish Chronicle in the Poppleton Manuscript', *Innes Review*, xxxii (1981), 7. There appears to be a dearth of literature on Scottish treaties. The earliest surviving English treaty is that of Dover in 1101, though, as in the case of Scotland, the existence of earlier treaties can be inferred. See G. P. Cuttino, *English Medieval Diplomacy* (Bloomington, 1985), 3.

31. Snorri Sturluson, *Heimskringla: History of the Kings of Norway*, trans. Lee M. Hollander (Austin, 1967; henceforth *Heimskringla*), 681.

32. See now Rosemary Power, 'Magnus Barelegs' Expeditions to the West', *SHR*, lxv (1986), 107–32.

33. G. Turville-Petre, *Origins of Icelandic Literature* (Oxford, 1953), 169–75.

34. Ibid., 84–85; Svend Ellehoj, *Studier over den aeldste norrone historieskrivning* (Copenhagen, 1965).

35. R. Th. Christiansen, *The Vikings and the Viking Wars in Irish and Gaelic Tradition* (Oslo, 1931), passim.; Donald A. MacDonald, 'The Vikings in Gaelic Oral Tradition', in Fenton and Pálsson, *Isles*, 265–79.

36. Cowan, 'Icelandic Studies', 117.

37. *Heimskringla*, 675.

38. *Islensk Fornrit, Orkneyinga Saga*, ed. Finnbogi Gudmundsson (Reykjavik, 1965), 98; *Orkneyinga Saga: The History of the Earls of Orkney*, trans. H. Pálsson and P. Edwards (London, 1978), 80–81. On portage in the area see Hugh Cheape, 'Recounting Tradition: A Critical View of Medieval Reportage' (henceforth Cheape, 'Recounting Tradition'), in Fenton and Pálsson, *Isles*, 197–223. It is worth noting that in 1325 Robert Bruce cut a track at West Loch Tarbert to facilitate portage (Nicholson, *Scotland*, 113).

39. A. O. Johnsen, 'The Payments from the Hebrides and the Isle of Man to the Crown of Norway 1153–1263', *SHR*, xlviii (1969), is not entirely convincing.

40. *Book of Clanranald* (henceforth *Clanranald*), in Alexander Cameron, *Reliquiae Celticae: Texts Papers and Studies in Gaelic Literature and Philology*, edd. A. MacBain and J. Kennedy (Inverness, 1894), ii, 155. The *Book of Clanranald* is itself a kind of saga and is deserving of more serious consideration than that afforded it by Duncan and Brown, 'Argyll and the Isles'. Cf. Cheape, 'Recounting Tradition'.

41. *Chronicle of the Kings of Man and the Isles*, edd. George Broderick and Brian Stowell (Edinburgh, 1973; henceforth *Chron. Man* (Broderick and Stowell)), 18. The edition by P. A. Munch (Christiana, 1860), revised by Rev. Goss for the Manx Society (1874) has also been consulted throughout.

42. 'The Earliest Stewarts and Their Lands', in Barrow, *Kingdom*, 337–9; Barrow, *Anglo-Norman Era*, 64–70; Barrow and Royan, 'James Stewart', 167–8.

43. *Clanranald*, 155. Somerled's rebellion was piously regarded as an example of MacDonald treason in the 17th century. When that 'grand rebell Somerled . . . raised a great army of Islanders and others [and] made a horrible devastation over all the main land of this kingdome' the Campbells were to the fore in resisting him and in ensuring that he 'suffered due punishment at Glasgow for his proud treasonable attempts'! Letter of 1661 in which the Campbells, at that time themselves accused of treason, protest their loyalty to previous Scottish monarchs. *Letters to the Argyll Family* (Maitland Club, 1839), no. 36.

44. *Chronicle of Melrose*, in Anderson, *Early Sources*, ii, 254.

45. There are many examples of this attitude in the 16th. and 17th. centuries, Alasdair Macgregor of Glenstrae being one (Edward J. Cowan, 'Clanship, Kinship and the Campbell Acquisition of Islay', *SHR*, lviii (1979), 132–57, at 151.

46. Duncan and Brown, 'Argyll and the Isles', 195, 203; Barrow, *Anglo-Norman Era*, 68.
47. *Chron. Man* (Broderick and Stowell), 26; Anderson, *Early Sources*, ii, 378–93.
48. *RMS*, ii, no. 31760; *Paisley Registrum*, 125.
49. Anderson, *Early Sources*, ii, 393.
50. Duncan and Brown, 'Argyll and the Isles', 199–200.
51. *HS*, 150.
52. Ibid., 152.
53. Ibid., 152–3.
54. Barrow, *Bruce*, 42.
55. Duncan and Brown, 'Argyll and the Isles', 204–5.
56. Anderson, *Early Sources*, ii, 555–8.
57. Antonia Grandsen, *Historical Writing in England c. 550–c. 1307* (London, 1974), ch. 16 *passim*; Knut Helle, 'Anglo-Norwegian Relations in the Reign of Hakon Hakonsson (1217–63)', *Mediaeval Scandinavia*, i (1968), 109–11.
58. Matthew Paris, *Chron. Maj.*, quoted in Anderson, *Scottish Annals*, 360–1. Interestingly, *Chron. Melrose* states that Alexander died while on his way to 'pacify' the Isles (Anderson, *Early Sources*, ii, 558).
59. *HS*, 271; Anderson, *Early Sources*, ii, 556–7.
60. *RMS*, ii, no. 3136; Dowden, *Bishops*, 198.
61. Duncan and Brown, 'Argyll and the Isles', 208–10.
62. *Paisley Registrum*, 175.
63. *HS*, 286; *Chron. Man* (Broderick and Stowell), 42.
64. Duncan and Brown, 'Argyll and the Isles', 211–12.
65. Ibid., and n..
66. Young, 'Walter Comyn', 143.
67. *HS*, 307.
68. Duncan, *Kingdom*, 588 and n..
69. *Scots Peerage*, vi, 243. A Malise of Strathearn was named as one of the Scottish envoys to Norway in 1264 (*CDS*, i, no. 2373).
70. This is Kermac Macmaghan of *ER*, i, 19. He was the ancestor of the Mackenzies and the Mathesons: see William Matheson, 'Traditions of the Mackenzies', *TGSI*, xxxix–xl (1942–60), 193–228. According to *HS*, 340, the Scottish raiders on this occasion indulged in the sport of *gallcerd* (tossing babies upon spearpoints); the practice had originally been associated with the Vikings.
71. *HS*, 342.
72. *CDS*, i, no. 2320.
73. Maurice Powicke, *The Thirteenth Century 1216–1307* (Oxford, 1953), 591.
74. Brøgger, *Ancient Emigrants*, 169.
75. *CDS*, i, no. 2320.
76. No less an authority than Sir Maurice Powicke finds Henry's designs in Scotland 'mysterious' (*Thirteenth Century*, 591). It seems fairly obvious that he was intent upon the overlordship of Scotland but was thwarted

by a combination of the Scots, his problems in England and by Alexander himself.

77. *ER*, i, 5–6; Brøgger, *Ancient Emigrants*, 172–3.
78. Hakon's expedition may be traced in *HS*, 340–67; Anderson, *Early Sources*, ii, 607–42.
79. *Paisley Registrum*, 128–9.
80. *Foedera*, i, 336.
81. *CDS*, i, nos. 2041, 2185.
82. *ER*, i, 5.
83. Duncan and Brown, 'Argyll and the Isles', 203, n. 5.
84. *ER*, i, 24.
85. Young, 'Walter Comyn', *passim*.
86. Fraser, *Lennox*, i, p. li.
87. *Paisley Registrum*, 132.
88. Ibid., 121.
89. *APS*, i, 372.
90. *Scots Peerage*, vii, 245.
91. *HS*, 366.
92. This has already been expertly done by Richard Lustig, 'The Treaty of Perth: a Re-examination', *SHR*, lviii (1979), 35–57.
93. J. Sephton, *The Saga of King Sverri of Norway* (London, 1899), 249, 251.
94. *HS*, 164.
95. Ibid., 262.
96. *King's Mirror*, 236.
97. Peter N. Riesenberg, *Inalienability of Sovereignty in Medieval Political Thought* (New York, 1970), *passim*.
98. *Chronicle of Lanercost*, quoted in Anderson, *Early Sources*, ii, 680.
99. RCAHMS, *Argyll*, i, *Kintyre*, nos. 309, 310, 314, 316; ii, *Lorn*, nos. 276, 281, 282, 286, 287, 290, 292; iii, *Mull, Tiree, Coll and Northern Argyll*, nos. 332, 333, 335, 339, 345. See also J. G. Dunbar and A. A. M. Duncan, 'Tarbert Castle: A Contribution to the History of Argyll', *SHR*, 1 (1971), 1–17; W. Douglas Simpson, *Dunstaffnage Castle and the Stone of Destiny* (Edinburgh, 1961), esp. 19–21.
100. E.g. *Monroe's Western Isles of Scotland and Genealogies of the Clans 1549*, ed. R. W. Munro (Edinburgh, 1961), which stresses the fertility of the islands.
101. Eli Sagan, *At the Dawn of Tyranny: The Origins of Individualism, Political Oppression and the State* (New York, 1985).
102. Ibid., p. xx.
103. Anderson, *Early Sources*, ii, 604; *HS*, 331.
104. Fergusson, *Alexander III*, 12.

6

THE ARMY OF ALEXANDER III's SCOTLAND

Geoffrey Barrow

Five years before his sudden and unlooked for death in 1249, Alexander II mustered the army of his kingdom at Caddonlea near Galashiels (the customary rendezvous for a Scottish expeditionary force heading southward) and led it across the Border and through Northumberland as far as Ponteland.[1] Henry III had become alarmed at developments in Scotland since the death in 1238 of his sister Joan, queen of Scots. Alexander had not only married *en secondes noces* a French noblewoman, Marie de Couci, who had borne him an heir, the future Alexander III, in 1241; he had connived at the lawless activity in the Irish Sea of William Marsh (*de Marisco* — son of Geoffrey Marsh a former justiciar of Ireland), who had turned pirate, established a headquarters on Lundy and was preying on English shipping and finding refuge in Scottish harbours;[2] and he had permitted the building of two castles, Hermitage in Liddesdale, the work of Nicholas Soules, and Caerlaverock by the mouth of the Nith, built either by John Maxwell or his son Aymer Maxwell, an increase of the hitherto slight Border fortification which the English king regarded as needlessly aggressive and provocative.[3] Henry III and his former brother-in-law certainly seem to have been prepared for war in 1244, and when the Scots reached Ponteland about the middle of August only seven or eight miles separated them from the English king and his host assembled at Newcastle upon Tyne. But wiser counsels prevailed. The English king's brother, Richard of Cornwall, and the archbishop of York, Walter Gray, were among the great magnates, English and Scots, who persuaded the two kings to patch up their quarrel and dismiss their forces.[4] There had, after all, been no war between the two countries since 1216, and in the event the Anglo-Scottish peace was to endure for eighty years, a remarkable record for two realms which had often been mutually hostile in the past and would after 1296 be perpetually at odds till well through the sixteenth century.

Whatever prompted withdrawal on Alexander II's part in 1244 it was evidently not anxiety lest his army might prove insufficient. Not only had the Scots deliberately advanced some thirty-six miles into English territory, but we possess an eye-witness account of their troops via the pen of Matthew Paris, the St Albans historian, which proves that the English had genuine respect for their opponents.[5] A well loved and popular king (so runs this account) led an army consisting of a thousand *armati*, knights and men at arms — that is, 'professional' warriors mounted on trained horses and equipped with body armour and superior weapons, and one hundred thousand foot soldiers inspired by a common desire to defend their native land. The cavalry, it is true, did not possess horses of the Spanish, Italian or other exceptionally good breeds; and the total of infantry must be greatly exaggerated (perhaps fivefold?). Nevertheless, we need not doubt that the army with which Alexander II confronted Henry III in 1244 was, as Matthew Paris puts it, 'numerous and powerful' (*numerosus valde et fortis*).[6]

It is in no way surprising that Matthew Paris distinguishes between the Scots cavalry and infantry. Contrary to what may still be a lingering belief, the normal thirteenth-century army was a mixed force of horse and foot. What Matthew's account does not make clear is that in 1244 and, indeed, for another fifty years and more the Scots army was in effect two armies, on the one hand a body of knights and more lightly armed but nevertheless mounted soldiers, who performed their 'free service', 'knight service' (*liberum servitium, servitium militare*), in respect of their estates held explicitly for the service of knights or sergeands, on the other the 'common army' of the realm consisting of quotas of able-bodied men who were mustered compulsorily from the country as a whole, or from particular regions, on the basis of so many men from each basic unit of land assessment such as the ploughgate, davoch and ounceland.[7] Because of this fundamental dichotomy, the proportion of cavalry to infantry in Scotland was always likely to be lower than in a country such as England where, although the cavalry might render its service in response to strict feudal obligation, the infantry was likely to consist of whatever levies of local men the sheriffs and commissioners of array could muster and hold together by a mixture of threats and cajolery.[8]

While the essential duality of the Scots army, dating from the reign of David I, seems to have endured till the close of the thirteenth century, at least two converging forces were at work by the mid century which would have a reunifying effect, so that by c. 1300 the army would be more or less what it must have been two centuries earlier, a truly national force diversified by its weaponry and military skills rather than by its method of recruitment. In the first place, the concept of the king's forinsec service became homogenized. Whereas in the twelfth century and for much of the reign of Alexander II forinsec service in its military aspect had been synonymous with 'common army' or 'Scottish army' (or its equivalent south of Forth),[9] while knight service and serjeanty service were referred to separately, from the later thirteenth century we find record evidence of 'the forinsec service of one quarter of a knight' or the like[10] and even of knight service in the common army of the lord king.[11] What seems to have happened is that knight service was no longer thought of as exotic and uncommon; its chief characteristic was now merely the fact that it was owed away from the estate and must be performed for the king or the realm, not for the vassal's lord. It was, however, still distinguished from 'common army' by the fact that it was owed by a particular individual in respect of a particular estate, usually indeed constituting the chief or only render due from the vassal in return for which he held that estate from his lord.

Secondly, the practice of 'feudalizing' forms of military service less expensive and elaborate than knight service seems to have become more common during the thirteenth century.[12] By knight service we mean the readiness for peace-time castle ward and wartime campaigning of a man and his horse (or indeed horses), well protected by body armour and thoroughly trained over a lengthy period, the man armed with sword, lance and mace or short-shafted axe, and guarded by a long shield, the horse protected by a covering of boiled leather, or some form of mail. By common army service we envisage the turn out, essentially for emergencies, of men with comparatively little body protection save perhaps for a simple 'hard hat', quilted 'jack' or jerkin and gloves, equipped with a long-shafted spear or an axe with a curved blade, and a relatively small targe-type shield.[13] This being so, we may see that the scope for various kinds of intermediate military service was considerable. Surviving record covering the period from William the Lion's reign to Robert I's tells of a man on foot in the king's army, a young man with haubergel, a mounted sergeand with a haubergel, a mounted archer with a haubergel, a mounted archer or simply an archer or archers.[14] There can be little doubt that an archer or bowman, whose effectiveness demanded considerable training and skill, ranked higher than a spearman, and this would explain why before c. 1213 land in Buchan could be granted for the 'free service' of an archer:[15] non-free service would normally involve spearmen or axe men only, although there were almost certainly exceptions in the case of particular areas, such as the Forest of Selkirk, where common army service was probably normally performed by archers.[16] In Walter of Guisborough's famous account of the battle of Falkirk (1298)[17] a prominent role in the *exercitus Scottorum* is assigned to the bowmen (*viri sagittarii*) from Selkirk Forest commanded by Sir John Stewart, brother of James, fifth Steward of Scotland. These 'notably tall men, handsome of figure' were surely fighting as part of the general obligation of military service, even although their expertise would have been greater than that of the ordinary rank and file spearmen (*lancearii*). At Kilsyth too (in 1304) we hear of as many as ten archers being required as a vassal's service to the earl of Fife,[18] and this looks like an attempt to fix and feudalize what had previously been a territorial common army service based on the local assessment unit.

It is hardly rash to guess that the process of merging the strictly feudal force with the common army, hastened though it undoubtedly must have been by the long war of 1296–1328, was already under way in Alexander III's reign. Thus in 1286, immediately after the king's death, the Guardians issued a summons for army service due to the 'royal dignity' (i.e. the crown during the vacancy of the throne) throughout the realm, whether this was 'free service' or 'Scottish service', all summoned being required to bring victuals for forty days and to be at twenty-four hours' notice to go wherever directed for the defence of the realm and its liberty.[19]

In a national emergency, therefore, as in 1244 or 1286, it seems that a pooling of 'feudal host' in the strict sense and common army, the product of an obligation for compulsory military service, was practicable and necessary. How far either the feudal or the national obligation extended to service furth of Scotland is unclear. Both feudal and common army service were called upon by William the Lion for his campaigns in the English northern counties in 1173–4,[20] but it might have been claimed that the territories which the Scots invaded were lawfully within the king of Scots' dominions — either because William I chose to regard Henry II's re-arrangement of the frontier in 1157 as invalid or because the 'Young King' Henry had granted him the northern counties as an inducement to support the great revolt against his father.[21]

The considerable flurry of military activity across the border in 1216 and 1217 is harder to interpret, since our chief source is the *Melrose Chronicle* which uses several different expressions for the king of Scots' armed forces without explaining precisely what is meant by them.[22] In February 1216 Alexander II, in retaliation for King John's savage onslaught upon the south east of Scotland, led his whole army (*cum manu valida et exercitu suo universo*) to Carlisle. We may be fairly certain that at least an element of 'common army' was involved here, for the chronicler laments the fact that in spite of strict royal prohibition some Scots — at this date the word still means men from either Galloway or the country benorth Forth — plundered and devastated the daughter house of Melrose at Holm Cultram. Returning home with their booty, more than 1900 of these marauders were drowned in the River Eden. The picture is of a horde of fierce foot soldiers, probably Gallovidians to whom raiding in Cumbria was not unfamiliar.[23] In the following summer the Scots king crossed the west march once again, capturing the city but not the castle of Carlisle. As in February so in July Alexander II led a 'whole army' (*exercitus universus*), but that this did not include the common army, at least of his whole realm, is made clear by the Melrose writer's statement that the Scots were left out, the king taking 'supplies' (*expensas*) from them in lieu of service. This was evidently the aid in hides referred to in two brieves issued by the king in favour of Arbroath Abbey.[24] In February the Scots had confined their operations to English Cumbria, to which Alexander II laid claim, but in his summer expedition King Alexander marched south as far as Dover to rendezvous with Louis, son and heir of the king of France. Hence, almost certainly, the use of the common army on the first invasion and its exclusion from the second. Nevertheless, the force which Alexander led to Dover was reckoned 'large' by English observers, and could be termed *exercitus universus* and *omnis exercitus suus* by the Melrose chronicler.

In May 1217 the Scottish king embarked yet again on an invasion of England, hoping it would seem to implement the promises he had won from Louis of France and the irreconcilable Magna Carta barons that he would have possession of the English northern counties.[25] He brought a *universus exercitus* into Northumberland and laid siege to the castle of Mitford, west of Morpeth, for a week before withdrawing. Hearing that the keepers of the land between Tees and Tweed, Philip of Oldcoates and Hugh Balliol, had threatened a counter-invasion of Scottish territory, King Alexander raised 'a general army' (*generalis exercitus*) of English, Scots and Galloway men and came back into Northumberland on 5 July, but although this host seems to have been larger than that employed in May and obviously included the common army we are not told what if any campaigning it undertook. It must have been withdrawn before September, because by then the Scots king had mustered his third expeditionary force of the year, this time described merely as an 'army'. The king had brought this force only as far as Jedburgh when he heard that his ally Louis of France had made the treaty of Kingston (12 September 1217) with the supporters of the boy king of England, Henry III. The news prompted Alexander to discharge his army. Instead of invading England, the Scots king travelled peacefully to Northampton, where he did homage to King Henry for the earldom of Huntingdon, held of the king of Scots by Alexander's uncle David. It seems therefore that in 1216 and 1217 both the feudal army and the common army were mustered and deployed, sometimes together, but that the common army was limited to invasions of territory over which the Scottish crown claimed lordship.

In 1244 Alexander II could no longer lay claim to Northumberland, the right to which he had explicitly abandoned by the treaty of York in 1237.[26] But he could represent his invasion of English territory as defensive action in the face of an imminent attack by Henry III.

Half way between the emergencies of 1244 and 1286, in 1263, the king of Norway's large-scale descent upon the western isles and western seaboard of Scotland presented Alexander III with a challenge which he may to some extent have deliberately provoked and in any case could not ignore.[27] In the face of the powerful Norwegian threat involving raids on the Scottish mainland (especially the plundering and burning of the shores and islands of Loch Lomond),[28] there could of course be no question but that the Scots' military effort was defensive, even although Hakon Hakonsson's expedition had been prompted by Scottish aggressive gestures towards the islands going back at least to Alexander II's abortive campaign in the summer of 1249.

What is harder to be sure about is whether the Scots king adopted essentially the same combination of feudal and conscript levies to meet the Norwegian challenge of 1263. A number of entries in the sadly fragmentary exchequer roll extracts for 1264–6 show measures taken to meet the emergency, one at least demonstrating the king's personal interest.[29] But these entries largely relate to the provisioning and garrisoning of royal castles, the most striking being the earl of Buchan's activity at Inverie on the north shore of Loch Nevis, where there was evidently a castle.[30] The stationing of troops at Inverie surely implies that the Scots had substantial naval forces at their disposal, for the place is scarcely accessible from the landward side. The need to reinforce castle garrisons involved providing not only food and munitions but also money wages, for the specialist crossbowmen and the more miscellaneous sergeands employed were evidently paid. This was possibly because the obligatory period of unpaid service was too short to meet the national need or possibly because the obligatory service, whether feudal or common army, simply did not produce enough men.

When we come to the only major military engagement of 1263, the battle of Largs, we are faced by a startling discrepancy in those surviving sources which are most nearly contemporary. The *Chronicle of Melrose*, in a passage written before 1271,[31] plays down the role of the Scots army and rather surprisingly awards none of the honour or glory to King Alexander. Instead, the Melrose writer states that as the king of Norway himself affirmed he was repulsed not by human forces but by the power of God (*virtus divina*), which broke up the Norwegian ships and inflicted death upon their army. This of course refers to the storm which blew on 30 September and 1 October, causing the Norwegian ships lying between the Cumbraes and the Scottish mainland to drag their anchors and forcing several of the ships ashore.[32] The Melrose account then goes on to say, here surely straining the image of direct divine intervention, that (on 2 October) God attacked those Norwegians who had gathered to plunder and laid them low 'by means of the foot soldiers of the country' (*per pedissequos patrie*).[33] It is unfortunate that the chronicler chose the word *pedissequus*, which ought strictly to mean 'footman' in the sense of servant or attendant;[34] but there can hardly be any doubt that the Melrose writer intended the word to mean a common foot soldier.

There is equally no reason to doubt that these foot soldiers would have been part — perhaps, if *patria* is to be understood in its familiar sense of 'local countryside',[35] only the Strathgryfe, Cunningham and Kyle levies — of the common army of Scotland. The sheriff of Ayr, probably Walter Stewart, earl of Menteith,[36] and the sheriff of Lanark, Alexander Uvieth (or Unieth),[37] would have shared responsibility for mustering and positioning these levies with the local magnates, chief of whom was Earl Walter's brother Alexander (of Dundonald), fourth Steward of Scotland — to whom, indeed, the person responsible for the account of the battle of Largs in Walter Bower's version of the *Scotichronicon* gives much of the credit for the outcome.[38]

On the Norwegian side, we are lucky to have the extremely detailed saga of King Hakon.[39] Its author had to cope with the awkward fact that what had obviously been intended to be an epic of praise for a victorious warrior king had instead to record a somewhat humiliating Norwegian withdrawal, followed two months later by Hakon's death at Kirkwall. Nevertheless he faced the awkwardness boldly and provides detail which even when it does not show the Norwegians in the most favourable light is far superior to the Melrose chronicler's pious and jejune banalities. It is only from *Hakon's Saga* — as far as contemporary sources are concerned — that we learn what we would otherwise expect, that the Scots army contained a substantial cavalry force — five hundred knights, indeed, if the saga is accurate.[40] That at least some of this mounted force found scope to fight on horseback is shown by the saga's vivid description of one young Scottish knight called Ferus (or Perus) whose helmet was all gilt and set with precious stones and whose body armour matched this splendour.[41] 'He rode boldly against the Norwegians, through their ranks and back to his men', before being attacked and brought low by Andrew son of Nicholas.[42] The form 'Ferus' might suggest Fergus, a favourite personal name with the knightly family of Ardrossan;[43] but that we should prefer the alternative Perus — for Piers or Peter — is strongly indicated by the statement in Bower that the only (notable) Scottish casualty at Largs was the knight Peter (de) Curry.[44] Peter or Piers Curry was no doubt a descendant of Peter de Curri, vassal and tenant of the Steward for lands in Mauchline parish at the beginning of the thirteenth century.[45] This young knight may have made a specially brave show, but according to the saga writer the Scots cavalry as a whole were well armed and equipped, their Spanish (i.e. high quality) horses protected by mail coats and having fine trappings.[46]

The saga also gives us valuable detail about the Scots infantry. They were, it says, 'a great army of foot soldiers, well-equipped with weapons, mostly bows and Irish axes';[47] they must also have included slingers (later deployed against the Scots, with deadly effect, at Falkirk), for the saga reports that in the initial engagement the Scots 'attacked hard, and threw stones'.[48] These troops would of course have been the *pedissequi patrie* laconically mentioned by the *Melrose Chronicle*. Walter Bower may not have possessed much information about Largs, although he believed that the Norwegians came with 160 ships and 20,000 warriors and he knew that on his way to anchor off the Cumbraes King Hakon had attacked the castles on Arran and Bute.[49] He was more concerned to relate a miraculous story of the Fife knight Sir John Wemyss having a vision in which Saint Margaret appeared leading four doughty knights who were identified as the kings Malcolm Canmore, Edgar, Alexander I and David I, all armed cap a pie, ready to defend the realm.[50] This story, coupled with Bower's statement that a serious battle was fought at Largs in which the leader on the Scottish side was Alexander the Steward and in which the knight Peter Curry fell,[51] suggests that in Bower's mind at least the conflict was not limited to infantry. As we shall see later,[52] there is evidence at once more objective and more contemporary than Bower to support the clear statement of the Norwegian saga writer that many knights took part on the Scottish side. For the moment we may feel we are on safe ground in assuming that in 1263, as in 1244 and 1286, the Scottish realm met a major military emergency by calling out the common army and the knights and sergeands who owed service for their estates.

To say that the tendency to bring the common army and the feudal host together was already noticeable in Alexander III's reign is not to say that contemporaries had ceased to see these two elements as distinct. Two documents, one dating a few years before the reign,[53] the other one year after,[54] speak of knight service ('half the service of one knight in the army', 'the free service of one knight') as something separate and different from 'Scottish service', for which the king's barons and knights were responsible, though it may well have been performed in practice by their tenantry.[55] From c. 1260 we have a charter[56] in which the granter confirms arrangements for the king's forinsec service to be performed on the beneficiary's behalf 'whenever it might happen that the knightly army and the Scottish army should be activated in the lord king's service either together (*communiter*) or separately (*per se*)'. Discussing this text in 1977 (published 1980)[57] this author noted that it was unfortunate that an earlier document in which these arrangements were apparently specified had not survived. In the intervening period another charter[58] has come to light — available, alas! only in a defective copy — which must be closely contemporary in point of date and seems to specify just such arrangements as we may imagine to have been set forth in the document now lost.

The charter which has recently come to light records a grant by Gilbert of Cleish to his nephew John of Pitliver of fifteen acres at Cleish — specified as Abraham's Toft plus whatever was required to make it up to fifteen acres, as well as a little other land and pasture rights — to be held in fee and heritage, for an annual render of one pound of cumin payable on 29 June. Beside this annual rent, John of Pitliver was required to perform whatever forinsec service of the lord King was due from fifteen acres, as long as he did not accompany Gilbert in the army.

Gilbert, we know, was a knight,[59] holding Cleish, presumably as a knight's fee, of the earl of Fife.[60] If John of Pitliver accompanied his uncle in the army that meant that he was assisting him to perform the knight service he owed, and the charter says that if this happened John would be exempt from forinsec service. But whenever the common army of the lord king was mustered, John was to serve in that army, in his own person and on his own horse, along with Gilbert and at Gilbert's expense. This arrangement is closely parallel to an early thirteenth-century bargain[61] by which Simon, son of Robert, held Scroggs in Tweeddale of David, lord of Lyne, on condition of performing the king's forinsec service, mounted on his own horse but having whatever was needed to support him and his horse for the campaign provided by the lord (including a remount should this become necessary). It is hardly rash to suppose that a considerable number of such bargains were struck by lords with their lesser free tenants in order to ensure that the 'Scottish army', 'common army' or forinsec service was adequately performed in respect of the lands of which they were feudal superiors. Such arrangements would cover the ordinary muster of the common army, though they would not provide any substitute for a universal call-up 'when every man must go forth to defend his head'.[62]

It is unfortunate that we have so little firm information with regard to the relationship between unpaid and paid military service, the duration of unpaid service in any one year, and the relationship between actual performance, whether in person or through a substitute, of physical or bodily service under arms and the contribution of aid (*auxilium*) and victuals. Occasionally a vassal will be burdened with the service of both men and victuals but it is not uncommon to find merely food required, specifically 'in the common army of the lord king'[63] or 'in the lord king's army'.[64] Aid appears to have been a burden distinct from the requirements to provide food,[65] and may perhaps best be seen as a demand by the king for either money or offerings in kind to meet a special emergency, not necessarily military. It is not easy to find instances in Alexander III's reign, but, as has been noted already, his father levied an aid in hides in 1216[66] to meet the extraordinary expenses of his march to Dover to join forces with King John's English and French enemies.

We know that at least on some occasions Alexander III had to pay wages to his troops. The practice was understandably rare in thirteenth-century Scotland and, indeed, remained so until the sixteenth and seventeenth centuries. The Norwegian emergency of 1263 may have been the only occasion for paying cavalry and foot soldiers to arise during the reign, but it is likely that specialists such as crossbowmen (*balistarii*)[67] and sentries (*vigiles, homines vigilantes*)[68] were normally in receipt of wages. In the exchequer rolls for 1264–6 we find notes of various payments to such specialists, but what is more interesting is that Walter, earl of Menteith had to maintain 120 sergeands — presumably men-at-arms or mounted troops, archers and sword or axe men — in Ayr castle for three weeks,[69] wages amounting to £80 were paid to sergeands for 'three terms' (quarter or half-year periods?) ending on 11 November 1264,[70] liveries amounting to nearly £50 were paid to the king's sergeands by the chamberlain,[71] and a sum of £180 16s 8d (271 merks plus 3s 4d) was paid out also by the chamberlain in wages to knights (*feodis militum*, the context making it clear that here 'fees' has the modern sense of payments or wages rather than the familiar 'knight's fees').[72] Although the exchequer record unfortunately fails to specify the number of knights, the total points to more than a mere handful, for example of household knights, and offers strong independent support for the mention of a sizeable force of Scots knights in the saga of Hakon.[73]

There are many points of great importance with regard to the army of Alexander III's Scotland where the evidence is tantalizingly insufficient or even fails us altogether. But the overall picture is of a system of military recruitment which worked well and was not ill-adapted to the needs of the Scottish kingdom in the second half of the thirteenth century. When in the 1290s a much graver crisis threatened than anything confronting Alexander III the *exercitus Scottorum*, overwhelmed in 1296, victorious in 1297 and defeated, honourably and by no means decisively, in 1298, was to prove more resilient and adaptable, ultimately more successful, than the evidence we possess for 1249–86 might lead us to expect.

NOTES

1. *Chron. Melrose* (Stevenson), 156; *Chron. Bower*, ii, 74 (where 'Penteland' should be 'Ponteland').
2. F. M. Powicke, *King Henry III and the Lord Edward* (Oxford, 1947), ii, 740–59, Appendix B, 'The murder of Henry Clement and its consequences', gives the fullest account of the careers of Geoffrey and William Marsh.
3. Paris, *Chron. Maj.*, iv, 380; *Chron. Bower*, ii, 74. Hermitage, evidently the castle located by Matthew Paris in Lothian, does not seem to be recorded

before 1296 (Bartholomew Cotton, *Historia Anglicana*, ed. H. R. Luard (Rolls Series, 1859), 311–12), and appears again in a record of 1300 (*CDS*, ii, no. 1165). The castle located by Paris in 'Galloway' (at this period the larger Galloway would certainly have included the valley of the Nith) seems to have been Caerlaverock. Aymer Maxwell was sheriff of Roxburgh in succession to Nicholas Soules, c. 1248 (Fraser, *Douglas*, iii, no. 285; Raine, *North Durham*, no. 139; *Midlothian Chrs.* (Soutra), no. 31), and was sheriff of Dumfries and justiciar of Galloway in 1264 (*ER*, i, 16; Barrow, *Kingdom*, 138). Henry III also had grounds for concern in that two other leading Scots lords, Walter Lindsay and John Comyn of Badenoch, had built strongly fortified houses, in effect small castles, in North Tynedale, respectively Dally on the Chirdon Burn (1237: *CDS*, v, no. 12) and Tarset at the foot of the Tarset Burn (1244: *Close Rolls, 1242–7*, 221).

4. *Chron. Melrose* (Stevenson), 156; Paris, *Chron. Maj.*, iv, 380.
5. Ibid.
6. Ibid. For the reported use of 'Spanish' horses by the Scots in 1263, see below, p. 139.
7. *Highland Papers*, ii, 227–45; Barrow, *Anglo-Norman Era*, 166.
8. Michael Powicke, *Military Obligation in Medieval England* (Oxford, 1962), 118–33; M. Prestwich, *War, Politics and Finance under Edward I* (London, 1972), 99–105.
9. *Highland Papers*, ii, 227–45; Barrow, *Anglo-Norman Era*, 166.
10. *Cal. Inquisitions Post Mortem*, iii, no. 366, 'forinsec service of 1/4 knight's service' (1296; possibly infected by English influence); *RMS*, i, App. I, no. 3; Stringer, *Nobility Essays*, 194 (SRO, GD 124/1/1112), probably c. 1300; and cp. *Lennox Cartularium*, 39 ('forinsec service of the lord king when it arises i.e. the third part of the eighth part of one knight's service'; late 13th/early 14th century?).
11. *RRS*, v, no. 281 (1325); cp. *Lennox Cartularium*, 47.
12. Barrow, *Anglo-Norman Era*, 139–41. To the examples there cited may be added Walter the Steward's infeftment of Gilbert son of Gilbert in three pennylands in Bute for the service of one archer in the common army of the king of Scotland (Stirling, Central Regional Archives, Bundle 384/1/1, 1309 x 16); SRO, GD 148/1; and *Lennox Cartularium*, 56.
13. Information on the weapons and protective clothing and equipment of soldiers in the reign of Alexander III is generally unsatisfactory and there is scope here for an important piece of research. Statements in the text are based chiefly on references in contemporary chronicles and administrative documents together with the evidence of acts of parliament from 1318 onward (see especially *APS*, i, 473–4, 752; cp. ibid., ii, 10–11, *temp.* James I). See also K. A. Steer and J. W. M. Bannerman, *Late Medieval Monumental Sculpture in the West Highlands* (RCAHMS, 1977), 23–9 and plates 2–6, 8, 17–24; and *Scottish Weapons and Fortifications, 1100–1800*, ed. D. H. Caldwell (Edinburgh, 1981; henceforth, Caldwell, *Weapons*), esp. 10–20, 253–314 and 391–8.
14. Barrow, *Anglo-Norman Era*, 140; Barrow, *Kingdom*, 314.

15. *Aberdeen-Banff Coll.*, 407–9. The implication of the phrase 'free service' in this charter seems to be that the tenant had bargained with his lord to offer a bowman's service specifically in return for the estate in question. Had the service been merely a contribution to the common army, it would not have been free and would probably have been referred to in general terms.

16. See *Kelso Liber*, ii, no. 471, where the military service due from the barony of Bowden in 1327 is specified in terms of archer service. Robert I's legislation of 1318 (*APS*, i, 474) prescribes that every man possessing goods to the value of a cow must have a good spear or a good bow with a sheaf of twenty-four arrows.

17. *Chron. Guisborough*, 327–8.

18. *CDS*, ii, no. 1457.

19. *Formulary E*, no. 89.

20. Lawrie, *Annals*, 132–4; Barrow, *Kingdom*, 286–8.

21. Lawrie, *Annals*, 123–4; *RRS*, ii, 7; G. W. S. Barrow, 'The Reign of William the Lion, King of Scotland', in *Historical Studies*, vii (ed. J. C. Beckett, 1969), 28, 36–7.

22. *Chron. Melrose* (Stevenson), 122–32.

23. Compare Ralph Diceto's vivid description of Gallovidians recruited by William I in 1173 (Lawrie, *Annals*, 133–4): 'athletic, naked, remarkable for baldness, equipped at their left side with knives formidable to armoured men, skilled at throwing spears even from a distance and holding their long spears aloft like a standard when advancing to battle'.

24. *Arbroath Liber*, i, nos. 110, 111; *Chron. Melrose* (Stevenson), 122–3.

25. For the events of 1217 see *Chron. Melrose* (Stevenson), 130–2.

26. Stones, *Relations*, [20].

27. Barrow, *Kingship and Unity*, 116.

28. Anderson, *Early Sources*, ii, 617–26, especially 625–6.

29. *ER*, i, 5, 10–12, 18, 24. For the king's interest in expeditious work, see ibid., 31.

30. Ibid., 18–19.

31. *Chron. Melrose* (Stevenson), 190 (cf. *Chron. Melrose* (Facsimile edn., ed. A. O. Anderson *et al*, London, 1936), p. lxii).

32. Anderson, *Early Sources*, ii, 626–8.

33. *Chron. Melrose* (Stevenson), 190.

34. *A Latin Dictionary*, ed. Lewis and Short (Oxford, 1975), s.v., gives 'male attendant, footman, man-servant, page, lackey'. *The Revised Medieval Latin Word List*, ed. R. E. Latham (London, 1965), gives *pedesecus*, 'follower, attendant'.

35. Ibid., s.v., 'district, neighbourhood'.

36. *ER*, i, 5.

37. *CDS*, i, no. 2677; *Kelso Liber*, no. 190; *ER*, i, 30.

38. *Chron. Bower*, ii, 98.

39. Anderson, *Early Sources*, ii, 608–42, gives the relevant passages in translation. The best critical edition is that of Marina Mundt, *Hakonar*

saga Hakonarsonar, Norwegian Texts, 2 (Oslo: Norwegian Historical Source Institute, 1977).

40. Anderson, *Early Sources*, ii, 630.
41. Ibid., 632.
42. Ibid.
43. *CDS*, ii, no. 1668; T. Pont, *Cunninghame Topographized*, ed. J. Dobie of Crummock and J. S. Dobie (Glasgow, 1876), 58–61.
44. *Chron. Bower*, ii, 98.
45. *Melrose Liber*, i, no. 75; cp. no. 70.
46. Anderson, *Early Sources*, ii, 630. The statement about Spanish horses contrasts interestingly with Matthew Paris's information in 1244, cited above, p. 133.
47. Anderson, *Early Sources*, ii, 630. For axes see Caldwell, *Weapons*, 259–306, and especially at 262–72 and 305, where the author deals with weapons which might possibly have been called 'Irish axes' in the thirteenth century.
48. Anderson, *Early Sources*, ii, 630.
49. *Chron. Bower*, ii, 97.
50. Ibid., 97–8.
51. Ibid., 98.
52. Below, p. 142.
53. *Highland Papers*, ii, 121–3.
54. *Moray Registrum*, no. 263.
55. Ibid.
56. *Coupar Angus Chrs.*, i, no. 60.
57. Barrow, *Anglo-Norman Era*, 164–5.
58. Below, Appendix, pp. 146–7.
59. SRO, GD 254/1 (8120).
60. *Dunf. Reg.*, no. 145.
61. *Glas. Reg.*, i, no. 87.
62. Barrow, *Anglo-Norman Era*, 168; *Kinloss Recs.*, 130.
63. Fraser, *Colquhoun*, ii, 272–5; *Lennox Cartularium*, 19–21, 23, 53 (adding 2/3lb. of pepper and 2/3lb. of cumin), 57, 78, 96–7, 99 (all involving cheese).
64. NLS, MS. Adv. 34.6.24, pp. 248–9 — unspecified 'food for one man in the lord king's army'; *Lennox Cartularium*, 84, 85, 'as much food in the lord king's army as is due from one quarter of land (i.e. quarter arachor) in the earldom of Lennox'. In the latter case the charter grants land to support a horse sufficient to transport the food.
65. Aid (*auxilium*) is frequently but not invariably specified alongside army service or Scottish service, and seems normally to have been regarded as distinct from such service. See, e.g. *Highland Papers*, ii, 123; *Lennox Cartularium*, 80.
66. Above, p. 136.
67. *ER*, i, 5 (Ayr), 12 (Aberdeen), 30 (Roxburgh).
68. Ibid., 5 (Ayr), 24 (Stirling).

69. Ibid., 5.
70. Ibid., 10.
71. Ibid., 11.
72. Ibid., 10.
73. Anderson, *Early Sources*, ii, 629–30; above, p. 139.

APPENDIX

Gilbert of Cleish grants to his nephew John of Pitliver fifteen acres of land at Cleish (Kinross-shire) in fee and heritage for one pound of cumin annually payable on the feast of SS Peter and Paul (29 June); with specification as to how military service is to be performed. Undated, but probably c. 1252–3:

Omnibus[1] sancte matris ecclesie filiis etc. — Gilbertus de Cles sal[utem]. Noverit universitas vestra me dedisse etc. — confirmasse et assensu heredum meorum Johanni de Petliver nepoti nostro[2] pro homagio et servicio suo [quindec]im acras terre in territorio de Cles, scilicet toftum Abrahe et residuum superius et inferius ex parte australi et [aquilon]ari eiusdem crofti usque ad quindecim acras [compl]etas, et illam portionem que adiacet contigue . . . parti orientali, et communem pasturam ad . . . [v]accas cum sequela earum et ad sexaginta oves . . . et ad tres sues fetas cum sequela earum infra predictam villam de Cles et extra. Tenendas et h[abendas predicto Johanni et] heredibus suis de me et heredibus meis in feudo et hereditate, libere, quiete et pacifice cum omnibus libertatibus [et] aisiamentis ad tantam pertinentibus terram infra predictam villam de Cles et extra. Reddendo inde annuatim, mihi et heredibus meis, unam libram cumini ad festum apostolorum Petri et Pauli pro omnibus serviciis et secularibus demandis, faciendo et[3] forinsecum servitium domini Regis quantum pertinet ad quindecim acras terre, si dictus Johannes mecum [non ierit] in exercitu. Si autem mecum ierit, quietus erit de forinseco [servicio]. Et cum communis exercitus domini Regis con[gregatus fuerit di]ctus Johannes in propria persona et proprio equo mecum ibit in illo exercitu sumptibus meis. Et sciendum est . . . [quod mol]et bladum suum ad molendinum meum de Cles ad tricesimum vas. Ego[4] vero et heredes nostri[5] . . . cum omnibus pertinentiis dicto Johanni et heredibus suis predicto servicio contra omnes homines in perpetuum warran[tiza]bimus et defendemus. Hiis testibus Domino Roberto abbate de Dunf[ermelyn], Domino Johanne de Haya, Domino Merleswano, Domino Philippo vicario de Kilconq[r], Edmundo Irinside, Duncano filio Mathei et multis aliis.

NOTES TO APPENDIX

1. Punctuation is editorial, save that the dashes and dots represent the copyist's abridgements and failure to read his original, respectively. Passages in square brackets are supplied editorially.

2. Sic.
3. Sic, for etiam?
4. F. 52ᵛ.
5. Sic.

Heading: Copiata ex autographo penes Alexandrum Jeffrey W.S., Edinburgh
       1813

Source: National Library of Scotland, MS. Adv. 26.3.3, f. 52ʳ⁻ᵛ.

The date of Gilbert of Cleish's charter cannot be determined more narrowly than 1240 x 53, the limit-dates of Robert of Kenleith's tenure of office as abbot of Dunfermline. But since Duncan, son of Matthew, lord of Crambeth, is found as late as 1272 (*Dunf. Reg.*, no. 319) a date nearer 1250 than 1240 seems probable. The charter may be close in date to an agreement of 12 March 1253 between Sir Gilbert of Cleish, knight and Duncan of Crambeth (with his brother, Patrick) anent the marches between Cleish and Crambeth (or Dowhill): SRO GD 254/1 (8120).

7

ECCLESIASTICAL ARCHITECTURE IN THE SECOND HALF OF THE THIRTEENTH CENTURY

Richard Fawcett

It would be misleading to suggest that the architecture attributable to the long reign of Alexander III has an entirely distinct character of its own. Several of the major building operations under way in the course of his reign had been started, and their designs thus at least partly determined, well before 1249, whilst the main lines of artistic thought pursued by the masons who found such munificent patronage from both clerics and laity were to a great extent developments on established themes. It may be added that there are few indications that Alexander was himself a major instigator of ecclesiastical building campaigns. Nevertheless, the period during which he occupied the throne must be reckoned important for its number of high quality building operations, and beyond this the events which followed his death resulted in one of the most defined *caesurae* in the history of European ecclesiastical architecture. For these reasons it is perhaps justifiable to consider the architecture produced between 1249 and 1286 as having at least as coherent an identity as that of any reign since David I.

Amongst the various building campaigns in progress at the time of his succession were operations at a number of Scotland's most prestigious foundations, including St Andrews Cathedral and Dunfermline Abbey. At the former the construction of Scotland's largest and most important cathedral, started in or soon after 1160, was still in progress, and was only to reach a completed state during the episcopate of William Wishart (1271–9).[1] Regrettably, insufficient work of the second half of the thirteenth century has survived to allow detailed conclusions about its design and the impact it may have had on contemporary architecture. It may be suspected, however, on the evidence of the south aisle wall and the responds of the internal elevation incorporated in the west wall, that the design of the later parts was so largely conditioned by the earlier phases of construction that it had only limited lessons to offer masons in search of fresh stimulus.

148

But if the overall design was preconditioned there can be no doubt that the quality of the work was of the highest order, as has been amply shown by fragments found in the course of various works in this part of the cathedral.[2]

Greater freedom was probably allowed to the mason who designed and constructed the St Andrews west front on its present line in the time of Bishop Wishart, following the collapse of its predecessor during a gale.[3] Although its vertical emphasis may have been compromised by the low vaulted narthex placed in front of it, within what had originally been intended as the western bays of the nave, it must have been one of the most imposing essays in facade design of medieval Scotland. The central section, corresponding to the main vessel of the nave, was defined by strong polygonal stair turrets, and was pierced by the lavishly moulded processional entrance; the aisle ends were decorated by wall arcading. However, much of what is now seen post-dates a devastating fire in 1378, which necessitated extensive repairs to the upper parts of the front, and rebuilding of parts of the nave.[4]

At Dunfermline, the thirteenth-century work has survived in an even more fragmentary state than at St Andrews, so that we know very little of its overall design. From what was recorded of the plan before William Burn's parish church was built on the site of the choir in 1819,[5] it may be seen that the prebytery was extended two bays beyond the chord of the romanesque apse, with a lower axial chapel at the east end. The purpose of this extension was presumably both to accommodate the monastic choir more spaciously and to house the body of St Margaret more fittingly within a distinct part of the building. The lower portions of the east walls of her chapel are the only parts of the extension to survive, and they point to a design of considerable sophistication, not unlike the choir aisles of Carlisle. There was blind arcading along the lower walls and a system of bay division by vaulting shafts. Nevertheless, the papal ruling of 1249 that no new consecration was necessary[6] suggests that the scope of the work was more limited than has often been thought, and that much of the original romanesque choir must have been retained.

If we can learn relatively little from St Andrews and Dunfermline, it is now at Glasgow Cathedral that the finest architectural achievements of the thirteenth century in Scotland are best observed, in a building which has survived largely intact. Glasgow is the product of a complex sequence of building campaigns, and is of great interest for the way in which the architectural evidence illustrates that successive bishops were each in turn prepared to abandon the work of their predecessors in order to provide their diocese with what they saw as an appropriate cathedral church. Despite these changes, the structure has an immediate impact of quite majestic harmony.

A fragment in the south-western corner of the crypt, belonging to the work dedicated by Bishop Jocelin in 1197,[7] probably formed part of a cruciform reconstruction of the eastern arm of the church which had been dedicated by Bishop John in 1136.[8] But it appears that soon after Jocelin's death, before his reconstruction was even completed, it was being modified. At the same time work was started on a new nave, the lower walls of which were eventually incorporated in the nave we now see. This operation may be dated from the design of its base course and internal wall shafts to the early thirteenth century, and may be attributable by a process of exclusion to Bishop Walter (1207–32). Yet work on this project was itself to be postponed when Bishop William Bondington (1233–58) turned his attention once again to the eastern limb. This he started to rebuild to a more spacious plan, in keeping with the current architectural preference for a larger choir and presbytery contained within a separate limb of the building. This was the turning point in the sequence of operations which ultimately resulted in the virtually complete reconstruction of the cathedral in the course of the thirteenth century. The work at Glasgow was the most important building campaign from the second half of the century of which we have detailed knowledge, and it provides important information on the range of ideas which were accessible to masons working in Scotland; the successive phases will be discussed separately so that they can be seen within their immediately contemporary contexts.

The plan of the building was probably determined by 1242 (see Figure 2d, p. 179), when the faithful of the kingdom were exhorted to contribute to the work during Lent.[9] Its essentially Cistercian disposition, with a square ambulatory and eastern chapels, is unusual for a cathedral, although Archbishop Roger's choir at York, of the third quarter of the previous century, may have had an earlier and simpler version of this plan type.[10] It has recently been convincingly argued that the type may have been introduced into Scotland through Cistercian channels from the Yorkshire abbey of Byland to the Midlothian house of the order at Newbattle.[11] For Bishop Bondington the attraction of such a layout was probably quite simply the easy access it afforded to a feretory for the body of St Kentigern, placed in the customary position behind the high altar.

Plate 1. Glasgow Cathedral choir. *Crown copyright: Historic Buildings and Monuments, Scotland.*

At Glasgow the sharp eastward fall of the ground meant that construction of the choir proper had to await completion of the superb crypt which underlies it, so that if the planning of the eastern limb predates the reign of Alexander the choir itself was probably largely erected whilst he was king. As with the majority of greater churches under construction during the mid-century, the internal elevations were of three distinct storeys, with careful articulation into bays and storeys by wall shafts and string courses. The continuing impact on Scotland of architectural ideas developed in the northern parts of England, and the likelihood that many of the leading masons working here were still drawn from that area, is seen in both the overall design and in many of the details of Glasgow. As had been the case in the nave of Holyrood Abbey, started some thirty years earlier, the relationship between the arcade and triforium stages betrays something of the far-reaching influence of Lincoln Cathedral (see Figure 1a, p. 178). Reconstruction had started in St Hugh's choir there in 1192, and had reached the nave by the time work was started at Glasgow. The twin pairs of triforium openings to each bay of Glasgow, with simple plate tracery piercings in the tympana, show the same basic pattern as in the choir of Lincoln, and the luxuriant growths of stiff-leaf foliage on the arcade caps may also show a debt to that source.

However, the Glasgow mason's design reveals an awareness of more recent variants on the Lincoln theme, in the details of the triforium, such as had been developed at Rievaulx Abbey in north Yorkshire; but, at the same time, he also shows the growing willingness to follow a creatively independent line that was becoming evident in the buildings of other masons working in thirteenth-century Scotland. Around the second decade of the century the designer of Holyrood, for example, whilst following Lincoln closely in many respects, had nevertheless elected to employ more massive piers than had been used at Lincoln. He chose to give them a solid stepped profile relieved by engaged shafts in the angles and on the leading faces, the appearance of which was less removed from romanesque types than were the slender piers surrounded by disengaged shafts with which the more adventurous English masons were experimenting. Although the heavier piers at Holyrood were perhaps prompted by a degree of nervousness at the problems of supporting a high vault, since few other Scottish churches had vaults over their main spans at that time, the Glasgow mason also chose to design more sophisticated variants on the stepped profile pier even though vaults were to be placed over only the lower lateral spaces.

Plate 2. Glasgow Cathedral choir arcade cap. *Crown copyright: Historic Buildings and Monuments, Scotland.*

The decision to cover Glasgow's choir by a timber wagon ceiling, with a horizontal springing point at the wall head, rather than by a stone vault requiring arched junctions with the wall, also called for a clearstorey design in which neither Lincoln nor Rievaulx could provide guidance. Except in the narrower end sections each bay was given a triplet of arches of equal height, corresponding to the windows on the outer face of the wall passage at this level, and with a narrower blind arch to each side. The resultant continuous but punctuated arcade of equal arches has some analogies with the slightly earlier nave clearstorey at Jedburgh Abbey, with which Glasgow had close links since one of the abbey's founders had been Bishop John (c. 1114–47).

The outstanding calibre of the Glasgow choir mason is abundantly evident in his ability to synthesise and build upon ideas from a wide variety of sources. His inventiveness is particularly noteworthy in the design of the three-light plate traceried windows in the choir aisles (see Figure 3a, b, c and d, p. 180). Although an unbiased assessment might be that their architectural interest rather outweighs their aesthetic charm, that architectural interest is nonetheless very high, since relatively little plate tracery has survived in Britain as a whole, and the group at Glasgow remains perhaps the largest and most ingenious. As with other features of the design it is possible that Lincoln may have been a major source of ideas: the nave triforium there has some of the most complex surviving examples of such tracery apart from Glasgow, whilst its west window may once have contained one of the largest fields of plate tracery ever attempted, before being replaced by later tracery.

Perhaps the most unexpected feature of Glasgow is the so-called Blackadder Aisle. If, as has been said earlier, the plan of the choir is unusual in a thirteenth-century cathedral, this great single transeptal aisle is even more so. From the plinth course it may be seen that the layout of the transepts and nave had been dictated by the foundations and lower walls set out in the campaign which has been attributed to Bishop Walter, and the lack of projection of the former must have created some inconvenience for the cathedral clergy as more altars came to be required. The decision to throw out a widely projecting arm with a main floor on the same level as the transept, raised above a crypt, has been generally assumed to have been taken by Archbishop Blackadder around the turn of the fifteenth and sixteenth centuries, on heraldic evidence. However, a recent study of the architectural details of its crypt,[12] which was the only part of this extension to be completed, has suggested that, as was argued in the last century by John Honeyman,[13] the walls of this projection are in fact earlier than the time of Blackadder. Close inspection reveals that the external heraldry is likely to be secondary to the shell, but contemporary with the vault, which is itself certainly attributable to Blackadder on heraldic grounds. Beyond this, the similarity of the piers, responds, wall ribs and window reveals to their counterparts in the choir and its crypt is so very close that it is difficult not to conclude that they must be the work of the same mason, whereas the relatively much later date of the vault covering the aisle is indicated by the marked differences between its rather heavy ribs and those of the more deeply cut wall arches built along with the responds. In passing it may be noted that it was possibly this aisle which inspired the construction of a related asymmetrical transeptal aisle at the Benedictine abbey of Iona later in the century. In both cases it was probably the cult of the 'resident' saint which prompted the start of the work, although in neither case does initial enthusiasm for the project appear to have extended to its being completed as originally conceived.[14]

Work on Glasgow was to continue to the end of the century, with the resumption of building the upper parts of the transepts, laid out along with the nave in the earlier years of the century, even before the choir was fully completed. But at this stage it is necessary to leave Glasgow in order to bring into consideration some of the other operations under way during the same years that the choir was rising. Of the major churches started around the central decades of the century the one which may now be seen to have approached Glasgow most closely in the quality of its architecture was the cathedral of Dunblane. After being elected to his virtually derelict diocese in 1233, the Dominican Bishop Clement set about an energetic campaign to rescue its finances, of which the chief instrument was to be a papal mandate of 1237.[15] Construction of his cathedral was probably started soon after this, and it may be seen from the continuity of the plinth course, so far as the restoration of 1889 has not placed its reliability in question, that the whole building was planned and laid out in one operation. But the work is unlikely to have been completed before the later decades of the century.

The plan (see Figure 2a, p. 179) was for an elongated aisle-less choir, with a two-storeyed lean-to range along much of its north side to house the ancillary offices of chapter house, sacristy and treasury. To the west of this is a nave flanked by an aisle on each side, the southern one incorporating a twelfth-century bell tower to the east of its mid-way point. Such a plan was little more than parochial in scale by comparison with most of its English and European peers, and economy was manifestly a factor in its adoption. However within its limited scope an effect of considerable dignity was achieved through the quality of its architecture, and variants on the same plan were also employed in other major Scottish churches, including the cathedrals of Dunkeld and Brechin.

Although the tower is the only part of the structure we now see which pre-dates the operation instigated by Clement, the discernible sequence of the building may suggest that an existing choir was retained in use for some years. From the design of the windows and vaulting it seems that the first part of the new cathedral to be completed was the north choir range, which was followed by the nave and finally by the choir. Since the east wall of the nave was provided with high windows above the choir arch it seems that the choir as first designed was to have been a lower structure than we now see, and that the initial scheme was superseded by one which gave rather greater emphasis to the eastern limb. Despite the fact that the tracery which now fills the great windows in the southern flank and east wall of the choir belongs to Sir Robert Rowand Anderson's restoration of 1889, their containing arches are original, and their large scale and moulded detail suggest they were built towards the end of the thirteenth century, when the vogue for such vast windows became prevalent.

Examination of the nave of Dunblane, where work is likely to have started around the mid-century, suggests that the operation did not proceed entirely smoothly and that there were perhaps as many as three phases to the work. The most striking feature of the interior as we now see it is its elegantly lofty two-storeyed arrangement (see Figure 1e, p. 178). Tall arcades, carried on piers of characteristically stepped and shafted profile, support a clearstorey which has a continuous screen of arches along the inner side of its wall passage. By contrast with the arcades the walls of the aisles appear a little uncomfortably low. But, following a study of the masonry at the east end of the south aisle, the suggestion has recently been made that the arcades were initially designed to have been of about the same height as the aisle walls, and that the aisles were at first to have been covered by stone vaults.[16] Above the window rear arch at the east end of the aisle are curved lines of thin stones which are clearly not the relics of a hood mould since they do not run concentrically with the arcs of the rear arch. The likelihood of their having belonged to a wall rib instead is suggested strongly by a number of stones beneath them on each side which, most unusually, are roughly cut with two faces at right angles to each other at the junctions of the walls. From their position and form these stones appear most likely to have been cut back from the *tas-de-charge* and supporting corbels of vault springings. The start of work on a vault at this point is also supported by the character of the masonry above those stones identified as having belonged to a wall rib, which may be interpreted as infilling of the seating of vault webbing. Complementing this evidence of an abandoned scheme for a vault are indications that the eastern arcade respond originally only rose to the height of the suggested vault springing, along with the curious way in which an additional order was added to the respond above this level, rather awkwardly carried on a corbel.

There is now no way of knowing if the first design for the nave would have been for a three-storeyed elevation, with a triforium corresponding to the roof space over the aisle vaults, as at Glasgow, although it is

Plate 3. Dunblane Cathedral nave. *Crown copyright: Historic Buildings and Monuments, Scotland.*

tempting to suspect that this was the case. But against this it must be said that in Scotland, as elsewhere, several leading masons of the mid-thirteenth century were showing a wish to eliminate the dark middle stage of the triforium, for which the modified design of Dunblane is itself the best evidence, and it may be that the first design at Dunblane was also for two storeys.

Two variants on a method by which the triforium stage could be omitted from buildings with vaulted aisles, and with aisle roofs which thus had to rise above the level of the arcades, are to be seen in the two transepts of the Valliscaulian priory of Pluscarden, for example, which may be at least in part contemporary with Dunblane (see Figure 1c and d, p. 178). There the clearstorey passages and their inner arcades were extended down in different ways to just above the main arcade heads, so that the blank area of walling corresponding to the aisle roof space was reduced in impact by being relegated to the back plane of the wall. It is possible that some similar arrangement was at first envisaged for Dunblane. However, with the decision to omit the vaults over Dunblane's aisles this problem was removed there, and it was feasible to place the clearstorey windows directly above the handsomely heightened arcade arches.

In the modified design the inner screen of the clearstorey at Dunblane at first consisted of an unbroken arcade of two arches in each bay, corresponding to the windows on the outer face of the wall. But in the course of construction a further modification was introduced by the insertion of tracery into both the screen openings and the windows, and this tracery is of particular interest because of its hybrid nature (Figure 3e, p. 180). The importation into England from France in the course of the 1240s of bar tracery, in which the forms are defined by curved bars of stone rather than being simply voids cut into stone plates, was to be a major turning point in the history of British ecclesiastical architecture. In Scotland the earliest firmly documented examples of the use of such tracery were, as we shall see later, in the 1270s.[17] However, at Dunblane the tracery introduced into the upper levels of the nave and the triplet of windows on the west front may represent an earlier, albeit slightly garbled, attempt to assimilate such ideas. Within these openings the twin light heads are formed by curved bars, as in orthodox bar tracery, although the main element of the tracery field, a quatrefoil or cinquefoil, is still cut through a plate. It is true that the plate is reduced to a minimum, so that there are additional voids at its flanks and base, but it is still essentially a plate. The date of this hybrid cannot be known with certainty, although it seems unlikely that the stage of operation at Dunblane which contains it could have been reached before the late 1250s or the 1260s.

Before moving on to consider those buildings in which true bar tracery is employed, reference must be made to a number of other churches which were probably rising in the earlier years of the reign of Alexander III. One of these is the nave of the Cluniac abbey of Paisley where, although most of what is seen inside is fifteenth-century work dating from the abbacies of Lithgow (1384–1433) and Tervas (1445–59), the outer aisle walls and west front incorporate earlier work of a variety of dates. The west front has been radically altered by the insertion of three large windows in two tiers, at the time the main body of the nave was rebuilt; but its design is still essentially of the thirteenth century and shows some analogies with that of Dunblane.

At both, the elevation of the front is a direct expression of the cross-section of the building behind, with strong buttressing giving clear vertical expression to the central part, although at Paisley the outer corners of the aisles are more massively marked than at Dunblane, by angle turrets. Similarly, at both, the central entrance doorway was given strong emphasis by multiple-shafted jambs carrying moulded, rather than carved caps and with elaborately moulded arch orders; in each case the doorway is flanked by a single decorative blind arch on either side. Such similarities are what might be expected in buildings of comparable scale which are not far apart in date, and there is no reason to assume that there was any more direct linkage between the two.

It is possible, however, that there may be a more direct link between Paisley and Glasgow. The lay entrance on the north side of Paisley nave, over which was later placed Abbot Lithgow's porch, is afforded emphasis by lavish mouldings to the three orders of jambs and arches, with a rich display of stiff-leaf foliage to the caps. Despite being heavily begrimed and rather damaged, these caps show something of the same highly finished but slightly mechanical brilliance that is to be seen in the larger arcade caps of Glasgow Cathedral choir. It is consequently tempting to suspect that at least one of the masons at Paisley may have been drawn from the nearby cathedral lodge.

Stiff-leaf foliage which would seem to be of a mid-century date may be found at a number of other buildings, and several fine fragments have been unearthed at St Andrews Cathedral. Amongst examples still to be seen in place are those in the choir of Dunkeld Cathedral. According to the invaluable account of the cathedral's construction contained in Alexander Myln's lives of its bishops, the choir of Dunkeld was built from its foundations by Bishop William Sinclair (1309–37).[18] But, despite the confusion introduced to the evidence afforded by Dunkeld through Archibald Elliot's restoration of the choir in 1814, there can be little doubt that the wall arcade which runs around parts of the lower walls is of the thirteenth rather than the fourteenth century, and much of the upper walling including the window arches may also be of the thirteenth century. The quality of the foliage decoration on a number of the arcade caps shows some variety, although for the most part it is so badly damaged that it would be hazardous to attempt any firm conclusions about its relationship with that at other buildings. It may be said, however, that the mouldings of the trifoliate arches carried by the caps show considerable finesse, and indicate the presence of no mean master mason.

In a better state of preservation are some excellent carved capitals in the vaulted ground floor stage of the north-west tower at Brechin Cathedral. The stone from which these caps were carved was rather friable and thus discouraged deep undercutting, whilst there appears to have been some loss of detail as a result of penetration of dampness. Nevertheless, the quality of at least two of the caps may be seen to be sufficiently high to invite comparison with some of the better mid-century examples of such foliage decoration in England. Completion of the tower would seem to have been interrupted, possibly by the troubles which followed the death of Alexander III, and its upper stages may perhaps be associated with references to work on a belfry during the episcopate of Patrick Leuchars (1351–c. 83).[19]

The ground stage of the tower which contains the caps seems likely to post-date the construction of the adjacent nave. But the architectural evidence for the chronological relationship between the two parts has been extensively disturbed, first by an insensitive reconstruction of the nave aisles in 1806, and later by an attempt to restore more than a little of their character by John Honeyman in 1900. However, the inner nave walls with a simple clearstorey above the arcades, and the lower part of the west front, are evidently thirteenth-century work, although the form of the arcade bases may have suffered a degree of transformation at some stage. On balance it seems more likely that the arcades, if not the west door, date from the earlier part of the century and are thus outside the scope of this study.

Brechin also has a fragment of one other important building of the thirteenth century, the chapel of the Maison Dieu Hospital. It can be approximately dated by the foundation charter of William Brechin to around 1267.[20] Despite being small in scale, the details of the chapel's surviving part show a high degree of refinement. Both the external reveals and the rear arches of the individual lancet windows have carefully proportioned mouldings, whilst the south doorway is given emphasis by an effective combination of an unbroken and a supported order.

Another building which calls for a mention at this point is the church of the Augustinian priory of Inchmahome, on the Lake of Menteith. Construction is likely to have been started not long after the foundation by Walter, Earl of Menteith, in about 1238. But the building shows signs of modifications to the first designs which, as at Dunblane, may point to interruptions in the operation, and it is unlikely that construction of the parochial nave was under way before the middle years of the century. Attached to an aisle-less choir with a sacristy against its north flank, the nave had a single aisle on its north side, with a squat tower over the western bay of the aisle. From the awkward way in which the tower fits into its bay, and the lack of correspondence between the piers of the arcade and either the tower or the buttresses of the outer aisle wall, it may be seen that no tower was envisaged in this position when the arcade was built, although it is integral with the aisle wall. There were evidently yet further changes of mind when the south wall of the nave was built, since it is far from parallel with the north side of the church, in spite of provision being made for a more regular junction with the west wall when that wall was built. It may be that the south wall as it now stands represents a later modification, contemporary with the rebuilding of the conventual buildings.

As was only too frequently the case with less well-endowed foundations, economy must have been a consideration in the building of this church, which was relatively small and entirely unvaulted. Nevertheless, the north arcade has well detailed piers which show some similarity with Glasgow in both their stepped section with engaged shafts and also in the provision of sub-bases with an attractive concave flare rather than the more usual chamfer. The greatest architectural flourish of the priory church was the west front, with a central entrance doorway below a three-light window of unknown form. The soft grey stone from which the dressed masonry of the lower part was cut has weathered badly, and has lost much of its detail, although its original quality is still readily apparent. As usual at this period, the doorway is deeply recessed, with four richly moulded orders in the arch, carried on

Plate 4. Inchmahome Priory nave. *Crown copyright: Historic Buildings and Monuments, Scotland.*

a complex sequence of engaged shafts in the jambs. To either side of the doorway, and extending out to the buttresses which frame the central section of the front, is a pair of blind arches supported by triplet shafts, with shallow quatrefoils or trefoils between the arch heads. The richness of this front by comparison with the rest of the church has led to the extraordinary suggestion that it may originally have been made for another church of greater architectural pretensions, and was simply reused at Inchmahome;[21] but this would seem to be an unwarrantably ingenious interpretation of the evidence.

For the latter part of the reign of Alexander III our main sources of information are three major building campaigns, at the cathedral of Elgin, the Cistercian abbey of Sweetheart, and, of course, at the cathedral of Glasgow. At Elgin the cathedral had first been laid out in about 1224, when papal permission was given for the see to be transferred there from Spynie.[22] In its initial form it was a cruciform structure with an aisle-less choir, aisled nave, and transepts devoid of eastern chapels. On the indications of the plinth courses it would seem that it was only after the building had been set out that the magnificent pair of western towers was also determined upon, and at some stage a chapel was added against the eastern bays of the south nave aisle adjacent to the transept. Further major alterations and additions were undertaken in the later decades of the thirteenth century, and it is these which are of immediate concern. The reason for their reconstruction was almost certainly a fire which Bower records as having taken place in 1270.[23]

The additions took the form of an eastward extension to the choir and presbytery and its lateral augmentation by flanking aisles. Leading off the northern of these was built an octagonal chapter house, one of only three polygonal chapter houses of English type known to have been built in Scotland. The additions also involved the lateral expansion of the nave by the construction of outer chapel aisles, incorporating the earlier outer chapel on the south side, and making Elgin the first Scottish church to have such double aisles. In the western bay of the new outer south aisle a deep porch was placed over the main lay entrance. Our understanding of the precise details of all this work, particularly in the nave and chapter house, has been rather clouded by the further extensive work which was necessitated by the earl of Buchan's destructive raid in 1390, although the broad outline is clear enough.[24]

As in Bishop Bondington's campaign at Glasgow, a major concern of

Bishop Archibald (1253–98) at Elgin must have been the provision of an eastern limb which could fully and fittingly accommodate both the canons' choir and the high altar with the ceremonial area around it which was called for by the rites of Sarum. The expansion involved, including the flanking aisles and their eastern chapels, probably virtually quadrupled the original floor area of the building east of the crossing, and must have been a costly operation (see Figure 2b, p. 179). However, perhaps a little surprisingly, existing masonry was retained where possible, resulting in something of an asymmetrical appearance which may have been less evident when the choir was furnished and in use. On the north side the wall of the first choir survived the fire of 1270 with relatively little damage and it was consequently retained, incorporating tantalisingly incomplete evidence which points to that choir having been lower than the nave to its west, and having been lit by elevated windows incorporated within a continuous wall arcade.

It was only on the south side that the mason responsible for the extensions was able to design an entirely new elevation, and even here his work was carefully attuned to that in the nave. From their junctions with the two western towers it may be seen that the nave elevations as built after 1224 were of two storeys, with a clearstorey running immediately above the arcade: as first built, the flanking aisles, like the high spaces, were unvaulted. In the course of the new work, well-detailed tierceron ribbed vaults appear to have been provided above all the lateral spaces of aisles and chapels, but a two-storeyed elevation was nevertheless adopted for the choir (see Figure 1f, p. 178), with a similar expedient as at Pluscarden for masking the blank area corresponding to the aisle roof by extending the clearstorey passage down below the level of the windows. The results in the choir of Elgin still provide eloquent testimony to the skills of the master mason in his ability to respond to the problems of incorporating old work, of attuning new to old, and of making allowances for an irregular bay system.

The culmination of the new eastward extension at Elgin was the spacious three-bay prebytery. To give due prominence to this area the aisles were only partly extended along its flanks in the form of shallow single-bay chapels beyond the choir entrances on each side, leaving clear two full bays of the presbytery. As a consequence the area was flooded with light through windows in its east, north and south sides. On the north and south sides the windows were in two tiers, with lancets forming a continuation of the clearstorey at the upper level and larger windows below. The eastern wall was pierced by two rows of five

Plate 5. Elgin Cathedral east front. *Crown copyright: Historic Buildings and Monuments, Scotland.*

lancets, at levels corresponding to the arcades and clearstorey. Above this would have been windows rising into the roof, but their original form is uncertain, since the fragmentary wheel window which we now see there was only placed in that position after the fire of 1390. The blind lancets to either side of the gable may point to there having been a further tier of lancets.

From inside the ruined cathedral the composition of superimposed lancets in the east wall is extremely satisfying, although it is from the outside that its attractions are most evident. Nevertheless, it must be said that the basic design of the east wall is rather conservative. Tall gables pierced by ranks of grouped single lights have a long history in Scotland and England. For Elgin, with its massive octagonal buttress turrets at the angles of the presbytery, the most immediate analogies are with such as the east gable of the north Yorkshire Benedictine abbey at Whitby, of around the second decade of the thirteenth century. What marks Elgin as being later are the more complex groupings of five rather than three lancets, and the bar tracery which was placed both within the lower lancets and the wider ground floor windows of the flanks.

It has been said earlier that such tracery was introduced into England from France in the 1240s, probably at the French oriented lodge of Westminster Abbey. A form of hybrid tracery introduced in the nave of Dunblane Cathedral around the 1250s or 1260s has already been referred to, but the earliest true bar tracery in Scotland, within adequately dated contexts, of which Elgin is one example, is to be found in the 1270s. In the east wall the tracery, which is now only known from its stubs and from early views, took the form of a subordinate arch below the lancet heads of the window, above which was a small circlet (see Figure 3f, p. 180). In the flanking two-light windows the tracery was a permutation on this theme, with a third circlet between the two lights (see Figure 3g, p. 180).

Interestingly, the tracery employed at Elgin was not one of the earliest types, presumably because the mason was aware of more recent developments outside Scotland. However, one church not far from Elgin still shows evidence of having had large traceried windows of a type which had been developed earlier than those of Elgin, although this does not, of course, mean that they need have been earlier in date within their Scottish context. That church is Pluscarden Priory, the transepts of which have already been briefly discussed. It is unfortunate that we have no firm building dates for Pluscarden, since its architecture may well have played a significant role in the importation of new ideas to the area. The transepts show indications of having been built over a period of several decades in the mid-century, and the choir would seem unlikely to have been completed before the end of the third quarter of the century. Evidence of extensive damage and consequent rebuilding in all surviving parts of the church has traditionally been associated with the earl of Buchan's rampage through the area in 1390, although the documentary confirmation of this, as of so much else at Pluscarden, is lacking. As first built the choir had large windows of a scale similar to those in the choirs of Dunblane and Dunkeld. The stubs of tracery retained within later masonry when the size of the window openings was subsequently reduced show the windows in the flanking walls were of four lights grouped in pairs beneath sub-arches, with circlets contained by the sub-arches and a third circlet between them (see Figure 3i, p. 180). This was a type of tracery which had been employed at Amiens Cathedral in north-eastern France in the 1220s, and two decades later in the chapter house of Westminster Abbey. It, and variations upon it, was to be one of the staple types of British bar tracery for several decades.

Related tracery was introduced at Glasgow Cathedral in one window of the south choir aisle, which would seem to have been the last to receive its infilling, and also in the south transept and west front there. An approximate date for this phase of the work at Glasgow is suggested by a document of 1277 referring to a gift from the Lord of Luss for timber to be used in the bell tower and treasury.[25] This suggests that work on the eastern limb was nearing completion, and could well indicate that work was already sufficiently advanced on the construction of the transepts — on the foundations and lower walls set out in the first years of the century — for thought to be given to the central tower. The details of the mouldings and windows of the transept point to a new mason being in charge of the works by that stage, who was aware of the magnificence and changed sense of scale which could be created by vast traceried windows. The choir mason had, indeed, used very tall windows in the eastern gable wall, which rose above the arcade separating choir and ambulatory; although there is some reason to believe that the four great lancets he designed for that position were not originally so deep, externally at least, as since nineteenth-century restorations. But in the transepts the master mason chose to open up the wall as fully as was feasible, whilst still taking care that his work should not contrast too markedly with that of his predecessors.

At the level corresponding to the aisles he formed a pair of two-light windows in each gable wall (see Figure 3h, p. 180); from this, incidentally, it is evident that the idea of building the main storey of the 'Blackadder Aisle' on the south side must by then have been abandoned. Above these he constructed a single window in each transept rising through the levels of triforium and clearstorey into the roof above. These windows were heavily restored by Edward Blore in the mid-nineteenth century,[26] although their forms before then are shown in engravings by James Collie of 1835.[27] The south transept window was of five lights, and was essentially like that in the four-light windows of Pluscarden with the addition of a single central light between the sub-arches (see Figure 3j, p. 180). The north transept window was of six lights, but was of rather less complex design, with simple groupings of three graded lights within a pair of sub-arches (see Figure 3l, p. 180).

A date in the 1270s for the Glasgow transepts, as suggested by the document of 1277, is supported by a fine group of related windows at Sweetheart Abbey. This abbey was founded for Cistercian monks by Devorguilla Balliol in 1273,[28] and it seems likely that construction of the church was started virtually immediately. The adherence of the Scottish Cistercian province to the earlier architectural precepts of the order is admirably shown in both the design and the planning of the church, despite the fact that elsewhere in Europe the order was by this time tending to part from the principles promulgated by St Bernard. Sweetheart's plan is of the characteristic 'Bernardine' form, with a rectangular presbytery flanked by transepts with eastern chapels, a structural nave long enough to accommodate the two choirs of monks and lay brethren, and a narrow lean-to western narthex (see Figure 2c, p. 179); so far as we know, only Newbattle and Kinloss amongst the Scottish Cistercian houses departed from such a plan. Beyond this the builders of Sweetheart also followed earlier Cistercian practice in rejecting a triforium stage and made no attempt to articulate the wall surface in any other way (see Figure 1g, p. 178), although their brethren at Dundrennan had succumbed to the lure of a middle storey about a century earlier. A possibly grudging acceptance of early ordinances against bell towers is shown by the way the central tower only rose slightly above the surrounding roofs of choir, nave and transepts.

Yet, if the Cistercian letter is followed to this extent, the spirit was certainly flouted in the magnificent display of traceried windows within the choir and transepts (see Figures 3k, m and n, p. 180), and perhaps to a lesser extent in the quality of the moulded and carved detail. The east window is similar to the south transept of Glasgow, although with additional embellishment, and the flanks show other variants on themes found at Glasgow. But there is one window type in the western bay of the two flanks which is of some additional interest for the looser grouping of circlets in the tracery field. Such designs have their origins in the royal domain of France as early as the 1230s,[29] but in England they were being used in buildings of about the same date as Sweetheart, showing its mason to have been aware of current usage south of the border. Tracery of this sort, in the freer interaction it allowed between the constituent elements, points the way to the greater fluidity of design which was soon to follow, although in Scotland these later developments were to be postponed by the hiatus which came soon after Alexander III's death. In passing, it may be mentioned that some of these windows have the curiosity that the form pieces which make up the tracery field have a different moulding section from that of the mullions.

In the western limb of Sweetheart, which contained the two choirs of the monks and lay brethren, the aisle windows have been lost, whilst the great west window has been reconstructed on more than one occasion. Changes in the design of the clearstorey windows after the second bay of the nave indicate a pause of some sort in the course of the operation: in the two eastern bays there are groupings of three individual lights, corresponding to the inner openings at this level, whereas the later bays have single semi-circular windows containing five graded lights. But the details, particularly of the foliate caps of the inner openings, suggest that this pause is unlikely to have been of any great duration, a fact which is also supported by the continuity of the design of the piers and arcade arches.

Despite the Cistercian restraint of its inner two-storeyed elevations, the nave of Sweetheart is of great value for showing how masons working in Scotland were retaining contact with recent trends south of the border. It is in the design of the piers, second only to that of the windows, that the awareness of current trends is most clearly shown by the Sweetheart mason. The piers themselves no longer have a stepped profile with angle and leading shafts, as had been employed in the majority of churches so far discussed. Instead they are of a type which has the appearance of bundles of conjoined shafts: the four largest shafts, to which added emphasis is given by broad fillets, are on the cardinal axes, and between them are pairs of lesser shafts. In the piers which had earlier been used in the choir of Glasgow, for example, the flat faces of the stepped section core had still given some expression of

Plate 6. Sweetheart Abbey nave. *Crown copyright: Historic Buildings and Monuments, Scotland.*

the planes of the supported wall, and consequently offered an appearance of sturdy strength. The Sweetheart piers are certainly no less sturdy, but the curved faces create an impression of greater ease of support due to their more plastic modelling. In looking for the origins of such piers it might be argued that their design harks back to prototypes in earlier Cistercian buildings in Scotland and northern England. At such as Dundrennan and Glenluce, for example, variants of bundled shaft piers based on examples used in Burgundy, the original home of the order, had been employed.[30] But the Sweetheart piers are significantly different from those earlier examples, and are rather of a type which was becoming part of the general architectural vocabulary of England in the later thirteenth century. It is perhaps above all the broad fillets emphasising the axes of the leading shafts which show that no debts were owed to the earlier houses of the order in this respect, and that it was instead to more recent work that the master mason was looking.

The modernity of Sweetheart is also shown in the details of the caps and bases of the piers, in which the individual mouldings are more fleshily rounded, less undercut, and are grouped in greater concentrations than had been the case in the choir of Glasgow or the nave of Dunblane. This change is most easily observed in the bases. At most of the mid-century churches which have been considered the upper base mouldings are of the type which had such deep cutting between their two main rolls that it is often described as 'water-holding', whereas at Sweetheart the upper mouldings consist of a sequence of three rather thick rolls, one above the other, with no undercutting between.

The general change of moulding design which took place around this date is of great value in attempting to understand the sequence of building in the nave of Glasgow Cathedral, for which there are no documentary pointers. As has been said, the plan was dictated by the abandoned campaign instigated in the first years of the century. Although Bishop Bondington had diverted the available resources from the nave to the choir, some work does seem to have been undertaken on the nave as the east limb was nearing its conclusion and work moved on to the transepts.

The mouldings of the south and west doorways, with their sequences of three-quarter shafts and quadrant hollows, bear comparison with parts of the choir, whilst the west window, despite over-restoration around 1850, is clearly of the same type as those inserted in the transepts during the 1270s. Of greater importance for the evidence it provides of the continuity of work from the transepts to the nave is the design of the nave piers. Despite the heavy reworking many have undergone, the form of the bases is essentially authentic, and the water-holding profile above a concave flared sub-base shows little change from the type established in the eastern limb. The piers themselves, of octofoil section composed of four filleted axial shafts alternating with four angular shafts with diagonally set arrises, are foreshadowed in the responds incorporated in the crossing piers, as are also the capitals with multiple mouldings down their bells.

On this basis it is evident that the design of the nave was already in hand when the transepts were under construction, and there is no good reason to doubt that the operation was prosecuted with due speed once the transepts were complete. There are, nevertheless, some changes of detail above the arcades which could point to a further change of mason at this level: this is seen particularly in such features as the triforium bases which, like those of Sweetheart, are made up of sequences of rolls. However, as will be seen when the tracery is discussed, there is nothing in the nave which is not consistent with a date in the later decades of the thirteenth century.

The mason who completed the nave of Glasgow was faced with greater problems than had been his predecessors, since not only was the plan fixed, with its tight rhythm of bays, but so also was the overall height. It was within these restrictions that he had to design his elevations, and it is perhaps not surprising that his solution has not received universal acclaim, although on closer inspection it is both more satisfying and interesting than first appears. The most striking feature of the elevations is the way in which the triforium and clearstorey stages are linked by embracing arches, with two of these arches corresponding to each of the arcade bays below (see Figure 1b, p. 178). Consequently, although the arcade bays are in fact narrower than those in the choir, they do not seem excessively so because of the contrast with the much closer spacing of the upper storeys.

Linkage of the upper storeys in this way had been first devised at the Welsh cathedral of St Davids towards the end of the twelfth century, and there is at least a temptation to suspect that the design for the nave at Glasgow as formulated in the early thirteenth century may have been for something of this type. However, experiments to reduce the impact of the triforium stage by subsuming it within the clearstorey, or by omitting it altogether, did not stop there. Indeed, the problem was one which was given much thought in many of the more advanced

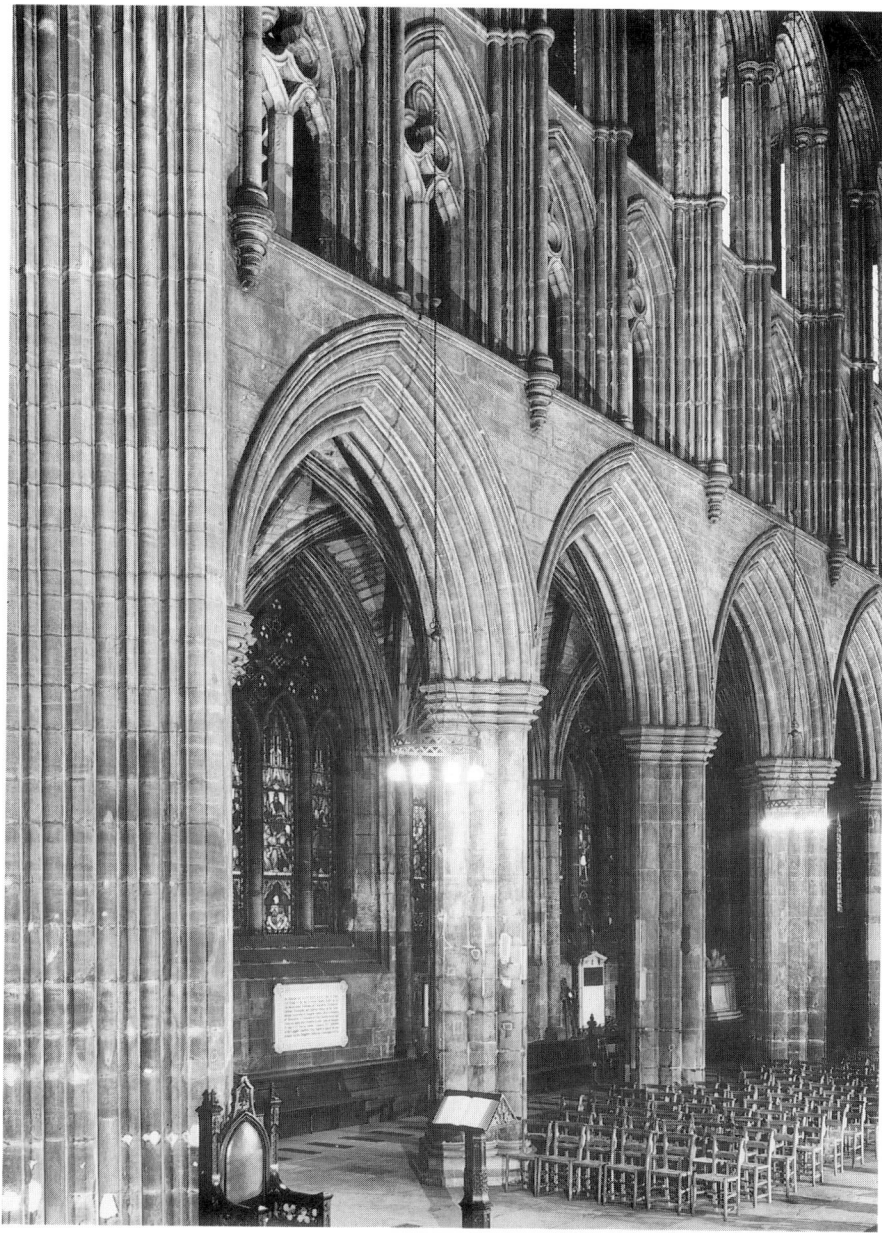

Plate 7. Glasgow Cathedral nave. *Crown copyright: Historic Buildings and Monuments, Scotland.*

architectural centres of thirteenth-century western Europe. In England some of the most interesting experiments on these lines were made in the western and northern parts of the country, whilst in Scotland reference has already been made to the solutions developed at Pluscarden and Elgin. It is within this broader context that the design of Glasgow nave should be viewed. That the nave was a creation of its time may be seen by comparison with the slightly later nave of York Minster, started in the 1290s, where a further variant on the theme of direct linkage between clearstorey and triforium was attempted, although there it was based directly on French prototypes.

For further support of a date in the later decades of the century for Glasgow's nave, we may look to the design of the tracery (see Figure 3o and p, p. 180). Apart from the great west window, tracery is used sparingly in the nave, and is confined to those openings in which it would make the greatest impact: the south aisle wall and the triforium. In the north aisle, perhaps because there was no entrance on that side, and in the clearstorey, the individual lights are simply extended up to the arch of the window. In those openings with tracery it is of a type which, south of the border, would be dated to around the last quarter of the thirteenth or the earlier years of the following century, in which the tracery field is occupied by single or grouped lobed figures without containing circlets. As is also the case in some of the presbytery windows at Sweetheart, certain features of the design and construction of the tracery show a slight awkwardness of handling which suggests the mason was not entirely sure of his ground. But from their design there seems no good reason to place their construction beyond the later years of the thirteenth century, although it is certainly a possibility that completion of Glasgow, as also of Sweetheart and Elgin, was interrupted by the political crisis at the century's end.

As will be gathered from what has been said so far, it is in the major buildings that our main source of knowledge of the ecclesiastical architecture of this period is to be found. By far the greatest proportion of the funds available for church building was by this time being devoted to the religious houses and cathedrals; indeed, the often repeated statement that the thirteenth century was essentially 'the age of the cathedrals' is as true of Scotland as of anywhere else in Europe. Although it must certainly be borne in mind that the low survival rate of parish churches since the Reformation may give us an unbalanced picture, it seems very likely that the growing tide of appropriations of rectories in the thirteenth century must have had its negative impact on the construction of parochial churches.[31] Such architectural evidence as there is points to an increasing number of the parish churches built being simple rectangular structures, devoid of differentiation between chancel and nave. Some of these rectangular churches, such as Altyre in Moray and Skipness in Argyll, are of handsome proportions, and we know from the fifteenth-century example of such a church as Foulis Easter in Angus, that simple churches might be treasure houses of ecclesiastical art where there was an interested patron.[32] But it is not to such buildings that one looks for primary guidance on the changing patterns of architectural thought at this period.

It is true that in the wealthier areas a number of more ambitious parish churches were still built in the course of the thirteenth century. The nave of Crail in Fife, for example, was a spacious aisled structure of basilican section, with a clearstorey which bears comparison with that at Brechin Cathedral in its simple openings with trifoliate rear-arches. There are also indications that other Fife churches, such as Kinghorn, may have been conceived on a similarly spacious scale, whilst further west the surviving aisle at Lanark clearly was part of a building of some pretensions. Nevertheless, there are insufficient remains of adequately securely datable examples of parochial architecture from the second half of the thirteenth century to allow more than the most general conclusions to be drawn, and the information they provide adds little to what is known from the greater churches.

The troubles which followed the death of Alexander III in 1286, and of his grandaughter four years later, were to have a dramatic impact on the course of ecclesiastical architecture. It has been seen that the products of the relatively large number of major building campaigns under way in the second half of the century reveal the presence in Scotland throughout this period of masons capable of designing architecture of very high quality, albeit within financial restraints which prohibited the highest flights of fancy in either planning or scale. From the architectural relationships of their buildings it is evident that the majority of the masons working in the lowland areas had their roots in northern England, as had been the case in the twelfth and earlier thirteenth centuries, and it is perhaps not going too far to suggest that Scotland and northern England were still so closely linked that the political border between the two was architecturally negligible. That is certainly not to say that our churches did not reflect developments taking place elsewhere in Europe, although at this time such developments do seem to have reached Scotland initially through the medium of England.

However, the Wars of Independence were to result in the severance of many of these artistic ties with England, so that the later thirteenth century was arguably the last period until the eighteenth century when the architectural courses of the two countries ran essentially in parallel. The surviving documentation suggests that relatively little major church building was taking place throughout the greater part of the fourteenth century, and the *lacuna* indicated by the documentation is also pointed to by a marked shift of direction in architectural thought at the turn of the fourteenth and fifteenth centuries at the time that church building once again gathered new momentum. With the exception of the first phase of rebuilding at Melrose, which is likely to have been an exotic raised under English patronage, masons working in Scotland seem to have consciously chosen to reject English guidance. This was no doubt partly for reasons of patriotism, but it is also likely to have been because English patterns of architectural thought had become foreign through a long period when there had been little call for church building. As a consequence Scottish architecture in the second half of the thirteenth century gains an additional interest as representing a highly creative phase which was arbitrarily terminated through political circumstances, and which was eventually followed by architectural developments of a very different character.

NOTES

1. *Chron. Wyntoun* (Laing), ii, 258.
2. David Hay Fleming, 'Some Recent Discoveries in St. Andrews', *PSAS*, xl (1914–15), 209–32.
3. *Chron. Bower*, i, 360–1.
4. Ibid., 364, 371.
5. See, for example, the plan of 1812 in the Hutton Collection, NLS MS 30.5.23 12b.
6. *Dunf. Reg.*, no. 288.
7. *Chron. Melrose* (Stevenson), 103.
8. Ibid., 70.
9. *Glas. Reg.*, i, p. xxviii.
10. A. W. Clapham, *English Romanesque Architecture After the Conquest* (Oxford, 1934), 87.

11. Christopher Wilson in Colin McWilliam, *The Buildings of Scotland: Lothian* (Harmondsworth, 1978), 36.
12. Richard Fawcett, 'The Blackadder Aisle at Glasgow Cathedral, A Reconsideration of the Architectural Evidence', *PSAS*, cxv (1985), 277–87.
13. John Honeyman, 'The Cathedral Church', in *The Book of Glasgow Cathedral*, ed. George Eyre-Todd (Glasgow, 1898), 226–74.
14. For Iona see RCAHMS, *Argyll*, x, *Iona* (1982), 80–85.
15. Theiner, *Monumenta*, no. 91.
16. Richard Fawcett, 'Dunblane Cathedral: Evidence for a Change in the Design of the Nave', *PSAS*, cxii (1982), 576–8.
17. Richard Fawcett, 'Scottish Medieval Window Tracery', in *Studies in Scottish Antiquity*, ed. D. J. Breeze (Edinburgh, 1984), 148–96.
18. Myln, *Vitae*, 13.
19. David MacGibbon and Thomas Ross, *The Ecclesiastical Architecture of Scotland* (Edinburgh, 1896–7), ii, 204.
20. *Brech. Reg.,* i, no. 3.
21. J. S. Richardson, *Inchmahome Priory, Perthshire* (Official Leaflet; Edinburgh, 1947).
22. *Moray Reg.*, nos. 26, 57, 58.
23. *Chron. Bower*, ii, 112.
24. *Moray Registrum*, no. 303.
25. *Glas. Reg.*, i, no. 229.
26. Blore's drawings are in two collections: London, Victoria and Albert Museum Department of Prints and Drawings, 8724, 1–38, and Glasgow, Mitchell Library, D527941.
27. J. Collie, *Plans, Elevations, Sections, Details and Views of the Cathedral of Glasgow* (London, 1835).
28. Cowan and Easson, *Religious Houses*, 78.
29. Robert Branner, *St Louis and the Court Style in Gothic Architecture* (London, 1965), 18.
30. Peter Fergusson, 'The South Transept Elevation of Byland Abbey', *Journal of the British Archaeological Association*, 3rd series, xxxviii (1975), 155–76, at 161.
31. I. B. Cowan, 'The Appropriation of Parish Churches in *Historical Atlas*, 37–38.
32. M. R. Apted and W. Norman Robertson, 'Late Fifteenth Century Church Paintings from Guthrie and Foulis Easter', *PSAS*, xcv (1961–2), 262–79; David McRoberts, 'The Fifteenth Century Altarpiece of Fowlis Easter Church', in Anne O'Connor and D. V. Clarke, *From the Stone Age to the 'Forty Five'* (Edinburgh, 1983), 384–98.

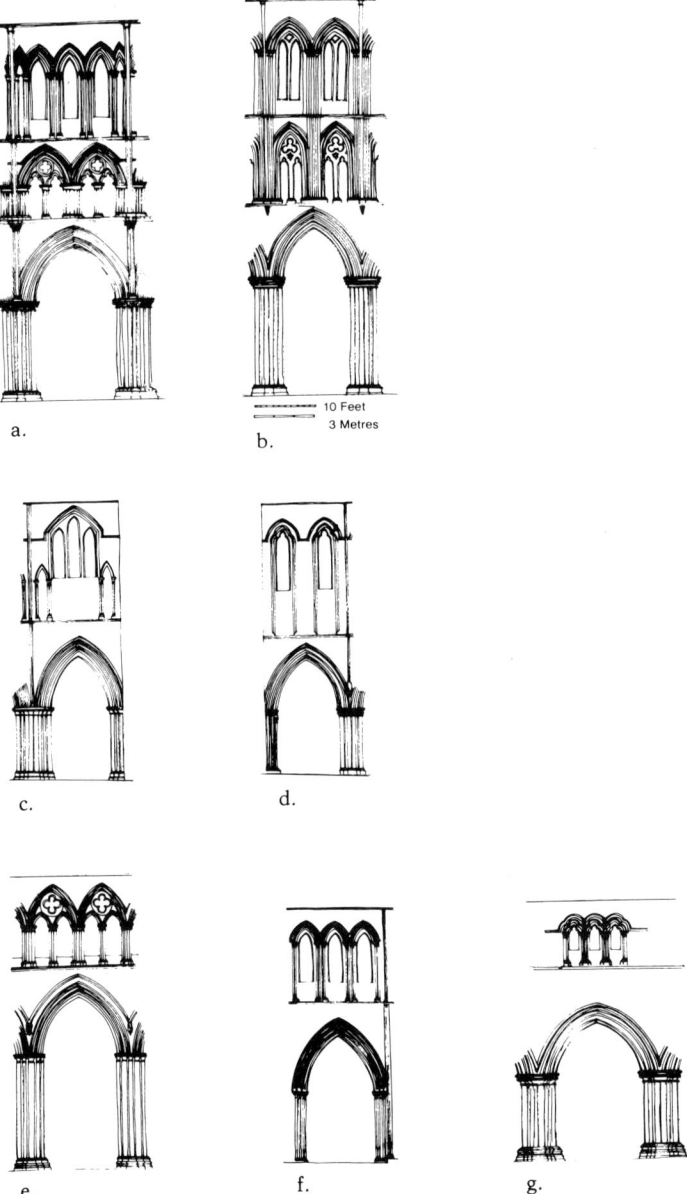

Figure 1. Comparative sketch elevations of major churches in the second half of the thirteenth century: (a) Glasgow Cathedral, choir; (b) Glasgow Cathedral, nave; (c) Pluscarden Priory, south transept; (d) Pluscarden Priory, north transept; (e) Dunblane Cathedral, nave; (f) Elgin Cathedral, choir; (g) Sweetheart Abbey, nave.

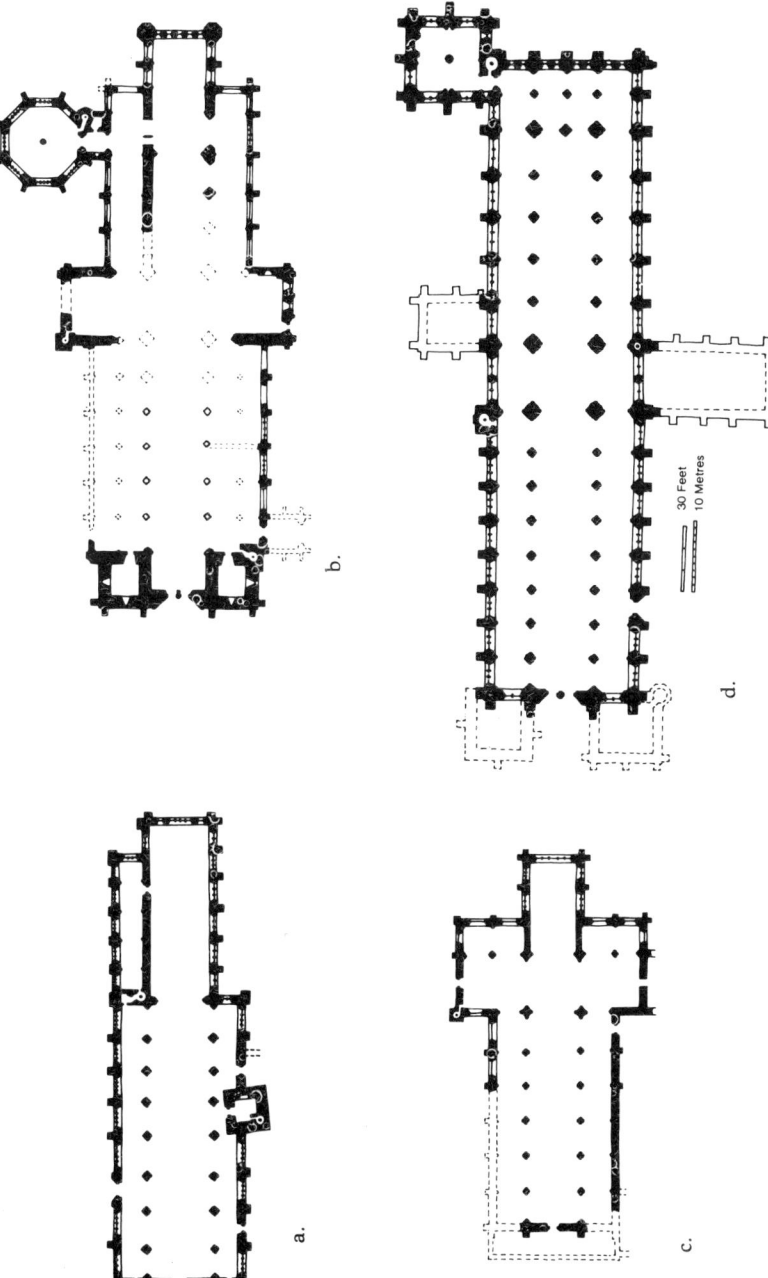

Figure 2. Plans of major churches: (a) Dunblane Cathedral; (b) Elgin Cathedral; (c) Sweetheart Abbey; (d) Glasgow Cathedral.

Figure 3. Window tracery in the second half of the thirteenth century: (a, b, c, d) Glasgow Cathedral choir; (e) Dunblane Cathedral, nave; (f, g) Elgin Cathedral, presbytery; (h) Glasgow Cathedral, transepts; Elgin Cathedral, chapter house door; (i) Glasgow Cathedral, west front; Sweetheart Abbey, north transept; Pluscarden Priory, choir; (j) Glasgow Cathedral, south transept; (k) Sweetheart Abbey, east window; (l) Glasgow Cathedral, north transept; (m, n) Sweetheart Abbey, choir; (o) Glasgow Cathedral, nave triforium; (p) Glasgow Cathedral, nave south aisle.

8

ALEXANDER III: THE HISTORIOGRAPHY OF A MYTH[1]

Norman H. Reid

For long it has been customary to treat the reign of Alexander III as a kind of 'golden age'. It is curious to note, however, that most of the early narrative sources actually give little justification for this. The contemporary *Chronicle of Holyrood*, for example, gives only the barest note of his accidental death, and no details at all of the events of his reign; the *Chronicle of Melrose*, also contemporary, dwells more upon the inglorious minority period than on the rest of the reign, and ascribes little of note to Alexander himself; even Fordun, in the body of his narrative, gives us little reason to expect the astounding eulogy which follows his account of Alexander's death. Clearly, the imagination of generations of historians has been stirred by something other than merely the events of Alexander III's reign. What, then, has made Alexander III so revered, and how has this long-standing reverence affected the interpretation of his reign in modern times? This chapter seeks to answer these questions through a study of the treatment of Alexander III's reign in a selection of historical writings from the last seven centuries.

There are several contemporary Scottish works. *The Chronicle of the Kings of Scotland,*[2] one version of which ends in 1251 and must have been written within a few years thereafter, makes mention of the king's 'coronation', and of his knighting and marriage in England in 1251. Referring to the first change in the council of Alexander III, it adverts to the fact that 'the devil has sown discord among the nobles', a noteworthy allusion to the God-given peace and unity which a well-governed realm enjoys.[3] Later versions of the same chronicle also advert to Alexander's death, one of them adding:

He was beloved of God and man, and endeavoured to keep the nations of his land always at peace; and none of his predecessors was able to hold the kingdom with so great peace and so great rejoicing.[4]

181

The *Chronicle of Melrose* is a fuller source. On the minority, it takes a strongly pro-Comyn and anti-English line, blaming Alan Durward (rather than the devil) for the dissension in the governing community. While there is little comment on the actual conduct of rule, the contention is clear that the Durward faction was acting towards 'the dishonour of king and kingdom' (*dedecus regis et regni*).[5] The chronicler notes the Durward party's seizure of the fruits of the see of St Andrews, an ungodly act, and their consequent excommunication. He thus implies that the Comyn seizure of the king at Kinross in 1257 was a righteous use of force, in order to re-establish just and godly rule. In the following year Alexander III took personal control, and called his host 'in order to subjugate his rebels and excommunicate traitors to himself'.[6] Also of interest to this study is the description of the acquisition of the western isles by Alexander III. The Norwegian expedition of 1263 is given very little detail, but the chronicler does ascribe the failure of Hakon's venture to divine rather than human power and claims that Hakon did likewise.[7] The discussion of the treaty of Perth,[8] although highly coloured by exaltation of the Melrose monk to whom is ascribed the complete negotiation, makes the restoration of peace between and within the two kingdoms the sole aim of both kings.

The fullest English sources for Scottish affairs in this period are the *Chronica Majora* of Matthew Paris (for the earlier part of the reign) and the *Chronicle of Lanercost*. Matthew Paris notes that Alexander III was 'raised to the throne' by the nobles of Scotland,[9] a clear expression of the authority lent to the king by the community. He makes mention of Alexander's response to Henry III's request for homage for Scotland in 1252:

> . . . he had come thither in peace and for the honour of the king of England . . . and not to reply to him about so difficult a question. For he had not held full deliberation or suitable counsel concerning this with his chief men, as so difficult a matter demanded.[10]

Protection of the integrity of the kingdom was one of the most fundamental duties of the king, and it is noteworthy that here Alexander performs that duty through appeal to the parallel responsibility of acting through the good counsel of the community. Writing of the events of 1257, Paris implies that Alexander had taken rule into his own hands, but since the king of Scotland, Alexander, — from whose youth the greatest benefit was hoped for the kingdom of Scotland, — misgoverned too unbecomingly, promoting and following foreigners and exalting and appointing them over his native subjects, the inhabitants and natives were indignant, and to prevent his breaking out in worse ways they placed the king himself and the queen under custody again . . . until . . . they should have removed to a distance all the foreigners. And thenceforward the nobles of Scotland held the reins of their kingdom with greater freedom and safety.[11]

In the same passage the queen is upbraided for bringing the English intervention upon the country. Coming from an English chronicler, this is a remarkably sympathetic comment, and a noteworthy allusion to the rights of the community in government.

The *Chronicle of Lanercost* is undoubtedly the best contemporary English source for Scottish affairs in this period. Although probably not actually compiled at Lanercost, it is undoubtedly of northern English origin, and was written during the reign of Edward I. In contrast to some other sources, it gives the lie to any impression that under Alexander the land prospered in uninterrupted welfare and plenty: for example, under the year 1256 the chronicler tells us that the weather in England and Scotland was so bad that the crops were almost entirely lost, causing famine in the following year.[12] Perhaps Lanercost's greatest contribution to our theme, however, is his personal antagonism to Alexander III. He is prepared to believe those who blamed Alexander for the death of his wife and children, who died *pro peccato, ut creditur, patris.*[13] He reiterates this sentiment later: the deaths of his children were attempts by God to make Alexander amend his sinful ways. The chronicler is, however, prepared to give Alexander some credit; he says, for example, that in his invasion of Man in 1275 Alexander made efforts to win peace with the Manxmen. Godfrey, King of Man, was offered 'the peace of God and the King of Scots', but the offer being turned down, the Manxmen were routed in the ensuing battle.[14] The chronicler seems to imply that the righteous were victorious. Lanercost gives us more details of Alexander's death[15] than any other contemporary source, English or Scottish. He accuses the king of the sin of lust, which, persuading him to ignore the good counsel which advised him not to attempt to return to Yolande late on a wild night, cost him his life. (It should be noted that the chronicler has no love for Yolande, at whose door he lays the blame for many of Scotland's future woes.) Instead of any eulogy, Lanercost uses the death of Alexander as a moral tale: he paid no heed to the death of his first wife and children, amongst other warnings and portents sent by God, and refused to mend his ways; he was immoral, impetuous and irreverent.[16] Such a picture hardly coincides with the medieval idea of the perfect king — of blameless life and character, heedful of good counsel, pious, and interested in the welfare of his kingdom far above himself. Lanercost admits that many wept both over Alexander's death and over the grave consequences which it had for the kingdom, but qualifies this with the assertion that those who were closest to Alexander did not weep for him.[17]

The *Chronicle of Man* provides a new angle from which to view this reign with regard to the western isles. It almost completely ignores the major concerns of the sources we have so far studied: the minority period merits no attention here; Hakon IV's expedition receives little more than the barest reference, and even the Norwegian cession of Man and the other islands to Scotland in 1266 is not mentioned. It does, however, open our eyes to the islesmen's own attitude to their position: despite Scottish claims to the contrary, they did not consider subjection to either Scotland or Norway a reality until it was forced upon them. For this reason, the Scottish invasion of 1275 is given detailed treatment.[18]

Hakon's Saga gives us a different view again. Its ambivalent attitude towards events in the west has been amply demonstrated elsewhere in this volume,[19] but it leaves no room for doubt that the Scots kings were the aggressors. Alexander III's first embassy regarding the isles, in 1261, came 'more with fair words than with faith', and was detained over the winter, because of its discourtesy in attempting to leave without warning or permission.[20] In the following year we hear details of the development of the dispute which finally led to the expedition of 1263. The earl of Ross had attacked the islands with great ferocity, and it is made clear that these attacks were a continuation of the expansionist policy which had been initiated by Alexander II: Alexander III 'meant of a surety to lay under him all the Southern Isles'.[21] From the detailed description of the expedition itself, it is worth noting that the saga adds no weight to the accusation in some of the Scottish sources that Hakon was intent on conquering Scotland; on the contrary, he acted with an understanding of the difficult position in which many of the islesmen found themselves, torn between competing claims to their allegiance by two kings. He gave them time to decide which king to follow, and promised that if he came to agreement with the king of Scots he would seek atonement for any who supported him.[22] Negotiations were held, but, although there seemed to be little to hinder an agreement, none was reached and the Norwegians concluded that the Scots were playing for time.[23] At length, despairing of a peaceful settlement and short of supplies, the Norwegians turned again to harrying, notably in the Loch Lomond area. Shortly thereafter there occurred the great storm and the battle at Largs, which is minutely described. In contrast to later Scottish accounts, the saga does not ascribe decisive victory to either side, but nonetheless asserts that:

> In this voyage king Hacon had won back those realms which king Magnus barelegs had won from Scotland and the Southern Isles.[24]

In the following year, according to the fragment of *Magnus' Saga*, continued Scots aggression seemed to offer little hope of peace in the isles.[25] Eventually, however, further negotiations led to the treaty of Perth.

What, then, have the contemporary sources told us about Alexander's reign? The attention centres mainly on the turbulence of the minority period, the conflict with King Hakon, and the deaths of Alexander's family and himself. These emphases are natural; these were the aspects of the reign which were most memorable. Some of these narratives do, however, give us more; they tell us of their attitudes to the king and his rule. There is a fairly consistent lamentation over misgovernment by one side or the other during the minority. Perhaps the *Chronicle of the Kings of Scotland* is most representative when, without taking sides, it refers to the evil of discord in the community. Even the more partisan writers, such as the Melrose chronicler and Matthew Paris, agree that the minority was the antithesis of good rule. Leaving aside the *Chronicle of Lanercost* for the moment, there is also a fairly unanimous impression that the general conduct of Alexander's reign after his assumption of personal control reflected those qualities of kingly rule which were demanded by the expectations of the age; the *Chronicle of the Kings of Scotland* has him beloved of God and man, and holding the realm in peace and happiness; the *Melrose Chronicle* has him rightly subduing traitors, favoured by God over the Norwegian affair, and ambitious to win peace; Matthew Paris reminds us of the community's part in the wielding of power, and comments on Alexander's upholding of the integrity of his realm. *Hakon's Saga* also implies mutual respect. Just as it was honourable for Hakon to lead the expedition, it was honourable for Alexander to resist it; both kings pursued their actions out of a duty to promote the welfare of their kingdoms. The two were in conflict, and in the final analysis it lay upon God to favour one or the other.

Matthew Paris, on the other hand, makes reference to Alexander's bad rule. Whilst Paris implies that allowance should be made for the king's youthful inexperience, however, the Lanercost chronicler is less tolerant, and levels fundamental criticisms at the king. Lanercost's antagonism is interesting, for it does not seem to be a generalised anti-Scottish sentiment; he is far from critical of the Scots nobility after 1286.[26] Without knowing precisely where or by whom the chronicle was written, it is difficult to draw any firm conclusions about the roots of this antagonism, but it may be that the chronicler's striking dislike of Yolande is a key.[27] Her lineage cannot have endeared her to an English chronicler: the relations between France and England were not good in this period, and it should be remembered that by the time this was written the Scots may well have made the treaty of Paris with the French (1295) in alliance against the English dominion over Scotland. It is possible that the chronicler's general attitude to Alexander might have been coloured by the king's second marriage.[28]

The picture which we can draw of Alexander III, then, from the contemporary narratives is generally of a good king who lived up to the expectations of his position, and who led his country, largely at peace and in at least relative prosperity, after a minority which exemplified the need for good kingly rule. He seems to have been genuinely popular, although he was not without critics, and there is no reason to believe the impression that has sometimes been given in more recent times, that this was a flawless reign, in which the land knew unceasing, boundless joy and wealth.

We turn now to works which were composed in Scotland during the one hundred and fifty or so years following Alexander's death. The chronicle by John of Fordun is one of the most significant and invaluable sources for the history of Scotland in the period closely prior to, and during, the War of Independence. Writing in the third quarter of the fourteenth century, Fordun's treatment of our period is generally reliable and achieves a level of analysis quite unparalleled in any earlier Scottish source. His account of the reign begins with the dispute which took place at Alexander's inauguration[29] regarding the rectitude of inaugurating a king who had not previously been knighted. This dispute was of course a precursor to, and portent of, the divisions within the governing community which were to plague Alexander's minority. Fordun uses this episode as a platform upon which to build a homily regarding the importance of having a king ('a country without a king was, beyond a doubt, like a ship amid the waves of the sea, without rower or steersman'), and the requirement for the consent and acclamation of the community before a king can claim the right to rule. He goes on to describe the inauguration ceremony in great detail, doubtless in order both to assert the legitimacy of this king, and to stress the vital part played by the community in the creation of a king, and thus by implication in the conduct of his rule. The narrative continues with a description of the translation of the bones of Queen Margaret, the saintly ancestor of the new king, to her new chapel in the abbey of Dunfermline (to celebrate her canonization).[30] It then goes on to the realisation by the Scots magnates that the minority was going to be fraught with danger, and their consequent approach to Henry III for assistance and protection, resulting in the marriage of Alexander III to Henry's daughter, Margaret. Henry also knighted Alexander, and Fordun is full of praise for the English king's part in Scottish affairs.[31] There follows the fall of Alexander's first council with, shortly thereafter, severe strictures against the Comyn government which replaced it:

> . . . these councillors were so many kings. For he who saw the poor crushed down in these days, the nobles ousted from their inheritance, the drudgery forced upon the citizens, the violence done to churches, might with good reason say, 'Woe unto the kingdom where the king is a boy!'

> . . . judgement and righteousness in the kingdom of Scotland were slumbering.[32]

Once again the minority is portrayed as the antithesis of kingly rule, since changes in the government made the situation progressively worse as each party in turn tried to wreak vengeance on the misdoings of the other.

The first personal act of Alexander III reported by Fordun is the appeal by the king against the abuse of the rights and privileges of his crown which were represented by the enquiry of a papal legate into the disputed succession to the earldom of Menteith, a case which Alexander was ready to judge himself.[33] This is highly significant, for it shows Alexander to be a mature ruler, keen to dispense justice, and to protect the liberties of the kingdom. Under the year 1261 Fordun records the finding of an ancient cross at Peebles, and ascribes to Alexander the piety of founding a church on the site.[34]

There follows a section on Hakon IV's enterprise in the isles.[35] Not a great deal of detail is given, and the account is generally restrained: Largs is certainly not portrayed as a glorious victory, although the storm which drove the Norwegians on shore, at the mercy of the Scots, is described as an act of God, who naturally favoured those who righteously defended their land against foreign incursion. Following the failure of Hakon's quest, Alexander hastily sent forces to the isles to secure them for himself. It can be no coincidence that in naming the leaders of the Scottish expedition to the western isles, Fordun specifically mentions the earl of Buchan (a leader of the Comyns) and Alan Durward: the king had achieved a state of unity in which the leaders of the community could resolve their differences and work together for the common good. Heeding good counsel, King Magnus of Norway negotiated the cession of the isles to Scotland.

Perhaps in order to contrast Alexander III's firm and settled personal rule with the chaos of England in the grip of noble rebellion, Fordun goes on to describe the assistance lent by Alexander to his beleaguered father-in-law. Returning to Scottish affairs, and the defence of the rights and privileges of the realm, Fordun recounts the resistance by the king and clergy of Scots to the efforts of the papal legate Ottoboni to raise taxation from the Scottish church.[36] He continues with the clandestine marriage of Martha, countess of Carrick, to the young Robert Bruce,[37] which is presumably introduced as a backdrop to the birth of the son of the marriage, King Robert I, who is the hero of Fordun's narrative. There follows the death of Henry III, the attendance of Alexander and his queen at the coronation of Edward I, the subsequent death of Alexander's queen, and the later visit of Alexander to England to do homage for his English lands.[38] The requested homage for Scotland is not mentioned, but there are hints of a deterioration in relations between the two kings and their kingdoms. This theme returns (after discussion of the further papal taxation raised by Boiamund) with a dispute over the border which, despite negotiations, remained unresolved.[39]

Then begins the downfall of Scotland, with the deaths of the king's children. Prince Alexander was especially lamented, and was buried

> amid the boundless grief of the whole people, the tears and groans of all the clergy, and the endless sobs of the king and the magnates.[40]

Fordun has the gathering woes of Scotland compounded by the

tyrannous character of Edward I, whose ruthless conquest of Wales, barbarous treatment of the Welsh, and mispropriation of the papal taxation raised for the crusade are fiercely criticised. He admits that this outburst is included

> lest any foreign nation which may read the said history should, unchastened by the example of the Welsh, unwarily fall under the dominion of most wretched thraldom to the English.[41]

Finally, Fordun tells of the 'solemnly' conducted marriage of Alexander to Yolande, and then, without further comment or embellishment, simply reports the death of the king.[42] It is worth quoting in full the eulogy which follows:

> How worthy of tears, and how hurtful, his death was to the kingdom of Scotland, is plainly shown forth by the evils of after times. This king reigned thirty-six years. All the days of the life of this king, the Church of Christ flourished, her priests were honoured with due worship, vice was withered, craft there was none, wrong came to an end, truth was strong, and righteousness reigned. Moreover, rightly, and by reason of the merits of his uprightness, was he called king: seeing that he ruled himself and his people aright, allowing unto each his rights; and if, at any time, any of his people rebelled, he curbed their madness with discipline so unbending, that they would put a rope round their necks, ready for hanging, were that his will and pleasure, and bow themselves under his rule. By reason whereof he was looked upon with equal fear and love, both far and near, not only by his friends, but also by his adversaries, — and especially by the English. And all the time he lived upon earth security reigned in steadfastness of peace and quiet, and gleeful freedom. O Scotland, truly unhappy, when bereft of so great a leader and pilot; while — greater unhappiness still! — he left no lawful offspring to succeed him. Thou hast an everlasting spring of mourning and sorrow in the death of one whose praiseworthy life bestowed, on thee especially, such increase of welfare.[43]

W. F. Skene termed Fordun's chronicle 'the first detailed and systematic history of Scotland',[44] and it is certainly true that it offers a much fuller and more analytical approach than any previous Scottish source. In his treatment of the minority, it must be noted that he does not obviously take sides, both praising the leaders of the two sides, and condemning both parties for their misuse of power. The disgrace of the minority is used as a contrast against Alexander's firm personal rule, which demonstrates all good kingly attributes. In this way, the whole of the Alexander III episode in Fordun's work becomes an exaltation of kingship. Contrasts are introduced periodically in order to heighten the image — most notably in the depths to which Henry III's England dives when the nobility rebel against the king, and in the base barbarism and injustice which he ascribes to Edward I. Alexander is not portrayed as a hero, but the encomium which follows his death is nonetheless consistent both with Fordun's narrative and with the attitude of the contemporary sources, for he does not portray the reign as outstanding; rather, he says that Alexander was to be lamented because he exemplified those qualities which were sought in a medieval king.

Fordun seems to be the first writer to make a conscious attempt to paint a picture of an ideal king. This can be explained by an assessment of his purpose in writing. From his very earliest chapters, Fordun set out to provide a firm historical basis for the independence of the Scottish nation from England. In this, he was part of a tradition of Scottish propagandists who were active throughout the period of the wars of independence. By boosting the image of Alexander III, and more particularly of the strength of his kingship in the tradition of independent Scottish monarchs, and by making great play of the woes which followed upon the untimely removal of such support and leadership for the kingdom, Fordun strengthened the argument that the attempted imposition of English hegemony in the ensuing decades was aberrant and a travesty of justice. Furthermore, by reinforcing a tradition of good independent rule at this stage in history, Fordun gave a clear example of kingship to be aimed at, and achieved, by his hero, Robert I.

Skene suggests that this section of the work was written around the year 1363 (although it may have been expanded later).[45] In the thirty-odd years which had elapsed since the death of Robert I in 1329, Scotland had had another royal minority punctuated by further civil war, attempts by Edward Balliol to win the throne (backed by Edward III), and a personal rule cut short by David II's capture by the English at the battle of Neville's Cross in 1346. The king remained in captivity for eleven years, during which the government of Scotland was weak and disorganised in terms of administration, economy and enforcement of law and order. There was throughout the period considerable English interference in Scotland, both political and military, and particularly after 1356 there was strong pressure from the English king to have himself or his heir nominated as heir to the Scottish throne. After David II's release in 1357 there was a reimposition of firm rule, and a gradual recovery of the kingdom's finances, administration and law. From the end of the decade, however, there seems to have been increasing hostility towards the king, there were accusations of bad counsel, and the situation deteriorated so far that in 1363 rebellion broke out.[46]

Fordun's tale thus also carries a moral for his own times; the minority is to be identified with the present or potential situation, whereas the personal rule of Alexander III is the portrayal of things as they should be. Thus in Fordun we have the first elaboration of the 'myth' of Alexander III. Treated in the contemporary sources as a good king, a king to be admired, Alexander becomes, for the nationally propagandist and morally pedagogic purposes of Fordun, a true paragon of kingship.

Little more than half a century later, the myth had grown further. Andrew Wyntoun's *Orygynale Cronykil of Scotland* gives no details of Alexander's inauguration, but passes straight on to the translation of the bones of St Margaret, embellished with the tale of how her body could not be moved past that of her husband, King Malcolm Canmore.[47] In the passage regarding the marriage and knighting of Alexander III[48] Wyntoun comments that Alexander was bound to live by the counsel of Henry III, and that it was therefore at Henry's instigation that the Durward party fell from power. There follows a brief description of the various changes in the government of the minority, and then, after a notice of the birth of the king's daughter, an account of the Norwegian invasion, most of which is taken up with a description of a furious battle at Largs.[49] Wyntoun gives undoubted victory to the Scots; the Norwegian king escaped, however, and fled to Orkney, where he died, having first written to Alexander to tell him of the false and traitorous dealings of the islemen. There are royal, noble and ecclesiastical births, marriages and deaths, and, in terms similar to Fordun, an accusation of tyranny against Edward I.[50] Wyntoun notes a gathering of the king, his council and the 'estates' in 1285, which was intended to settle finally the long-running dispute over the earldom of Menteith.[51] In 1285 we have the second marriage of Alexander III, and then the note of his death which is followed by a eulogy even more elaborate than that provided by Fordun.[52] To paraphrase: he was missed because under him all Scots lived in honour, quiet and peace, on account of which he was called the 'Peaceable King'; he was strong in the faith, devout, pious and reverent, and protected the church diligently; he loved those who were virtuous, and loathed the vicious; he was just and equitable, and pursued the law keenly; he was honest, loyal and liberal to his courtiers, virtuous in government, and generous in alms; he insisted that a man, of whatever station, who could have an ox, should have land under the plough, and as a result the land was abundant with corn, and food was cheap, even in times of dearth (a situation which ceased suddenly after his death). Wyntoun ends his section on Alexander III with the short poem, possibly the earliest extant, and certainly one of the most famous in the Scots language.[53]

Whilst it is true that Bower's *Scotichronicon*, for much of its narrative, serves to 'inflate Fordun merely with florid Latinity',[54] it nonetheless adds to our understanding of the development of the 'Alexander myth'. The first passage which differs significantly from Fordun is that which deals with the inauguration ceremony,[55] in which Bower claims that the king was crowned and anointed. Following his quotation of Fordun's passage on the misery and oppression of the Comyn rule after 1251, Bower goes into a lengthy discourse on the concept of Christian kingship.[56] Bower, similarly to Lanercost, tells us of great dearth in the land. For the years 1258, 1261, 1267 and 1272, he gives details of famine, tempests (in 1267, the worst since the days of Noah), 'sterility of the land' and unwholesome (*infoecunditas*) conditions,[57] which do not enhance our image of a land burgeoning under great material prosperity. He adds detail to Fordun's treatment of the Norwegian invasion, most notably with his story of the vision of St Margaret and her sons, seen by Sir John Wemyss on the eve of the battle of Largs.[58] This is a symbolic offering of the victory into divine hands, and an emphasis both of the historic context of the struggle, and of the dynastic legitimacy of the king. Bower further inflates this episode with more historical information regarding the isles than was supplied by Fordun. He also gives us more details concerning Alexander's death.[59] Having described the king's fall, he allays concern regarding the suddenness of the death by saying that sudden death, after a good life, need not hinder the soul's passage to glory. In a short *cantus* he claims that for almost seven years after Alexander's death, the Scots were doleful, having neither king nor harvests. As in Wyntoun, we have here almost a hint of sacral kingship: on the death of the good king the land suffers in every way. Bower's eulogy[60] quotes Fordun, interspersing the earlier writer's lines with new material. He describes the king's character and appearance in glowing terms; he speaks of the peace and opulence of the people as a result of good, firm rule; he describes the ayres which took justice to the people of the land, and admires Alexander both for his willingness to mingle with the people, and for making laws for the benefit of all sections of the community. According to Bower, Alexander's peaceful and just rule created favourable trading conditions, and his legislation prohibiting exports was so successful that within a few years the trading community was so prosperous that the kingdom abounded with all good things. So rich was the country that Lombards offered to build a city on an island in the Forth. Bower then includes a short lament for the woes of the kingdom after the death of this most beloved king, and ends his narrative of Alexander III with the tale of Thomas the Rhymer's prophecy and a short passage on the transitory nature of human life.[61]

And so, in both Wyntoun and Bower, the myth of Alexander III takes another step forward. Like Fordun, they both paint a picture of a good king, but they go further: they both introduce the new idea that the realm was materially poorer after Alexander's death. It is Bower alone, however, in his fervour to increase Fordun's impact, who introduces the concept of the 'golden age'. Suddenly Scotland under Alexander III has not only a fine example of medieval kingship, who leads his realm in peace, justice and unity; but she has a king through the sagacity of whose legislation the realm becomes a mecca for foreign merchants who bring with them untold riches.

Like Fordun's, Bower's is a fervently patriotic work, intended to bolster the cause of Scottish independence. His additions to Fordun are of two main types: he provides information and detail which Fordun omitted, and he interpolates comment and moralistic tales. This gives rise to a curious inconsistency in Bower's work, for in his inflation of Fordun, Bower includes information which does not serve to enhance the image of a realm basking in the reflected glory of the archetypal good king. For example, he provides us with more detail than any previous source on the famine and hardships which repeatedly afflicted the country; in praising Gamelin, bishop of St Andrews (to which see, as abbot of Inchcolm, Bower was staunchly loyal), he even seems to imply that at times Alexander could be a *rex horrendus*.[62] Nonetheless, true to his purpose, Bower offsets the criticism by inflating Fordun's eulogy of the king, and, in order to give credence to the excesses of his praise, invents the idea of new legislation leading to material prosperity.[63]

It should be remembered that only a few years before Bower completed his work, Scotland had witnessed the murder of James I. As Bower wrote, the country was yet again in the grip of a period of turbulent minority, with a divided community; in the very recent past both plague and famine had afflicted the country. The threat of foreign domination had receded somewhat (although within Bower's lifetime James I had spent eighteen years in English captivity), but there was nonetheless a fiercely nationalist sentiment in the country.[64] Perhaps

Bower misunderstood the subtlety of Fordun's symbolic approach to Alexander III, or perhaps he deliberately abandoned it in favour of a plainer message for his own day. Whatever the reason, it is to the imagination of Walter Bower that we have to ascribe the decisive flourish in the myth of Alexander III.

Probably written shortly after the death of James II, *Liber Pluscardinensis* is fairly close in time to Bower's work.[65] For the period of Alexander's reign it is principally an abridgement of Bower, although it does introduce some new material. Pluscarden, in a much abbreviated description of the inauguration ceremony,[66] follows Bower in claiming that Alexander was 'solemnly and magnificently crowned, anointed and consecrated'. This writer also refers to the origin myth of the Scots, tracing their roots to Egypt and Greece, and outlining the great achievements of those two countries.[67] Now Alexander III has not only a lineage which is notable in terms of Scottish ancestry, but in addition has a dynastic link with the greatest civilisations of mankind. It is interesting that Pluscarden does not involve Henry III in the removal of Alexander's first council: that is done by the prelates, barons and other chiefs and leaders, giving good counsel, after the return of Alexander to Scotland. The new counsel, of prudent and discreet men, was elected by the three estates, on account of the tender age of the king.[68] The writer goes into some detail of the tyrannies and excesses of the discredited council. Quoting scripture, he explicitly equates actions against the king with actions against the people of the realm.[69] Particularly in the period up to 1263, the Pluscarden writer omits many of the ecclesiastical obituaries and appointments, and other incidentals included by Bower, and gives much less space to non-political affairs. The result is that this work becomes more monarcho-centric than the *Scotichronicon*, and centres more heavily on the internal politics of the reign. There is extra detail regarding the battle of Largs, which becomes even more of a victory for St Margaret and the Scots, and, as in Bower's account, is hailed as a liberation of the *patria*.[70] Even after 1263, when the affairs of England and the crusades gain more attention, this writer still achieves a different balance of material from Bower, occasionally providing unique details. For instance, he tells us that the legate Boiamund returned to Rome to seek a reduction in the level of taxation because he could see the poverty of the country;[71] and he relates that Alexander's homage to Edward I excluded the rights, privileges and liberties of his crown.[72]

Liber Pluscardinensis, then, retells Bower's story from a more consistently Scottish viewpoint, and one which perhaps serves to strengthen even further the positive aspects of Alexander's rule. In its summary of the reign,[73] the work is based almost entirely on Bower, borrows his invention of statute, and even exaggerates further the consequent abundance of the land (notwithstanding Boiamund's reaction to the country, noted above). In this writer we see the first of those who have used Bower to perpetuate the myth.

A mere glance at a few histories written between 1500 and 1800 is sufficient to demonstrate some of the influence exerted by earlier writers. The *History of Greater Britain* by John Major was published in 1521. Creditably perceptive and analytical for its early date, for the most part it follows the narratives of Fordun and Bower. Its interpretation of the material, however, adopts a much more restrained line. Major was an ardent advocate of union with England, and is thus very critical of the marriage of Alexander's daughter to the king of Norway; had she been married into the English royal house, an opportunity would thus have been found for uniting the kingdoms under one king, the advantages of which union he discusses at length.[74] He has a more critical attitude to the events as described in the older sources: he tells of the king's death simply, without great detail, and takes an almost antiquarian interest in the prophecy of Thomas the Rhymer, attributing it to 'our chronicles of this period', and taking pains to deny any belief in the story.[75] He makes little of the benefits of Alexander's rule, other than the equity of justice, which he evidences with Bower's account of justice ayres.[76] Major accepts that as a king Alexander was 'worthy to be placed alongside his father', but no claims are made about great bounty in the realm, or the perfection of Alexander's rule: the unsupported excesses of Bower's story are ignored, presumably because they were consistent neither with the facts nor with Major's thesis. To Major, this reign was above all a missed opportunity, for had the Scots acted differently, Scotland and England could have been united, and the calamity of the ensuing war could have been avoided.

The *History of Scotland* written by George Buchanan is less critical than Major in its use of source material. While basically following Bower, Buchanan is sometimes guilty of further exaggeration. Possibly using as his source Fordun and Bower's criticism of the first Comyn government, Buchanan becomes vehemently anti-Comyn. He claims that

When the king took the government into his own hands, he pardoned the
Cumins upon their humble submission, as if their crimes had been expiated
by the death of [Earl] Walter.[77]

His suggestion that this was because the king feared their power, and
wished no disturbance in the land when he was anticipating foreign
war, is not found in the earlier sources, and reminds us of the new
methodology of writers in this period: they were not telling a moral tale
for their readers, but were attempting more academic work. Buchanan
could view the early sources for a period such as the minority, and
expect, from a sixteenth-century perspective, that the Comyns would
have been punished once the king attained majority. Not finding this to
be the case it becomes necessary for him to analyse and explain the
omission. His treatment of the Norwegian invasion is entirely lacking in
sympathy for Hakon IV: here was an unprincipled aggressor 'who
sought an occasion for quarrel'.[78] In defence of the realm, Alexander's
achievement is therefore magnified. Following Fordun, Buchanan has
Hakon IV landing with twenty thousand men, who were first defeated
in battle and thereafter scattered by a storm.[79] In this humanist work,
we find no hint of divine (or saintly) intervention on behalf of the Scots:
the invasion was defeated by force of arms. In his summing up of the
reign, while accepting Bower's word that good legislation was
responsible for great economic prosperity, Buchanan finds it necessary
to support the argument by explaining why there is no corroborating
evidence of such legislation: he claims that 'neglect and age' had
rendered the laws obsolete and forgotten.[80]

Moving to the latter part of the eighteenth century, we come to the
Annals of Scotland written by Sir David Dalrymple of Hailes. This
work, which covers the years 1057 to 1371, is the first history which
we study here which is modern enough in its historical methodology to
cite sources as a matter of course. It gives detailed treatment to the
reign of Alexander III, and cites a wide range of sources, including
contemporary chronicles (both English and Scottish), Bower (cited as
Fordun), Wyntoun and other early histories. In addition, record material
such as *Foedera* and monastic records are used, primarily to corroborate
statements of the narrative sources, and to provide detail. The story
Hailes tells reflects Bower's narrative quite closely. It is noteworthy,
however, that he is careful to pick and choose material from all of the
sources: he mentions that Bower ('Fordun') gives character sketches of
many of the protagonists of his tale, but refrains from including them in

his text, and consigns them instead to a footnote;[81] he rejects the extremes of criticism lavished on one or other of the two main 'parties' during the minority, but instead adopts an approach which displays no obvious bias. His use of material is well exemplified in his treatment of the conflict over the earldom of Menteith, in which he cites Bower, *Foedera* and Wyntoun, synthesises the material to produce order out of the confusion, and places all of his details of the dispute, from beginning (1257) to end (1285), in one section,[82] irrespective of chronological context within his overall narrative. It is thus an interesting testimony to the influence of non-contemporary sources when Hailes, whilst admitting that the sources do not agree, describes the conflict at Largs as a major battle, in which he numbers the Norwegian losses at twenty-four thousand ('part of the crew of 160 vessels'). He is, furthermore, scathing of the cynicism with which this battle was viewed by another historian.[83] Hailes makes little of the circumstances of the king's death: he was 'riding in the dusk of the evening', and was thrown by his horse over a precipice[84] (a detail which is not found in any of the contemporary sources). In his summary of the reign, Hailes points out the benefits of acquiring the western isles, the peaceful relations with England, and the treatment of the church and clergy; he follows Bower in the story of the quarterly justice ayres, and in the ascription to Alexander of 'temperance and purity of manners'.[85] There is no mention of material prosperity, of legislation, or of general lamentation by the people following Alexander's death.

In view of the modern image of Alexander's reign, then, and remembering the Bower inflation of the 'Alexander myth', it is perhaps surprising that the works of the sixteenth to the eighteenth centuries do not, by and large, follow Bower in his excessive admiration of the reign of Alexander III. Their debt to Bower, and indeed to all of the other sources we have so far studied, is clear; but they have attempted to interpret the material, and have generally been critical of information which has appeared unfounded, or too obviously rooted in the purpose of the writer.

In the nineteenth century, particularly in its central decades, much publication was undertaken of documentary sources which had previously been largely inaccessible. This both stimulated historians, and enabled them to research more thoroughly, and, as a result, several eminent historians produced histories of Scotland towards the end of the century. Revisionist in their day, these became standard works, some of which have held their place in the core of modern Scottish historiography until very recent times. It is not possible in a short essay to examine all of the works produced in this period. Thus three well-known general histories have been selected, along with W. F. Skene's *Celtic Scotland*, as a reasonable sample of the scholarship of this period.

Skene's work concentrates on the north and west of Scotland, and it is thus hardly surprising to find that more than half of his narrative of the reign of Alexander III is taken up with the events of 1263. As for the rest of the reign, his versions of the king's inauguration and the translation of the relics of St Margaret are based on Fordun, and the minority is handled in only a few dismissive lines.[86] The evidence afforded by *Hakon's Saga* forms the basis of his description of affairs in the west, the Scots being the initial aggressors, and Hakon's expedition being intended as a 'rescue operation'. The account of the battle of Largs is balanced by use of Fordun, and the two conflicting sources are both quoted at length. Skene concludes that Hakon's expedition failed, leaving the isles 'at the mercy of King Alexander'.[87] After mentioning the treaty of Perth, Skene goes on briefly to narrate the deaths of the royal family, and the recognition of Margaret, 'Maid of Norway' as heir to the throne. He recounts the death of the king in an unacknowledged quotation from Hailes' *Annals*,[88] but declines any further comment on the king or his reign.

Andrew Lang's *History of Scotland* gives only a few pages out of his four volumes to Alexander III. He gives a much abbreviated version of Fordun's inauguration story, followed by a very standard treatment of the minority.[89] His short exposition of the Norwegian invasion and the battle of Largs[90] is again based on *Hakon's Saga* and Fordun. Most of the rest of the reign is seen in the context of relations with England, particularly the homage question, until, towards the end, he considers the theme of the deaths of the royal family and the need to secure the succession. His account of the king's death[91] is based mainly on Lanercost, but he makes no comment on the reign other than to dub Alexander III 'the last of the "Kings of Peace"' (presumably from Wyntoun), and to quote the fragment of verse first found in Wyntoun's chronicle.

The *History of Scotland* by John Hill Burton is a very much larger work than Lang's, and was one of the first in which it was accepted that the reign of Alexander III was a watershed at which to interrupt the chronological narrative in order to examine the society and institutions of the country. His contention that this period is so crucial to an understanding of Scotland's subsequent history is doubtless why he devotes a far higher proportion of his work to Alexander III's reign than did Lang. He discusses at length Bower's account of the inauguration ceremony,[92] coming to the conclusion that Bower was inaccurate in claiming that the king was crowned and anointed. He describes Alexander's marriage in detail, and discusses the ambitions of Henry III towards Scotland in this period.[93] For the minority itself, it seems that Burton was neither willing to believe nor to reconcile the accounts given by the contemporary sources without more corroborative evidence than was available to him:

> Any attempt to go into the details of the manner in which the country was ruled during this king's minority must of necessity become confused, because it is filled with intrigues and counterplots and efforts of personal ambition, while neither can the actors nor the policy they pursued be brought out so distinctly as to enable us to take an interest in them.[94]

He ascribes the events of the minority to the inherent instability of a throne occupied by a child giving rise to noble dynastic ambition, but does not linger, and goes on instead to the expedition of Hakon IV, which he prefaces with a brief history of the Norse involvement in the isles. He gives a fairly balanced assessment of the motives behind Alexander's attack and Hakon's defence of the isles, and is sceptical of those chroniclers who ascribe a great victory to the Scots, believing that the Norwegians were overwhelmed by 'a miscellaneous gathering of the peasantry'. The battle took place more by accident than design, and was an unfortunate twist of fate for Hakon.[95] Burton goes on, following the Fordun pattern, to discuss ecclesiastical affairs, and then turns to the disasters which dogged the later years of the reign. First was the death of Henry III. This left Scotland open to the ambition of Edward I, whose request for homage in 1278 is discussed at length.[96] The 'final calamity' of Alexander's death is noted with the tale of his fall (over a cliff),[97] and the narrative goes on to describe the events of the next four years before pausing for an examination of the state of the country, including the question of material prosperity. In discussing the architectural remains of the period, he makes the point that such buildings

> could not have been raised in a country where there did not exist riches. . . . I cannot but believe that, before the War of Independence, Scotland was a wealthy country for that day.[98]

Using that legislation of which there is record, and observations of trade and agriculture based on occasional references in documentary sources, he conjures up an image of a country which was better off than it ever had been before, or would be again for centuries to come.[99] He admits that his evidence is slender, and that his picture of wealth is based mainly on a 'general impression' gained from 'rummaging unmethodically among old documents', but tries to give it added weight by quoting a similar conclusion from an earlier work.[100]

Primarily a popular work, the history by Professor Peter Hume Brown, does not generally cite sources, but appears to have a clear enough debt to earlier works, particularly the contemporary chronicles, Fordun and Bower. He begins by quoting Wyntoun's description of Alexander as 'the peaceable king', going on to say that the early years of the reign did not give any clue of the benefits which were to follow them. Like some of the other historians of the period, he believes that the two parties of the minority were vaguely pro- and anti-English.[101] His short account of the inauguration[102] seems to be based mainly on Bower, and he cites Fordun as a source for the minority,[103] although he diverges markedly from Fordun's treatment of Henry III as a friend to the Scots in their time of difficulty. Hume Brown makes the apparently unfounded assertion, for instance, that the (anti-English) Comyns had popular support, and the meetings at the border in 1259 become a foiled attempt by the English king to seize Alexander and thus overthrow the Comyns.[104] Hume Brown's account of relations with Norway[105] does not accuse Alexander of instigating raiding in the isles, but does make Hakon's expedition a response to the depredations by the earl of Ross. Acknowledging the inconsistency of the source material, Hume Brown accepts the contemporary sources' assertion that it was primarily the storm which drove the Norwegians on shore, and that a minor, indecisive battle followed. Hume Brown's treatment of the church portrays Alexander as the upholder of Scottish ecclesiastical independence in the face of a grasping papacy.[106] He has little to tell us about the last ten years of the reign, other than the Scottish account of the homage given by Alexander III to Edward I in 1278,[107] and the 'lurid gloom' of the last years of Alexander. Accounts of the deaths of the king's children, portents of impending disaster, including the performance of the Dance of Death at Alexander's marriage feast (a story given to us by Bower), and other omens are followed by a detailed description of the king's death, including the by now usual embellishment that he fell over a cliff.[108] In summary,[109] Hume Brown claims that 'Alexander left

Scotland a prosperous and consolidated kingdom': he recites Bower's justice ayres story, and even includes Bower's invention of 'singular' mercantile legislation and the offer of the Lombards to erect 'factories' in the Forth. He then gives a brief account of the flourishing state of the country, and concludes with the fragment of poetry from Wyntoun, which he uses as evidence of 'the expression of popular feeling when fate was about to turn the gloomiest page in the nation's destinies'.

Several general points emerge from the late nineteenth-century works. Their interpretation of the newly available primary source materials, which put them on a plane above earlier writers, differs widely. For example, Hume Brown alone is vehemently critical of Henry III; Skene is more understanding than the others in his treatment of the isles; neither Skene nor Lang make any claims to Scotland's prosperity, while Hume Brown and Burton do so, but with wide variance in their justification of that viewpoint. These works also largely ignore those of the previous three centuries. Unanimously rejected are the grossly over-inflated claims of the eighteenth century regarding the battle of Largs, the more reasoned evidence of Fordun and the sagas holding sway. Hume Brown, adopting the anti-English sentiments of Fordun, Bower and the *Chronicle of Melrose*, cites further documentary evidence in his creation of a clear-cut popular anti-English sentiment in Scotland. The earlier writers' reasoned refusal to accept Bower's myth is abandoned by Hume Brown and by Burton, although the latter writer at least feels the need to find some evidence to support the basic contention of prosperity, and does not repeat Bower's wilder fantasies. In their quest to provide something new, Burton and, more particularly, Hume Brown, have stepped back more than four centuries. These late nineteenth-century works were to remain the central pillar of Scottish historical scholarship for many years, and were undoubtedly very influential, for it was the use of such works in schools and by the general public which created many of the romantic attitudes to Scottish history which still linger in the popular memory today.

Sir James Fergusson published his biography of Alexander III in 1937, but in style it seems to belong more in the nineteenth century; despite protestations to the contrary,[110] it is written in a deliberately archaic narrative style. His list of sources is restricted in the main to those we have studied, with the addition of some documentary collections — *Foedera*, Bain's *Calendar of Documents Relating to Scotland* and the *Exchequer Rolls*, and a miscellany of modern works, which, interestingly, includes only P. F. Tytler's work from the nineteenth-century histories. The first chapter is devoted to Scotland under Alexander II, and is undoubtedly included in order to provide a contrast with his son's reign. Following the late nineteenth-century line, it reveals that in this reign the country was poor, with little foreign trade, and that the nobles were Anglo-Norman rather than Scots, many owning lands on both sides of the border, creating conflicts of interest which led to the formation of pro- and anti-English factions.

Alexander III's reign is introduced by a series of biographical notes regarding some of the chief men of the kingdom at the time.[111] The ensuing treatment of the inauguration and translation ceremonies are taken wholly from Bower.[112] The narrative of the rest of the minority period also leans heavily on Bower, but is in addition fiercely antagonistic towards Henry III. Fergusson follows Hume Brown in asserting that the Comyns had popular support,[113] and details the persecution of Bishop Gamelin by the Durwards.[114] The seizure of the king by the Comyns in 1257 was motivated by fear that the country would be placed under interdict if it continued to be ruled by those who had been excommunicated over the Gamelin affair.[115] In the next year the king was able to assert personal authority, resulting in the compromise arrangement at Jedburgh, after which 'internal dissension vanished from the king's council'.[116]

The chapter which covers the years 1258 to 1263 begins with a recitation of events which again closely follows Bower's narrative,[117] and then turns to relations with Norway.[118] Alexander, frustrated by the failure of peaceful attempts to bring the islands under Scottish control, determined to subjugate the isles to the Scottish crown. Hakon therefore planned an expedition to bring the isles back under Norwegian hegemony. The account of the expedition itself is very detailed, and is based chiefly on *Hakon's Saga*, which it follows almost *verbatim* in places. The battle of Largs is given far more detail than in any previous writings, and, clearly, Fergusson has carried out topographical research with which to corroborate the written source material. His analysis is that the battle was forced on the Norwegians by the foul weather, and was in reality a series of skirmishes which did little damage to either side, but which left the Norwegians in relative disarray, forcing the retreat northwards. It follows some of the nineteenth-century histories in the assertion that there was no significant Scottish royal force in the area, basing this on a statement of the Melrose chronicler, and is critical of those writers (Buchanan, for example) who have inflated the scale of the battle.

Turning to the years 1263 to 1284, Fergusson places most stress on the further action and negotiation leading to the treaty of Perth,[119] before inserting a section which claims that 'at this time it [Scotland] was prosperous, richer than it had ever been before'.[120] He supports this contention with evidence of the value of land and amount of royal revenue, and gives the credit for the prosperity to the mercantile activities of the burghs. He makes considerable use of Bower's Alexandrian legislation concerning the turning of the idle to work and the breaking of new land, and of the king's consistent pursuit of justice for all his subjects. Bower's personal description of the king is repeated, and a character sketch[121] is concocted from the versions of most of the chronicles (excepting Lanercost, of course). The reign is summarised in glowing terms: welfare, peace and independence were Alexander's aims in government.[122] Issues such as the mission of Ottoboni, the Dunmore affair, and the continuing dispute over the earldom of Menteith are then considered,[123] after which Fergusson returns to the peace and prosperity, the loyal nobility and 'contented' peasantry, flourishing arts (architecture in particular), and patronage of music and medicine.[124] The years of decline, from 1274 onwards, receive predictable treatment.[125]

The final short section of the book is occupied with 'the death of King Alexander and the extinction of his house'. Once more, it is predictably detailed, reciting all of the portents of disaster which have been supplied by the chronicles, leading to a suitably florid account of the death of the king, the prophecy of Thomas the Rhymer, and a brief recitation of events through to the death of the Maid of Norway.

This book's ostensible purpose was to fill a gap in Scottish historiography. Laudable as the aim may be, the book does no credit either to its subject or its author. With the exception of the section on the battle of Largs, which at least makes some show of critical analysis, it is for the most part a simplistic recitation of a careful selection of contemporary and near-contemporary narrative sources, padded out with detail, as necessary, from documentary evidence.

If Fergusson's *Alexander III* is a depressing disappointment, the scholarship of the last few decades presents a decidedly brighter face. The ever-increasing amount of primary source material which has been made available, and the deeper understanding of the nature and potential of that material, has stimulated once again a flourishing revisionist school of modern scholars. The role of the late nineteenth-century historians in presenting the standard image of medieval Scotland was perhaps first seriously challenged in a general history by

W. C. Dickinson in his *Scotland from Earliest Times to 1603*, published in 1961. In his foreword Dickinson explained the 'real need' for a new history of Scotland to replace Hume Brown, which was then still the most generally accepted work.[126] In the following period, attention was particularly focussed on the society and institutions of the period, and the inestimable contribution made to that study by G. W. S. Barrow was drawn together in his invaluable *The Kingdom of the Scots* (1973). In the mid-1970s also, the two volumes of the Edinburgh History of Scotland dealing with the period to 1513[127] presented a magisterial synthesis of much recent work. Relatively little of this groundswell of revisionism dealt directly with the events of Alexander's reign, but neither were they ignored. D. E. R. Watt's article on 'The Minority of Alexander III of Scotland' (1971),[128] broke completely with the chronicle-type treatment of earlier writers, put the minority period into the contexts of previous baronial behaviour and of other European example, and studied the motives and actions of the protagonists in an effort to explain their causes and significance. Whilst more recent study has led some historians to different conclusions,[129] the contribution made to the historiography of Alexander III by Dr. Watt's article must remain undisputed.

The chapter providing a narrative of Alexander III's reign in A. A. M. Duncan's *Scotland: The Making of the Kingdom*[130] presents the reader with a well substantiated and penetrating picture of the reign. Gone from the political narrative is the simplistic notion of Scottish and English 'parties' in the minority; gone is the naive idea that those assembled for the inauguration of Alexander were surprised at the appearance of a bard to recite his genealogy; gone are the portents of disaster which heralded the king's death. The narrative is stripped bare of irrelevancies, in order to expose the significance of what remains. Duncan follows his narrative with an examination of the offices, institutions and methods of Scottish government, and of Scottish trade and economy.[131] It is refreshing at last to find an author who dismisses Bower's anti-export legislation as 'garbled nonsense'.[132] Duncan also examines the custom regarding succession, such a vital concern in the latter part of the king's reign. The book concludes with a summary of the real achievement of Alexander III and his predecessors: they created a harmony in the governing community which made effective the joint responsibilities of governing the country.

Scottish Society in the Fifteenth Century, a collection of essays edited by Jennifer Brown (1977),[133] represented another major step forward in the revision of our outlook on medieval Scotland. This book was a starting point for a great deal of subsequent work, particularly on the nobility of medieval Scotland. A new understanding of the role and motivations of the nobility has great significance for our interpretation of events, and many subsequent monographs, theses and articles have added substantially to our knowledge of the middle ages. Perhaps the most striking recent example of this is *Essays on the Nobility of Medieval Scotland*, edited by Keith Stringer.[134] In this work, several essays contributed to the study of Alexander's reign. The interest in, and understanding of, the medieval nobility is but one aspect of the new methodology of Scottish medievalists. The change has been in the range and understanding of source material, and it has affected every field of study.

In view of their influence on the public perception of history, some of the many 'popular' histories of the last few decades merit our attention. In the brief narrative devoted to Alexander III in R. L. Mackie's *A Short History of Scotland* (1930), he manages to have one of the factions of the nobility (presumably the Durwards) 'suspected of being in English pay';[135] Hakon's unexpected arrival in 1263 re-awakened 'a fear that had been dead for centuries';[136] and the battle of Largs is summed up as 'an indecisive skirmish', although it occupies almost half of the narrative. In his chapter on Scottish society in the period,[137] Mackie gives little support to Bower's myth, which he ascribes to hindsight, but upholds the romantic image of the 'conscientious king' leaving his realm bereft of leadership when his 'bruised and broken' body was found. Janet Glover's *Story of Scotland*, published thirty years later, refers to the 'brief but long-remembered golden age for Scotland',[138] but gives us very little information about it. Similarly, Professor J. D. Mackie's only significant comment on this reign is his description of 'The End of the Norse Peril',[139] the rest of the reign being largely ignored, with the exception of the king's death. Rosalind Mitchison, in her *History of Scotland* (1970) claims to have used 'the conclusions of modern research', and to have written the book partly with the specific intention of updating the popular images of Scotland's past. It is a pity, then, that it was 'worked at in isolation and kept away from authoritative criticism'.[140] Again the reign is largely ignored, with the exception of a short piece on the Norwegian expedition, and an examination of the 'golden age', a description which is found to be apt in the light of the prosperity of the burghs, which benefited from 'the "boom" found all over Europe in the thirteenth century'.[141]

As well as the 'serious' popular histories discussed above, recent decades have seen the expansion of a different genre of historical writing: general histories aimed at an entirely popular — even tourist — market. Such works have a vested interest in retaining the romantic image of Scotland's past, and it is unfortunate that this is so rarely achieved without compromising historical integrity. In John Prebble's *Lion in the North*, a misleadingly simplistic treatment of the minority[142] is followed by the final relaxation of 'the long threat of the Norsemen'[143] and Alexander's death, caused by his 'devotion' to Yolande: the king 'could not bear to be parted from her for an hour longer than was necessary', and gallantly died in the attempt to return to his love.[144] To be fair, Prebble accepts the contention that the golden age was created by hindsight,[145] but he nonetheless sees the reign as a 'glorious noon' for Scotland, and although his description of the land and society in the period[146] is colourful and flavoursome, it tells the reader little that could not have been read three quarters of a century before. *Flower of Scotland* by James Sharp (1981), whilst better than many in its use of modern research, still promotes the old idea of English and Scottish parties in the minority,[147] and, whilst its unexaggerated account of the invasion by Hakon IV[148] is welcome, it is noticeable that even here there is no attempt at all to understand the position and motivation of the various parties involved. This book, like so many others, is a recitation of events (including the king's fall over a cliff), not a work of history. That it provides a better recitation than many others in the field is to its credit, but whilst not actually bolstering the myth of the golden age, it does nothing to dispel it. Finally, even very recent works have not taken account of modern scholarship. One such, published in 1987, has little to say of Alexander, but enough for us to identify the ultimate sources:

> . . . for most of the thirteenth century Scotland enjoyed a golden age, especially under Alexander III.

> . . . It was under Alexander III that the Hebrides were regained for the Scottish crown as a result of King Hakon of Norway's ignominious defeat on the sands at Largs in Ayrshire in 1263.[149]

Professor Gordon Donaldson has commented that 'it takes a long time for the findings of scholars to filter through to the popular mind . . . a good error never seems to die'.[150] It is very noticeable how little the popular approach to the history of this reign has changed since 1930. The attitudes of those days, then in tune with contemporary scholarship, are still to a considerable extent current today, in the face of modern scholarship. It is a great pity that so many authors make no effort to disseminate the fruits of recent scholarship, but continue instead to feed the public on outdated, discredited notions.

The works of historians who wrote from the sixteenth century until the early part of this century were principally based on the medieval chronicles and their later inflations. Even after the publication of many of the documentary sources in the eighteenth and nineteenth centuries, Bower still reigned supreme as the most authoritative source for the history of Alexander III. It was not until well into the present century that the value of much of the documentary source material was recognised, and that study of this material deepened our understanding of its potential. This volume has examined all of the major areas traditionally studied in relation to Alexander III's reign. The picture we have at the end of the day is of a good king: almost thirty years of largely peaceful reign in relative prosperity, with legal and judicial machinery which appears to have worked quite well, amounts to a good record for any medieval monarch. But detailed study in the end bears out the original suspicion, gained from the contemporary narrative sources, that this, despite undisputed consolidation and development, was in itself an unspectacular reign.

The loss of the 'golden age' is no cause for lament; the Alexander myth has gone because it was an irrelevance and a hindrance to deeper study. The primary importance of Alexander III's reign lies in its position at a watershed of Scotland's history; a grasp of the true nature of this settled period is of vital importance to our understanding of the full significance of what followed. Much attention has been paid to the developmental aspects of the period of the Wars of Independence which were a direct result of the failure of Alexander's dynasty.[151] Without a thorough grasp of the nature of the reign which preceded the decades of turmoil, our understanding of the effects of those years must be severely limited.

The contemporary writers painted a picture of a good king and a stable reign; the early historians inflated this for their own propagandist purposes, and some subsequent writers, perhaps misunderstanding the nature of their source material, and with little opportunity to corroborate it, accepted the tale they were told. Whilst in the eighteenth century this view was challenged to some extent, the state of scholarship and the inaccessibility of alternative sources hindered a true redefinition of the reign. Some of the revisionist writers of the late nineteenth century seem to have been uncritical of the primary source material, and were partly responsible for a resurgence of the myth. Eventually in very modern times, the wherewithal to undertake more penetrating study has led to this reign taking its place in the revitalised historiography of medieval Scotland.

If Bower had not inflated Fordun, who had inflated the contemporary accounts; if Hume Brown had not accepted much of Bower's work when others did not, today we would not have had such a plethora of questions to ask. Historical study grows through the efforts of previous generations; its hunger is created by dispute, and its food is the discovery, evaluation and re-evaluation of source material. We have 'blamed' Bower for the myth, but perhaps we should instead congratulate him, for the concept of the golden age, nurtured by historians ever since, has pushed Alexander III to the forefront of Scottish history, and has been a catalyst for controversy. Together, Bower's enthusiasm and modern scholarship have at last gone some way towards finding the true nature and significance of Alexander III's Scotland.

NOTES

1. I am indebted to Dr. David Brown of the Department of Scottish History, University of Edinburgh, for his invaluable assistance with the completion of this chapter.
2. The chronicle is printed in full in M. O. Anderson, *Kings and Kingship in Early Scotland* (Edinburgh 1973), but is cited here from a translated extract in Anderson, *Early Sources*, ii, 562.
3. Expectations with regard to good kingly rule were quite clear in thirteenth-century Europe. Several philosophers had written extensively on the subject, and in Scotland political writings of the late thirteenth and early fourteenth centuries show that Scotland was fully in tune with current European thought. The basic requirements were that the king should have the right to rule bestowed upon him by the community, that he should have the physical and mental capability to rule, and that he should accept the good counsel of the community, maintain equitable justice, avoid unnecessary warfare, and uphold both the integrity of the kingdom and the ultimate sovereignty of God. A realm thus governed would be favoured by God, and would prosper. For further discussion of the theory in its application to Alexander III, see Norman H. Reid, *The Political Role of the Monarchy in Scotland, 1249–1329* (unpublished PhD thesis, University of Edinburgh, 1984; henceforth Reid, *Monarchy*), 35–42.

4. Anderson, *Early Sources*, ii, 687. This entry ends version G of the chronicle, which must therefore be very closely contemporary.
5. *Chron. Melrose* (Stevenson), 181.
6. Ibid., 183.
7. Ibid., 190.
8. Ibid., 196-7.
9. Anderson, *Scottish Annals*, 363.
10. Ibid., 365-6.
11. Ibid., 376.
12. *Chron. Lanercost*, 64-65; cf., however, Nicholas Mayhew's comments on the weather in the thirteenth century, above, p. 58.
13. Ibid., 97.
14. Ibid., 98.
15. Ibid., 115-17.
16. Ibid., 116 gives details of a jocular exchange between Alexander III and one of his barons regarding Judgement Day.
17. *soli illi genas lachrymis non madefecerunt qui ejus in vita amicitiis et beneficiis arctius inhaeserunt* (ibid., 117). Another hint that Alexander III was not universally revered is found in the chronicle by Thomas Wykes: 'of his death diverse men thought diversely' (Anderson, *Scottish Annals*, 384).
18. *Chron. Man*, 111.
19. See above, pp. 104-9.
20. *HS*, 327.
21. Ibid., 340.
22. Ibid., 349.
23. Ibid., 353.
24. Ibid., 363.
25. Ibid., 374.
26. *Chron. Lanercost*, 117 is very positive about the rule of the guardians after 1286.
27. . . . *accepit secundam uxorem rex Scotiae Alexander, filiam comitis de Dru, Yoletam nomine, sibi in dolorem et toti provinciae in perpetuum fere dampnum* (ibid., 114; see also ibid., 116, 118).
28. If xenophobia is indeed a factor in this chronicler's attitude to Alexander III, it may therefore be relevant that the king's mother, Marie de Couci, was also French.
29. For the account of the inauguration see *Chron. Fordun*, i, 293-5 (ii, 289-90).
30. Ibid., i, 295 (ii, 290-1).
31. Ibid., i, 295-6 (ii, 291).
32. Ibid., i, 297 (ii, 292).
33. Ibid., i, 298-9 (ii, 294).
34. Ibid., i, 299 (ii, 294-5).
35. Ibid., i, 299-300 (ii, 295). The subsequent action, and treaty of Perth, are found at ibid., i, 299-302 (ii, 296-7).
36. Ibid., i, 303-4 (ii, 298-9).

37. Ibid., i, 304–5 (ii, 299–300).
38. Ibid., i, 305–6 (ii, 300–1).
39. Ibid., i, 306 (ii, 301).
40. Ibid., i, 307 (ii, 302).
41. Ibid., i, 308–9 (ii, 303–4).
42. Ibid., i, 309 (ii, 304).
43. Ibid., i, 304–5 (ii, 309–10).
44. Ibid., ii, p. lxxviii.
45. Ibid., i, pp. xxx–xxxiii; ii, pp. lxxiii–lxxiv. Nicholson (*Scotland*, 205–6), has Fordun writing at the end of his life, between 1384 and 1387. Even if this assumption is correct, the points made below still stand.
46. See the detailed analysis of the reign of David II in Nicholson, *Scotland*, 123–83.
47. *Chron. Wyntoun* (Laing), ii, 250–1.
48. Ibid., 252–3.
49. Ibid., 255–7.
50. Ibid., 260–1.
51. Ibid., 263–4.
52. Ibid., 264–6.
53. Ibid., 266:

> 'Quhen Alysandyr oure Kyng wes dede,
> That Scotland led in luẅe and lé,
> Away wes sons off ale and brede,
> Off wyne and wax, off gamyn and glé:

> Oure gold wes changyd in to lede.
> Chryst, borne in to Vyrgynyté,
> Succoure Scotland and remede,
> That stad [is in] perplexyté.'

54. Duncan, *Kingdom*, 245.
55. *Chron. Bower*, ii, 80–82.
56. Ibid., 85–89.
57. Ibid., 93, 97, 105–6, 115.
58. Ibid., 97–102, particularly at 97–98.
59. Ibid., 128.
60. Ibid., 129–31.
61. Ibid., 131–2.
62. Ibid., 108.
63. The only reference to significant material prosperity which I have noted in contemporary sources is a passage in *Chron. Lanercost* (s.a. 1266) describing the wealth of Berwick in the mid 1260s. The opulence of one well-placed town cannot be taken as an indicator of country-wide prosperity, and indeed could be assumed to indicate a contrast with the rest of the land.
64. See the description of the minority of James II in Nicholson, *Scotland*, 325–52.

65. F. J. H. Skene's Preface to this work presents persuasive evidence to date the work 1461. See *Chron. Pluscarden*, i, pp. ix–xxxiii.
66. Ibid., 77, 80–81.
67. *Chron. Fordun*, i, 295 (ii, 290) also refers to the origin myth, but in less detail, and without further reference to the attainments of those countries. *Chron. Pluscarden*'s inflation is therefore highly significant.
68. *Chron. Pluscarden*, i, 84–85.
69. Ibid., 85.
70. The events of 1263 to 1266 regarding the isles are at ibid., 95–101; see especially ibid., 97: *patriam defensuri.*
71. *visa paupertate regni*: ibid., 107.
72. Ibid.
73. Ibid., 112–14.
74. Major, *History*, 189–90.
75. Ibid., 189, 190–1.
76. Ibid., 191.
77. Buchanan, *History*, i, 387.
78. Ibid.
79. Ibid., 387–8.
80. Ibid., 391.
81. Hailes, *Annals*, i, 201.
82. Ibid., 207–9.
83. Ibid., 213.
84. Ibid., 222.
85. Ibid., 223–4.
86. Skene, *Celtic Scotland*, i, 490–2.
87. Ibid., 493–5.
88. Ibid., 496.
89. Andrew Lang, *A History of Scotland from the Roman Occupation* (Edinburgh and London, 1900–1907), i, 121–2.
90. Ibid., 122–3.
91. Ibid., 125.
92. John Hill Burton, *The History of Scotland* (2nd edition, Edinburgh and London, 1873), ii, 21–24.
93. Ibid., 24–25.
94. Ibid., 25.
95. Ibid., 26–37.
96. Ibid., 40–41.
97. Ibid., 45.
98. Ibid., 105.
99. Ibid., 105–11.
100. Ibid., 110.
101. P. Hume Brown, *History of Scotland* (Cambridge, 1902), i, 118–19.
102. Ibid., 119.
103. Ibid., 120–4.
104. Ibid., 121, 123.

105. Ibid., 124–6.
106. Ibid., 126–7.
107. Ibid., 127–8.
108. Ibid., 129.
109. Ibid., 129–32.
110. Fergusson, *Alexander III*, p. x.
111. Ibid., 23–25.
112. Ibid., 23–32.
113. Ibid., 45, 52.
114. Ibid., 53–54, 56–60.
115. Ibid., 61.
116. Ibid., 66.
117. Ibid., 73–80.
118. Ibid., 80–114.
119. Ibid., 117–27.
120. Ibid., 127–39.
121. Ibid., 136–7.
122. Ibid., 137–9.
123. Ibid., 139–55.
124. Ibid., 155–8.
125. Ibid., 159–73.
126. W. Croft Dickinson, *Scotland from the Earliest Times to 1603* (revised edn. by A. A. M. Duncan, Oxford, 1977), p. vii.
127. Duncan, *Kingdom* and Nicholson, *Scotland*. For discussion of Duncan's treatment of Alexander III, see below, p. 204.
128. Watt, 'Minority'.
129. See, for instance, pp. 3–8 above.
130. Duncan, *Kingdom*, 552–94.
131. Ibid., 595–615.
132. Ibid., 603.
133. *Scottish Society in the Fifteenth Century*, ed. J. M. Brown (London, 1977).
134. Stringer, *Nobility Essays*.
135. Robert L. Mackie, *A Short History of Scotland* (London, 1930), 96.
136. Ibid., 97–98.
137. Ibid., 100–13.
138. Janet R. Glover, *The Story of Scotland* (2nd edition, London, 1977), 60.
139. J. D. Mackie, *A History of Scotland* (2nd edition, Harmondsworth, 1978), 43–45.
140. Rosalind Mitchison, *A History of Scotland* (London, 1970), p. ix.
141. Ibid., 35.
142. John Prebble, *The Lion in the North* (Harmondsworth, 1973), 55–56:

> 'Walter Comyn, Earl of Menteith . . . with his half-brother Alexander, Earl of Buchan, controlled the kingdom for the first six years of the young man's reign, never forgetting their own royal descent from Duncan I . . .'

'. . . a party sympathetic to England, led by Alan Durward, Justiciar of Scotland, and by Robert de Bruce . . .'

143. Ibid., 56–57.
144. Ibid., 57, 68.
145. Ibid., 57.
146. Ibid., 57–65.
147. Professor James J. Sharp, *The Flower of Scotland: A History of Scottish Monarchy* (Perth, 1981), 49.
148. Ibid., 47–48.
149. Michael Jenner, *Scotland Through the Ages* (London, 1987), 84.
150. Sharp, *Flower of Scotland*, Foreword.
151. See, for example, Barrow, *Bruce* and Reid, *Monarchy*.

INDEX

This index is very selective. Many names, places and topics to which the text makes only incidental reference have been omitted. References to individuals thus excluded will sometimes be found within the family entries, and bishops, earls and other office holders to whom passing reference is made may be found under their sees, earldoms or offices respectively.